ABOUT FALL CREEK BOOKS

Fall Creek Books is an imprint of Cornell University Press dedicated to making available again classic books that document the history, culture, natural history, and folkways of New York State. Presented in new paperback editions that faithfully reproduce the contents of the original editions, Fall Creek Books titles will appeal to all readers interested in New York and the state's rich past. Some of the books published under this imprint reflect the sensibilities and attitudes of an earlier era; these views do not necessarily reflect those of Cornell University Press.

For a complete listing of titles published under the Fall Creek Books imprint, please visit: cornellpress.cornell.edu.

A STRIPE OF TAMMANY'S TIGER

Louis Eisenstein
and
Elliot Rosenberg

Fall Creek Books
AN IMPRINT OF
CORNELL UNIVERSITY PRESS
ITHACA AND LONDON

First published 1966 by Robert Speller & Sons, Publishers, Inc.
First printing, Fall Creek Books, 2013

Library of Congress Cataloging-in-Publication Data

Eisenstein, Louis, 1915–
  A stripe of Tammany's tiger, by Louis Eisenstein and Elliot Rosenberg.
  xii, 300 p. 23 cm.
  Includes index.
  ISBN 978-0-8014-7884-0 (paper : alk. paper)
  1. Tammany Hall.   2. Politics, Practical—New York (State)—New York.
3. New York (N.Y.)—Politics and government—1898–1951.   4. New York
(N.Y.)—Politics and government—1951–

  F128.5 .E38   1966
  329.3/02/11   66029504

Cornell University Press strives to use environmentally responsible suppliers and materials to the fullest extent possible in the publishing of its books. Such materials include vegetable-based, low-VOC inks and acid- free papers that are recycled, totally chlorine-free, or partly composed of nonwood fibers. For further information, visit our website at www.cornellpress.cornell.edu.

To

Mom and Dad

TABLE OF CONTENTS

I	Once Upon a Tiger	1
II	Nurtured in Tammany's Realm	5
III	Ahearn the Elder: Squire of the Lower East Side	13
IV	Ahearn the Younger: Not by Breadbaskets Alone	32
V	Days of Grandeur and Grime	60
VI	Changing of the Guard: The White House, City Hall, Tammany Hall	76
VII	The Little Flower: Scent and Odor	92
VIII	Tiger? What Tiger? Do You See a Tiger?	117
IX	Years of the Meek "me-ow"	135
X	Fission in Fusion: The Little Flower Withers Away	154
XI	O'Dwyer: A Knight in Rusty Armor	167
XII	War of the Halls: City Hall Versus Tammany Hall	188
XIII	"Bashful Berty's" Last Stand	208
XIV	The Captains and the Kings Depart	223
XV	A Wagnerian Opera Without Music	241
XVI	Of Tammany Men, Reformers and Reformed Reformers	268

A STRIPE OF TAMMANY'S TIGER

Preface

This book is about politics, not political science. It is based on nearly a half-century in the field, a lifetime of activity within the framework of Tammany Hall. Although in no sense a text-book, a lordly format I happily leave to scholars, there are lessons here, the types of lessons that rarely peek out from the pages of more learned studies.

Politics is no pedantic abstraction. Politics is people. They cannot be reduced to simple formulas and statistical charts. Nor should they be. Politics is an amalgam of shrewdness and stupidity, of integrity and shame, of humility and arrogance, of loyalty and treachery. These strengths and frailties of mind and spirit do not fit snugly in a test-tube. They cannot be measured in the sterile atmosphere of a laboratory. Nor can a disinterested observer, magnifying glass in hand, explore the realm of political geography with the assuredness of a naturalist surveying his own back garden. There is a "feel" to politics, a dimension incapable of objective measurement and translation into technical jargon.

Modern political scientists may labor long hours to set up a body of "laws" about politicians and voters. But the annual unpredictability of human nature before Election Day has punched many a hole into these feeble efforts. Political science is not math or physics. Few apples would snub Newton's Law of Gravity by leaping back to their branches. But people do not behave like apples.

Politics, unlike political science, recognizes no "laws." However, there are "rules." Especially in the world of machine politics, they embrace all who play the game—strident reformers as well as party regulars. Many of these rules are demonstrated between the covers of this book. They are clear and simple. And by far the most important of them all is the Rule of Political Loyalty.

A man whose word is his bond, who honorably fulfills his commitments, sleeps easy at night. He knows his supporters and voters will stick with him through thick and thin. Conversely, a man whose word has the permanence of a wisp of smoke, who lightly discards his promises, must constantly sleep with one eye open. Opportunism may bring him temporary profit, but eventually he will reap a bitter harvest for his faithlessness.

The Rule of Political Loyalty is not respectful of rank. Whether a man be a county leader standing on the shoulders of his district leaders, or a district leader held aloft by his lieutenants, or a precinct worker rooted in a small constituency, a two-way bond of faith must govern his dealings. Loyalty downward is repaid by loyalty upward.

The rule also is not respectful of geography. It applies to the wards of Boston and Chicago and the parishes of New Orleans as well as to the assembly districts of New York. I have no doubt it equally applies to the thousands of Podunks scattered throughout the length and breadth of the country. Politics, as I noted earlier, is people. And people cling to similar values everywhere.

When the Rule of Political Loyalty is violated by men at the apex of a party's pyramid—Democratic or Republican—the foundation stones of that party inevitably erode and crumble. How this fate threatens my own party in New York will be explored on the following pages.

All too often, the riddle of raising the level of big city politics has revolved around vague talk of bringing a higher caliber of men into public life. But how do you define "higher caliber?" A university background may add to a man's store of knowledge, not to his common sense and sense of common humanity. Injecting a large dose of lawyers into a community's political bloodstream is no solution. A constituency is a tougher judge of a man's worthiness than any courtroom jury.

Intelligence may initially thrust a man into a position of public or political prominence, but intelligence alone will not be enough to keep him there. The most crying need in politics today is not for craft and glibness. It is for heart and soul.

Once Upon a Tiger

THIS IS THE STORY OF NEIGHBORHOOD POLITICS AS IT ONCE WAS, and never again will be, on New York City's Lower East Side. The Fourth Assembly District, base of the nation's melting pot, proudly wore the title of Banner Democratic District of the city and state. As such, it was a powerhouse in Tammany circles for decades. Its leaders always rode the Tiger and often gripped its reins. The Ahearns, father and son, ruled here as princes in an age when honest personal politics often filled a dishonest public framework. We shall never see its return or the return of their kind.

Admittedly, their story and the story of their successors—shallower men of synthetic public respectability but small private virtues—are depicted through biased eyes. I was a Tammany man for forty years. Through most of that period, the label held no shame. Today, in death, Tammany Hall is less a name than an epithet of contempt.

In disinterring some of the good that died with it, I do not deny the evil that helped bring on its fatal malady. Scandals were part of its history and they have been ably exposed by its foes. But there is another history, superficially glossed over by political undertakers, of neighborhoods where Tammany was far from a curse word. This story centers on old-style district leaders who loyally served their constituents and were faithful to their commitments. These men stitched fair principles on their hearts, not their exposed shirtsleeves. They cared not a whit for their press clippings nor wrote scholarly works on the responsibilities of political life. They did not lead two lives, one public and one concealed. They never smiled ingratiatingly and uttered pure, respectable ideas before large gatherings, then disappeared behind closed doors and knifed

1

each other in the back. The Ahearns and many of their contemporaries never betrayed a trust. Their word was their bond. This book is not absorbed with hazy codes of ethics and abstract philosophies. It is born of the conviction that a man's worth should be measured by his deeds, not his spoken words and newspaper clippings.

Tammany Hall declined and fell largely because it lost leaders such as the Ahearns. Its tragic illness was of its own making. Political analysts in academic towers have dragged in sociology and economics as the reasons for its final disintegration. No one can ignore the effects of the halt in large-scale immigration and the expanded role of government in providing for the general walfare. Yet these factors merely helped Tammany's demise along. They did not cause it. Where district leaders such as Louis De Salvio, Prosper Viggiano, Stephen Jarema, Frank Rossetti, Raymond Jones and Angelo Simonetti carry on in the old tradition, a thin stripe of the Tiger still survives. And it survives solely because these men regard their posts of political trust as sacred as any office of public trust.

A world of change has overtaken neighborhood politics. But this story cannot be told without frequently skipping back and forth between district clubhouses and Tammany headquarters. The dominant figures in the Hall's inner circle set the policies that guided the Tiger to its grave. The organization's general health affected each of its district limbs just as each district's aches and pains affected the entire organization.

Most assembly districts in this present post-Tammany period are politically arthritic. The typical mediocre leader today is a gatherer of statistics rather than a doer of acts. He has lost contact with his constituents and has lost the ability to translate their needs for elected officials. Once he steps twenty paces from his clubhouse, hardly a soul recognizes him. Many young people, steeped in the learnings of political science textbooks, may consider this diminished role a good thing. But when the district leader drew his hand away from the pulse of his neighborhood, elected officeholders lost their most valuable tool in finding out what the voters thought and felt. Public opinion polls are a poor substitute. All too often, Mayors and legislators succumb to the loudest pressure group rather than the silent majority.

The function of the precinct, or election district, captain has also evaporated into impotent smoke. Today his place is the lowest rung on the political ladder. In times past, though many young campaign workers find it hard to believe, the captain was king. Within my own congested domain of crowded tenements, I was friend, confidant, politician and social worker combined. I was the link between my people and their government.

One day a year, Election Day, I received my reward for these services. It was for me, not my party's candidate, that my constituents cast their ballots. And there were hundreds of captains scattered throughout the city who won similar rewards.

Scores of elected officials never fully appreciated the significance of the captain. Many were so influenced by their campaign oratory that the idea never sank in that the voter's principal political allegiance was to his captain. Maybe these candidates were misguided by the absence of the captain's name from the ballot form. I never knew for certain. But I did know that before a stodgy legislator raised his nose too high, he had to be set straight.

"The average Joe Jones in my precinct votes for me, not you," I would say. "He knows me well and he doesn't know you from a hole in the wall. When he needs help he comes to me, not you. I handle his problems, not you. And if there's a matter that's over my head, I can always get him through your door. After all, you won't see every fellow who wants to make an appointment. But if he mentions my name, you'll see him all right. That is, if you're interested in running for re-election.

"I'm always in my constituents' corner. And they know it. You can pour out all the pretty promises you please before election day. If it helps your ego, fine. But don't forget that every vote you pile up in my precinct is a vote for me, not you. You just happen to have your name on the ballot!"

For such blunt talk today, a captain would not draw raised eyebrows and startled glances, as I did. More likely, he would be laughed out of his club. The overwhelming majority of captains are no longer kings. They are not even knights on the political

chessboard. They are just insignificant pawns, collectors of peti-
tions and distributors of campaign leaflets. The captain has been
replaced by the mimeograph machine. The publicity release has
been substituted for his voice. The human and humane touch has
gone out of neighborhood politics. The role I filled for decades has
been abandoned.

This book is no autobiography. Nor is it intended as a fullscale
history of Tammany Hall. It is a highly personal glimpse into the
world of precinct, district and county politics, past and present. It
deals with several stripes of the Tammany Tiger and brings into
close focus some of the most forceful background figures in New
York City's political framework. Primarily, it is a forty year panorama of Tammany practices and personalities. And, regretfully,
events have shown that "change" is not necessarily synonymous
with "progress."

II

Nurtured in Tammany's Realm

I WAS A CHILD OF THE LOWER EAST SIDE AND I NEVER LEFT ITS womb. My parents arrived here late in the nineteenth century, long after the Mayflower's journey. For this they made no apologies. The Pilgrim ship sailed from Plymouth, England, and that is a long way off from western Galicia, where my ancestors had set down their roots. News of America and its opportunities traveled slowly in those years. But when it finally reached my parents' ears, they listened and they came.

It is fortunate they did. For their tiny village of Shendishiv—I have spelled it phonetically since it was too unimportant a place to appear on any map—was part of the old Hapsburg Austro-Hungarian Empire. After World War I it became Polish territory. Twenty years later, war blazed again and the Blitzkreig burned through it. Near Shendishiv the Nazis set up a new industry in a somewhat larger town. Some called it Oswiecim. Others called it Auschwitz. But whatever the spelling, its industry was death.

The old world my parents knew thus passed out of existence. So did the sons and daughters of my parents' friends, who would today be my own age. They were no doubt slaughtered during the early 1940s, for Shendishiv was a Jewish community. The village itself probably went up in flames during those grim days. If it did so at the time, few would have noted its passing. Maybe it survived as a living memorial, not a living place. The players, one way or another, had all departed the stage.

My parents first set foot on American soil at Castle Garden, on the southern tip of Manhattan island. Ellis Island had not yet become the converging point for Europe's lost souls. And the Statue of Liberty, which would welcome its wretched masses in the future, was still a French architect's dream.

5

Literature is filled with stories of the plight of humble immigrants. It abounds in tales of the shabby existence they led and the teeming slums in which they dwelled. My parents did not have to read such works as Jacob A. Riis' *How the Other Half Lives*. For years following their arrival, they *were* the other half.

My father was an industrious man, however. In time he set up a small suspender business on Attorney Street. It was a good business, a profitable business, but one that never made my family wealthy. The earnings that other men would have directed toward expansion, my father poured instead into the neighborhood synagogue. The synagogue, or "schul" as we called it, was the center of his new world. His store was merely the necessity that kept us clothed, fed and housed. In those days, income tax laws were a mirage. Charitable contributions were considered as blessings, not tax deductions. Therefore, my father's donations were usually anonymous as well as generous. He never became a rich or famous man. But he was a beloved and respected figure on the Lower East Side in a circle far wider than his own relations.

I was one of a family of nine. We grew up in the New World in almost an Old World setting. Our globe was bordered by Delancey Street in the south and Rivington Street in the north. Both were named after famous British colonial figures. But we, who lived there, rarely encountered any inhabitants of English stock. Before our time the neighborhood had been largely Irish and German. Now it was totally Jewish, a fact that will prove of enormous significance as this tale of neighborhood politics unravels.

Our first extensive contact with natives of pure American background came when we entered the city's public school system. Prejudice no doubt existed in those days just as it does today. But if a teacher of Anglo-Saxon descent smacked our hands with a ruler for misbehavior, we recoiled rather than resisted. On arriving home from school, we received a second slap from our father. He did not probe for the motives of the teacher, only the nature of our misconduct.

We knew little of the outside Protestant world. On our borders were clusters of Irish and Italians, settled in their own ghettoes. In coming years we would all find our niche in Tammany Hall, and each group would play a role in its development. For the moment, however, it was strictly an Irish-operated institution. This resulted from a simple fact of history. The Irish came here first. Besides, they spoke English, a tongue still alien to many other new arrivals.

As youngsters, we fought each other. Not for racial reasons, only because each group was "different." First the Italian boys battled the Irish boys. That struggle concluded, they would join forces and clobber us. When we were all exhausted we would make peace and return to school. There was never any permanent damage to body or spirit.

A journey to the waterfront to pick up ice had all the elements of a pioneer trek through Indian territory. It was a treacherous undertaking, but necessary. At the piers where ships unloaded, a large hunk could be purchased for a nickel. It could cool our icebox for days. Nearer to home, a hunk half the size could cost twice as much at a store. This price was beyond our meager ability to pay. So down to the waterfront we trekked, past block after block of hostile Christians. Sometimes they lay in wait. At other times we passed through their territory untouched. In either case, we returned with our hunks of ice to a hero's welcome.

In our little world the police played their distinct role. Though the patrolmen were almost all Irish, there was never any religious friction. They pounded the same beats year after year and knew everyone in their neighborhood including, of course, the local Tammany captain. They winked at the Sunday closing laws and lost not one bit of respect for their discretion.

They were looked up to by all the children on their beats. When, as youngsters, we boxed and wrestled in the streets, the blue-coated officer's attitude was that boys will be boys. They stood aside unless, of course, we were in danger of being flattened under a passing milk wagon.

Let some sinister-looking character enter the territory of his beat, however, and the policeman would be quick to pounce on him. "Why are you on this block? What's your business here?" would be the inevitable questions. And if the answers were hazy, the policeman would speed the fellow's departure. On hot nights we slept on our fire escapes with little cause for fear. Certainly crime existed. No society has ever completely eliminated it. But in the opening years of this century, parents on the Lower East Side could send their children down from the tenements at all hours and know they faced little danger to their safety. The same cannot be said today, despite the gradual disappearance of squalid slums and the rise of tall, immaculate apartment buildings.

The fireman was also a respected public servant—on or off duty. Come Saturday morning, battalion chief Patrick Walsh would tell his men: "The Jews in this neighborhood won't light their stoves Saturday, even in the middle of winter. It's against their religion. Saturday is their Sabbath. So if a bearded man asks you to go to his flat and put a flame on his stove, don't ask him why. Just do it." And the firemen, almost as uniformly Irish as the police, did more than they were asked, even if it meant climbing to the sixth story of a six-story tenement.

The fire engine house, horses and all, was quartered on the same block as my father's store and the synagogue. Each fall, with the approach of the Jewish New Year, Rosh Hashanah, the firemen would unravel their hoses and scrub down the walls of the synagogue. This was certainly a chore performed above and beyond the call of duty. It was worthy of more note than empty proclamations of brotherhood.

When the high holy days came, the neighborhood fell into silence. Nothing moved—not a pushcart, not a horse-drawn wagon, not a primitive automobile. Nothing. People could walk to the synagogue without a care about traffic. Every store for block after block was closed. Everyone wore his best clothes. In many cases this meant the outfit worn year after year only for religious holidays, graduations and marriages. For the extremely poor, and few were not, there was always a supply of matzoth and kosher food on festive occasions. The Fourth Assembly District leader saw to that.

His name was John F. Ahearn, a name that would mean much to me in later years. Like most Tammany district chiefs of his day, he was Irish. At the turn of the twentieth century, there were some 275,000 descendants of Eire in the city. But new waves of immigrants were pouring in from other lands including 145,000 Italians and about the same number of Jews. Although Irishmen still ruled

Tammany Hall, politicians were quick to realize what store signs clearly trumpeted. On the Lower East Side the Irish were steadily disappearing, and their places were just as steadily being filled by people from southern and eastern Europe. In the shadow of the Brooklyn Bridge, it was the Italian immigrant. In our own neighborhood, it was the Jewish settler at the end of his final exodus.

Leon Stand, father of one of my closest boyhood friends, Bert, became Mr. Ahearn's first Jewish lieutenant. Later, Bert would succeed his father and eventually become a powerful figure in the Tammany Hall hierarchy.

Mr. Ahearn, of course, spoke no Yiddish. And many of my parents' generation spoke no English. Jewish lieutenants, or captains as these political aides were called, became a necessary fixture at the local clubhouse if for no reason other than their indispensable use as translators. In a short time, assimilation into the club was complete. When Henry Goldfogle was selected by Mr. Ahearn as the district's first Jewish Congressman, the Yiddish-speaking community knew it had come of political age.

Many people still consider Al Smith as the sole worthwhile political product spawned on the Lower East Side. But scores can be named who never achieved Smith's fame, yet made a solid contribution to the city's political life and judiciary. Many were of my generation, and some were boyhood friends. Take the judicial branch, for example. Many of these names may be unfamiliar. But Irving H. Saypol, Saul S. Streit, Walter J. Bayer, Birdie Amsterdam, S. Samuel DiFalco, Saul Price, Joseph R. Marro, Arthur G. Klein, Jacob Markowitz, Harold Birns, Hyman Solniker, Daniel Weiss and Xavier C. Riccobono have all attained success on the bench and reflected credit on their Lower East Side upbringing. So have Louis J. Lefkowitz (later New York State's Attorney General), Bernard Newman and Jacob Grumet, who, for reasons I have never quite understood, became Republicans.

Politicians even during the first decade of this century respected the cultural background of all their constituents, not just those of their own religious and national background. Goldfogle regularly took part in the annual St. Patrick's Day Parade. And Barney

Downing, our Irish State Senator, never asked for pork when he ate at a kosher restaurant.

John F. Ahearn's own parents had taken root in the neighborhood shortly after the "spoils system" had been made respectable by President Andrew Jackson. Despite the changing complexion of the community, he still ruled as a prince among men. In other districts, the old Irish Tammany chiefs gave way to representatives of the new tides of immigration. But not in the Fourth Assembly District. Mr. Ahearn gave his Jewish constituency no cause to seek a change. While other quarters of Tammany were rent by ethnic conflict, peace and harmony prevailed here. When Mr. Ahearn passed on, his son, Eddy, succeeded him as leader. Both played the political game squarely, and both retained the confidence of their people till the day they died.

Politically, the Fourth Assembly District had always been Democratic, even before the birth of the Democratic party. This was a tradition from which it never wavered. During the forty years I spent in politics, it was Tammany's Banner Assembly District. The Hall could usually depend on an overwhelming majority for whatever names appeared on the Democratic ballot line. My own constituency became the Fourth Assembly District's Banner Precinct. And I became the district's Banner Captain.

I must admit, regretfully, that my father sometimes violated the tradition. Until Franklin Roosevelt's day, he departed from the straight Democratic ticket to vote for the Republican nominee in Presidential elections. He was often called upon to explain this heresy. "As a businessman I like to see aloof, respectable men in the White House, men who will keep the tariff up," he used to say. Then he would add with a twinkle, "But on the state and local level, we need humane men, people like ourselves, who understand the needs of the common man."

Any brief invasion of the Lower East Side's political history shows that "humanity" had always been associated with the Democratic Party. Long before the Fourth Assembly District was hacked out of the old "wards", as political districts were then called, candidates of the other parties faced a hopeless task on Election Day. Federalists here lost to anti-Federalists, for the Federalists planted the seed of the Republican Party and the anti-Federalists were the roots from which the Democratic Party sprang. When native-born bigots attached themselves to the Know Nothing Party in the 1830s, the neighborhood's Irish flocked to Tammany Hall. Their descendants never deserted it.

In 1860, Abraham Lincoln was swamped at the polls on a cold November day, for he ran as a Republican. No major virtues could possibly compensate for that political sin. After the Civil War, General Ulysses S. Grant produced a similarly anemic vote. Democrat William Marcy Tweed fared far better in his bid for minor public offices. So did Grover Cleveland, the first modern Democrat to reach the White House following the Reconstruction Period. Whether scoundrel or saint, a Democrat was assured of victory and the label Republican led to an inevitable sentence of defeat.

On the Lower East Side, the Democratic Party meant Tammany Hall in the 1800s, and few people in our section gave a second thought to the rantings and criticisms of outsiders. How could a man with a full stomach and a silk hat to his name presume to know what was best for his less fortunate fellow New Yorkers? Besides, the charges were usually levelled in the press or magazines printed in English. And few freshly-arrived immigrants had yet mastered this baffling language.

Tammany derived its name from a Delaware Indian chief. In a sense, the organization of my parents' day resembled the friendly Indian statesmen who greeted the Pilgrims. Peace pipes, not the bows and arrows of hostility, were their welcoming cards. Castle Garden and Ellis Island, of course, were no replicas of Plymouth Rock. They lacked the hallowed antiquity of that piece of stone. All newcomers, nevertheless, shared some problems in common.

The Pilgrims from England, set adrift in a new land, needed shelter. So did the latter-day Pilgrims from Italy, Poland, Austria-Hungary and Russia. Tammany Hall helped them get it—by finding them tenement apartments and even chipping in to pay the rent when necessary. These new Pilgrims, too, needed food to sustain them through the long winter. Tammany's braves could not teach them to plant corn, for there was no fertile soil. But jobs to earn their bread, and breadbaskets when no jobs were available, were well-received substitutes.

The English Pilgrims needed no passport to the New World. But those who followed them here needed naturalization and citizenship papers. Tammany's braves helped get them. In many ways the local Democratic machine provided aid and comfort long before the immigrant became a citizen and a voter. These favors did not fall on ungrateful shoulders.

Tammany also provided what little measure of entertainment these newcomers could enjoy. In this, the John F. Ahearn Association was typical of Democratic clubs throughout the city. Every summer it held an outing. For several hours the stench of the slums could be forgotten during a pleasant boat ride up the Hudson River. The aroma of fresh, green grass temporarily replaced the odors of the city streets. At night, a torchlight parade slowly wound its way from the boat landing up South Street to the Ahearn clubhouse on East Broadway.

Hundreds, at times thousands, took part. Shopkeepers along the route spread sawdust on their sidewalks in the shape of letters spelling out the Ahearn name. Wetted with gasoline, and ignited by match, the emblem burst forth into flames just as the marchers passed by. A good time was had by all.

Both old Pilgrims and new faced problems of government. The English Pilgrims developed the town meeting as a political device uniquely suited to their needs. This was necessary, for the area of their settlement was a political vacuum. The new Pilgrims, with equal initiative, encountered the difficulty of merging into New York City's political fabric, not designing one of their own. It was no less a task to adjust to America than to build it.

Tammany Hall served as mediator between the Established Order and its new subjects. If the "price" it extracted for this service was a vote for the Democratic slate on Election Day, the fee was far from exorbitant. And it was willingly and happily paid.

III

Ahearn the Elder:
Squire of the Lower East Side

At the juncture of East Broadway and Grand Street, in the heart
of the Lower East Side, a cold, impersonal bank stands today.
It is flanked by a small park where a few elderly folks gather to
absorb the sun's rays by day and the cool breezes by evening.
Extending eastward to the river are block after block of tall co-op
apartment buildings, built since World War II. Across the street
from the bank is a newly-erected, modernistically-designed public
school.

Little evidence remains that the immediate neighborhood was
the magnetic bottom of the nation's melting pot. And no surrounding block has been more altered than this one, where once
stood a three story brownstone bearing the number "290 East
Broadway".

The man most responsible for the area's architectural face-lifting,
Abraham E. Kazan, recently remarked, "I cannot help but laugh
when we are told that valuable historic buildings were destroyed by
the bulldozer. In this section of the city, the only building that one
may have in mind is the home of John J. Ahearn. If anything, I
take it that most of you would rather not remember that name nor
see that building."

The middle-class audience of the middle-income organization
which he addressed probably nodded in assent or even clapped
hands lightly and politely. But who and how many in the audience
could actually remember John F. (not *J.* as in the prepared text
of the speech) Ahearn, or his son Eddy, or the minor magic they
and their captains performed in generations past for bewildered

13

new Americans? In countless numbers these flocked to the club-house at 290 East Broadway, just two doorsteps away from the Ahearn home.

It is easy to flay the Tammany Hall organization of the early 1900s. Scandals surely abounded and there was certainly much worth flaying. But the Tammany Tiger had many stripes. Some naturally were black. Just as it would be unfair to damn the national Democratic Party because several tarnished demagogues have made it their home, it is equally unfair to cast stones at all who represented Tammany and carried its banner.

Nowhere was the banner held higher nor flown more proudly than here, in the Fourth Assembly District. True, it has not always remained so. During the late 1930s and throughout the 1940s, it became splattered by the same mud that dirtied the Tiger elsewhere. But while John and Eddy Ahearn reigned, 290 East Broadway was an address that brought dishonor neither to those who mounted the stone steps of the stoop seeking aid nor those who awaited them upstairs.

In a wide-open era when Richard Croker, leader of Tammany Hall, freely admitted he was working for his pocket all the time, and George Washington Plunkitt boasted he "seen his opportunities and he took 'em," the John F. Ahearn Association adhered to its motto of service, "Without Favor or Price". Both father and son saw their district's leadership as a weighty challenge, not as an unlimited vista for private gain. Neither Ahearn died rich.

The dark red brick building that housed the club was not an imposing one, indistinguishable from similarly constructed brown-stones surrounding it. To the casual passer-by it certainly did not appear to be a seat of political power. Having ascended the shaggy dozen stone steps leading to the narrow-framed entrance, the stranger might have turned back, convinced he was in the wrong building.

The main floor was almost bare and unfurnished. Just a handful of hard-back chairs and a table or two. The stranger might have noted the frayed, obviously well-worn carpet covering the wooden staircase. Many feet had plodded up that staircase to the top floor.

The lack of furniture might have puzzled the visitor, but only because he chose an inappropriate hour for his call.

Had he returned some Monday or Thursday evening between seven o'clock and the wee hours of the next morning, he could easily have seen the reason for this scantiness. There was no room for furnishings, only people. People literally crammed into the clubhouse, filling every available foot of space. The overflow waited their turn outside the building.

Thousands of new citizens and soon-to-be citizens found an impersonal government translated and interpreted here by the personal touch. The harshness of life in an unfamiliar New World was cushioned for newcomers who could not fill out citizenship papers or meet excessive rent payments and for those in need of jobs or peddlers' licenses. The club was a welcome oasis in a sea of uncertainty. Remember, many of these people, my parents included, had had their first view of the Republic from the porthole of a freighter's steerage section. All representatives of authority, especially those in uniform, were, from their experience, men to be feared rather than sought out.

Too often, Tammany leaders of those days were criticized for buying votes with a lump of coal in the winter and a hunk of ice in the summer. These charitable activities may still seem cynically motivated to current-day political scientists. No one would deny there were some district leaders who regarded politics as a business rather than a calling. At the turn of the century, however, who else offered aid? Certainly not the stiff, aloof Republicans. They earned respectability, not respect. And at the opposite corner, the Socialists were too busy preparing for the brave new world of the future to bother with the immediate needs of the present.

To where besides the Tammany clubhouse could a white-bearded, eighty-year-old patriarch go for assistance in securing a small state pension? Unable to speak or write a word of English, he would seek out our Irish leader.

Mr. Ahearn would give a comforting nod, then turn to me and say, "Louis, talk to this man in his own language. He didn't come here to see a show." Before the old man (the term "senior citizen" was as yet unknown) went home, he would have his problem dis-

cussed sympathetically, his pension application patiently filled out
and the seal affixed by a notary. His political loyalty might have
been anticipated in return. But it was a loyalty eagerly given, not
only by himself but also, at times, by his children and grand-
children.

In 1920, there was a severe housing shortage. "We had thousands of people," Eddy Ahearn once recalled, "whose rents were
being raised and who couldn't do anything about it. They came
to us.

"We formed a legal committee—all lawyers from the district
serving without pay. We defended 12,000 rent cases, believe that
or not, and we won them. The people down here don't forget
things like that."

The cold flats of the Lower East Side into which the poor poured
were not only grimy, uncomfortable and unhealthy. They were
also terribly expensive. "The real estate situation down here was
shot through with subleases," said Eddy. "It was a speculation.
Flats were scarce and a lessor could pass his lease on to someone
else at a profit, and the new man would push the rents up higher
still. Everybody who had a piece of paper on the house had to get
his cut out of the tenants.

"We showed all that up and we got a lot of backing. We put
forward legislation that curbed subleasing. It was the Democratic
votes at Albany that did it, but we showed the way."

Eddy's father, John F. Ahearn, shepherded his flock for nearly
three decades. He faced no bitter district fights to wrest the staff
from his grasp. In a section overwhelmingly Jewish in population
Mr. Ahearn's authority was never challenged along religious lines.
He ruled as a benevolent country squire, hardly the man to fit the
cartoonists' depiction of a greedy, cigar-smoking Tammany satrap.

A rock-like dignity in his face reflected the nature of the man.
We did not smoke or drink in his presence. Out of respect, we
addressed him as "Mr." at all times, just as he is described in this
book. Only a few old-timers of his own generation greeted him
as "John."

Above all, Mr. Ahearn was scrupulously honest in his personal
dealings. In an age when we have become accustomed to political

sharpsters who abide by "good government" principles publicly while privately trampling their associates in a mad dash to advance themselves, it is difficult to give proper weight to this almost obsolete quality. Though an unfortunate mark blemished his conduct as a public official, no one could ever question his conduct as a man. The word of John F. Ahearn was his bond.

When I met Mr. Ahearn for the first time in 1917, he was already in the twilight of life. He sat behind a pock-marked, chipped desk in a little cubbyhole of an office at the back of the clubhouse. I felt the addition of a few extra chairs to the two already there would have made it too cluttered to move about. There were no obvious trappings of authority. Yet few oak-laden, heavily paneled doors ever opened to throne rooms of greater influence in small domains.

Mr. Ahearn was the boss. Make no mistake about that. All elected Democratic officials from the district owed him their nominations. And nomination in our district usually guaranteed election. The Republican Party here was a fleshless skeleton, certainly no worthy opponent in the political arena.

When Monday and Thursday evenings rolled around, the district's Congressman, State Senator, State Assemblyman and Alderman were present and accounted for at the club. They had to be. No obligation was greater for any elected official than being available to the people who put him in office. Mr. Ahearn insisted on this, and it was a rule none dared violate. Only the need to be away in Albany or Washington was sufficient excuse for absence.

Mr. Ahearn also insisted that his lieutenants scrupulously fulfill their "contracts", as the varied assignments they were given were called. No promise that could not be kept was made. No promise was made that was not kept.

One evening shortly after I joined the club, a lawyer was given the task of representing a poor peddler the next morning in court. Two days later, Mr. Ahearn met the peddler and asked about the outcome. The peddler almost tearfully voiced his disappointment that no one from the club appeared with him before the judge. Mr. Ahearn fumed. The erring lawyer never was permitted to set foot in the clubhouse again.

Most "contracts" were farmed out to club members. The Congressman handled federal matters, either here or at Washington. The forte of the State Senator and State Assemblyman was Albany. The Alderman scurried about City Hall, his list of tasks checked off one by one as he worked his magic. Captains, each responsible for a precinct of about a thousand voters, handled the bulk of the work. The leader, however, took care of some matters personally.

I called on Mr. Ahearn one day with a friend whose goal was to wear a shiny policeman's badge. He had passed the intelligence portion of the exam with no difficulty. But two missing ribs, the result of an old injury, blocked his appointment.

"You go down to headquarters early tomorrow morning," said Mr. Ahearn. "Ask to speak to Captain ————. Don't worry. At one minute past nine, you'll be a patrolman."

He did—and he became one. Later, he rose to the rank of captain on his own.

John F. Ahearn was born April 18, 1853, close to the clubhouse he founded, nursed and led until his death sixty-seven years later. It was the core of his life's work. Seven days a week, rain or shine, he was available to his constituents. On warm weekends, an armchair on the sidewalk in front of the stoop became his "office".

He rarely left the neighborhood long enough for anyone to notice he was missing. Politics was not then a part-time hobby, to be conducted in a spirit of *noblesse oblige*. It was a full-time chore. Too many present-day reformers tend to treat humanity as an affectionate abstraction. Mr. Ahearn dealt with people close up.

The boss was a machine politician in the sense that he was part of the organization that ruled the city. He did not buck it. But he kept the less savory Tammany practices of other quarters out of his home district. Later, as Borough President of Manhattan, he would find himself unable to avoid these pitfalls. Thus, he was to become engulfed by a torrent not of his own creation.

Mr. Ahearn grew up in an era when William Marcy Tweed and his "Boodle Board" of Aldermen were stealing the city blind. Mayor Fernando Wood had already made his valiant effort to dispose of City Hall, but the deal had fallen through. He cut his political eye teeth while Richard Croker, Tammany's "Master of Manhattan", was salting away the fortune that would enable him to live comfortably abroad when the heat singed his whiskers here.

An Assemblyman while still in his twenties, Mr. Ahearn "advanced" to the chief clerkship in Essex Market Police Court. Now this may seem an unimportant job, not worth leaving the Assembly for. But it put Mr. Ahearn in a position where he could do a lot of good for a lot of people—while at the same time picking up votes for the Democratic column.

Many pushcart peddlers were hauled to the Police Court whose sole crime against society was ignorance of a simple city ordinance. On receiving word of their arrest, Mr. Ahearn would rush over from his office to the rescue. "What's going on?" he would ask. "Why are these men being held?"

"Well, Mr. Ahearn," the officer usually replied, "they've been caught selling merchandise without a license."

"Is that all?" Mr. Ahearn would say. "These are my people. They're my voters. What's their fine?"

On hearing it was two dollars, the chief would dip into his pocket, produce the price of justice and turn to the forlorn men in the lockup. Moments later, to the clanging of cell keys, the men would be released.

"You men can go home now," the policeman would lecture the relieved peddlers, "but get a license before you sell your wares. And you ought to thank your lucky stars and Mr. Ahearn for getting you out of this mess!"

Chances are they not only thanked their stars, they voted the row of stars on Election Day.

In 1889, Mr. Ahearn entered the State Senate. He remained there till 1903, when he won elevation to the Presidency of the Borough of Manhattan. He made a mistake in doing so. The machinery of this office, greased by corruption, was capable of sending any occupant skidding. Mr. Ahearn was no exception. In November, 1906, a pamphlet issued by the Bureau of City Betterment, called *How Manhattan is Governed,* severely criticized the management of borough affairs.

In view of the charges, Mr. Ahearn requested an investigation. This was conducted by the Commissioners of Accounts, with a young lawyer named John Purroy Mitchel as special counsel. The examination of the Borough President's office was minute and thorough. A comparison of the ledger balances and the actual inventories of storerooms in the Bureau of Public Buildings turned up many discrepancies. The books listed 228 whisk brooms in stock. Actually there were only 55. On the other hand, 19 wooden pails were listed in the ledger, while 33 were promptly found. The storerooms contained eight more ash cans than noted, but toilet paper was in short supply.

Of a more serious nature, Mitchel's report showed that contractors were not adequately supervised, street repairs were neglected and payrolls were padded. The blame was naturally placed at the feet of the Borough President.

The upshot was a hearing before New York State's Republican Governor, Charles Evans Hughes. On December 9, 1907, Mr. Ahearn was removed from office.

"It is not shown and it has not been claimed that he converted public money or property to his own use," admitted the Governor's report, "or has personally profited in an unlawful manner by his official conduct." Nonetheless, maladministration, remissness and grave abuses in the department had been definitely proven. These led to his ouster.

While not a party to corruption, Mr. Ahearn certainly knew what was going on under him. He was not stupid. But traditional party loyalty had bound his hands. In passing judgement in this incident, it would be well to remember that by taking the Borough President's job, Mr. Ahearn necessarily took on problems and political responsibilities that went beyond the borders of his own assembly district, where his authority was unquestioned. He entered wider political domains, where unwise accomodations with other party leaders led to disaster.

As for the intrepid counsel, John Purroy Mitchel, the investigation helped pave his way to the Mayorship seven years later. Like most reform Mayors, he guided the city along sound government principles. And like most reform Mayors, he was turned out of office after one term by a bored electorate. New Yorkers have always seemed to demand government *of* the people as well as *for* the people. Mitchel retreated far too often to luxurious surroundings and high society after working hours. He was defeated in 1917 in large part by the slogan, "Too Much Fifth Avenue and Not Enough First Avenue."

Throughout this period, and extending into the early 1920s, Tammany Hall was ruled firmly by Charles Francis Murphy. Murphy was born June 20, 1858, five years after Mr. Ahearn, and grew up in the Celtic surroundings of the Gas House District, just north of the Lower East Side. A broad-shouldered man with a good memory for friends and enemies alike, Murphy ran Tammany —and the city—with a good deal of shrewdness and common sense.

He seldom addressed public gatherings or appeared on convention floors. He preferred the seclusion of hotel suites for interviewing prospective candidates. He would no doubt have stared coldly and unresponsively at the image-making public relations men who freely bob and weave in and out of party headquarters today.

Unlike Mr. Ahearn, Murphy passed his closing years a wealthy man. He reputedly exacted a $2,000,000 excavation contract for a firm he controlled in return for granting the Pennsylvania Railroad permission to burrow into Manhattan. Allegedly through this and other uses of raw political muscle, he accumulated a small fortune. His country place on Long Island held a nine-hole golf course.

Murphy selected candidates for city and state offices like a commanding general deploying his troops. Most of his choices were wise ones. If he had missed base too often, he could not have survived as county leader for two decades. Governor Alfred E. Smith and United States Senator Robert F. Wagner Sr., father of Mayor Robert Jr., both owed their political rise to his good judgement.

Occasionally, though, he made choices he regretted. None caused him more grief than his acceptance of William Sulzer for the Governorship in 1912, partly at the urgings of Mr. Ahearn. Years later, Murphy would call the nomination of Sulzer "the greatest mistake of my political life."

Sulzer was popular on the Lower East Side. An Assemblyman for five years and a Congressman for eighteen, he had been considered a progressive member of Tammany. He endeared himself to our district's Jewish population during his Congressional tour of duty. He fought for repeal of our commercial treaty with Czarist Russia when persecution of the Jewish population there reached a crescendo. Was it not because of those very pogroms that many Russian Jews sought to exchange the terror of the Old World for the opportunity of the New?

The new Governor was an effective speaker, though a bit pompous and with a touch of vanity. Once in the state's executive mansion, however, Sulzer discarded his Tammany Tiger's stripes. It was an act of party treachery, for he did so after the election, not before.

"I am free . . . and shall remain free. No influence controls me but the dictates of my conscience," he declared. He proceeded to back up these words with rebellious deeds. He pressed for a state primary law upsetting the traditional convention system. Next, he refused to accept Tammany's man for the post of State Highway Commissioner.

This was too much for Murphy. "You may be the Governor," the leader reportedly scolded his politically prodigal son, "but I have got the legislature, and the legislature controls the Governor, and if you don't do what I tell you to do, I will throw you out of office." Sulzer remained unmoved.

Murphy had always held his district leaders responsible for the men they recommended for public office. He now turned to Mr. Ahearn with considerable annoyance and insisted, "John, you wanted Sulzer in Albany. You've seen the way things turned out. Now it's up to you to get him out."

The task was passed on to Aaron Jefferson Levy, as likeable a rascal as ever donned a legislator's toga. Levy's father had migrated from Czar Alexander II's Holy Russia during the 1860s. By the time of Aaron's birth on July 4, 1881, the elder Levy had become a prosperous merchant. The family's wealth vanished shortly afterward amidst a depression, so young Aaron took to the streets selling newspapers.

Eventually, he worked his way through New York University Law School and was admitted to the bar in 1903. He quickly established an enviable reputation at criminal law. Even Aaron's detractors admitted his brilliance. By 1908, he secured a seat in the State Assembly. Levy's liberal credentials there were impressive. He supported primary laws, direct election of United States Senators and women's suffrage.

Above all, however, he was loyal to his supporters and his superiors. Aaron did not personally dislike the Governor. But once his unpleasant assignment was outlined, he went diligently about the task.

The method of Sulzer's political and public demise was impeachment. In August, 1913, less than a year after taking office, the Governor was charged by a legislative committee with falsifying campaign expenditures. The next month, Albany was host to the spectacle of a court of impeachment consisting of the members of the Senate and Court of Appeals.

Aaron served as chairman of the Board of Managers. As such, he was the leading "prosecutor". His performance, if not noble in motive, was certainly impressive from a technical standpoint. Sulzer was found guilty of misrepresenting the use of campaign funds, perjury and suppression of evidence. On October 17, he was removed from office. The former Governor slipped silently into obscurity and died on November 6, 1941, almost a forgotten figure.

Levy's triumph led to a Municipal Court judgeship several months later. It was the beginning of a long judicial career. In the years ahead, he would get into hot water with several bar associations, Mayor Fiorello H. LaGuardia and the Citizen's Union over his conduct on the bench. Characteristically, he would cut his way through these unpleasantries and die, I am certain, a happy man. But these events rightfully belong to the future and will be told in a later chapter.

Nevertheless, one crisis faced by Levy that stemmed directly from the Sulzer affair might be noted at this point. In it, my father provided a helping hand.

Lower East Siders have long memories and, as I have mentioned, Sulzer was popular among the Jewish residents. In 1923, Aaron sought promotion to the State Supreme Court. The worried candidate approached my father, who was head of the Attorney Street synagogue.

"Mr. Eisenstein, what can I do?" he asked. "I need a big vote in this neighborhood to offset the uptown districts. But people still remember the impeachment. I hear there are whispering campaigns against me."

My father gave the problem some thought. Then an idea came like a spark. "Aaron," he snapped, "you're going to join the synagogue next week!"

"Why should I join the synagogue?" asked the puzzled Levy. "I always attend services anyway and make my contributions."

"Yes, I know," said my father. "But don't you see—in order to become a member, you must appear before the whole congregation and show your worthiness."

Slowly, the implications of the suggestion sank in. Here was to be his open "trial" before a Jewish "jury". If he were "acquitted" he would gain not only synagogue membership but, very likely, the Supreme Court judgeship as well.

The floor of a synagogue is certainly no place for politics. So the 500 people who jammed into the building that notable evening were not there, of course, to pass judgement on a man's qualifications for public office. And, naturally, the speech they heard and the probing questions they asked were merely to ascertain his character and spiritual standing. No unwarranted conclusions should therefore be drawn about the reasons for Aaron Jefferson Levy's elevation to the Supreme Court, now should they?

Whatever merit the later criticism of his judicial conduct had, it was impossible to dislike Levy as a man. Many years later, when my father reached old age, my family decided a move to Long Beach might act as a healthful tonic.

"Don't do it," Aaron chided, "the move will kill him. Here on the Lower East Side, he has set down his roots. Here he's a somebody. He's lived in the same house for fifty years. You don't tear a man from his roots unless he needs to set down new ones. Your father is happy here. Don't commit murder!"

Aaron Levy was a kind, humane, warm-hearted man. He was a good friend.

My father's neighborhood prominence accounted, in part, for my entry into politics. I was enlisted in the John F. Ahearn Association by an established member, Henry S. Schimmel, just as in future years I would bring many young fellows to the club for the first time. There was never any hesitation over the question of which of the two parties to join. On the Lower East Side, a Republican was a curiosity and a Republican clubhouse, a foreign embassy in hostile territory.

The core of the Ahearn club's strength, as the Ahearns themselves freely admitted, was the capability of its captains. Many textbooks on Government describe the precinct captain as the lowest form of political animal. When I joined the club in 1917, however, it was a position that commanded respect, not just a foothold in the door for ambitious lawyers. To his constituents, he was Humane Government, if not Good Government. His was the task of being available any day or night for a favor, not just Monday and Thursday evenings. He lived among his constituents and knew their problems. He suffered with them and shared their joys. "Captain" was a title of respect and, for those of us who became "Ahearn captains," a source of prestige well beyond the borders of our own Fourth Assembly District.

Like most youngsters still wet behind the ears, I did not immediately become a captain. As an apprentice, my tasks were at first menial. I ran errands, attended meetings and placed placards in the windows of local shopkeepers. Henry Schimmel, who remained a faithful friend and later became a respected judge, was running for the Assembly, and I was a soldier in his service.

This, too, was the year of America's entrance into the First World War. Before long, I would eagerly exchange my political private's stripes for a sailor's cap. It was not easy. Though a well-built youngster, I was shy of the required height and weight. Both the Army and Navy turned me down.

I sought out Mr. Ahearn and asked for his aid. He listened patiently, occasionally nodded, then searched the back of his mind for a name. "Tomorrow," he said, "go back to recruiting headquarters. See a Dr. ————. Eat a big meal tonight to put on a couple of pounds and don't worry about your height."

I spent 1918 as a Second Class Seaman. Unfortunately, Kaiser Wilhelm threw in the sponge before I was sent overseas. I thus

returned to the political wars without ever having had the opportunity to see the world.

Little change had overtaken the Lower East Side during the
war years, except the arrival of many more newcomers. Most became loyal Democrats. A few drifted over the restraining barrier
into the opposition camp. They did not become Republicans however. The traditional two-party system was almost unknown here.
The GOP elephant never undertook plodding safaris to hunt down
the Tammany Tiger. Faced with a simple choice between the two
major parties, our people followed a simple rule when they entered the voting booth. They voted the stars. They held to the
firm belief that the Republican Party was the party of the rich and
the Democratic Party was the party of the poor. Few on the
Lower East Side enjoyed large bankrolls.

There was a fiery threat during the late teens, though, from the
Socialist camp. It was short-lived, but lively. In fact, the Socialists
garnered a quarter of a million votes in one city-wide election.

Many new arrivals, especially to our district, came from East
European countries ruled by autocrats. Political opposition to
these regimes was stifled. Whatever criticism existed usually came
from men flying the Socialist banner, an act of courage as well as
radicalism. Since Jews were about the most oppressed group of all
in those unhappy lands, it is easy to see why many chose to transfer their loyalty to similar Socialist organizations here.

Socialist strength in New York City diminished and silently died
a natural death, largely through the growing up process. But the
Socialists helped along their own demise by not seeing the trees in
front of the forest.

These well-meaning visionaries directed their fire on the long-
range hopes of the young. They lit the torch of future reforms,
reforms that would eventually be realized under Democratic leadership in the 1930s. But the time was not yet ripe. They stirred discontent in an era that cried for relief before reform. They often
ignored the immediate needs of the people, especially the elderly.
We Tammany captains did not. There is such a thing as being a
Democrat by inheritance. By constant and concrete service to
these old folks, we earned not only their loyalty, but also harvested

the gratitude of their children, their nephews, their nieces and their in-laws. Our trump card in overcoming the Socialists was our ability to meet realities while our opponents were busily trying to merchandise dreams.

For six years, we did have a Socialist Congressman, and a good one. The worst that can be said of Meyer London was that he had a politically premature birth. Biographies have been written about his worthy labors. In 1914, he defeated Henry Goldfogle, was re-elected in 1916, lost to Goldfogle in 1918, beat Goldfogle again in 1920 and ended his checkered Congressional career by losing to Samuel Dickstein in 1922.

In December, 1917, London's "no" vote was the sole sign of dissent in the House of Representatives as America declared war on the Austro-Hungarian Empire. It was an act of both conviction and foolhardiness. It drew against him a formidable alliance indeed. His defeat in the following campaign was helped along by support given Tammany's candidate by such prestigious figures as Rabbi Stephen S. Wise, Jacob H. Schiff, Samuel Untermeyer and Theodore Roosevelt.

London was a man willing to take unpopular stands despite the personal cost. In this, he was a rare individual, a credit to the Lower East Side. Men of all political stripes mourned his tragic passing after an automobile accident.

By no stretch of the imagination were all Socialist campaigners either scholars or gentlemen. Our bouts with them each fall rarely went according to Hoyle. And the rough-and-tumble nature of these contests could not be blamed on our side alone, as has often been pictured in the press. The Socialists did not manage to elect a Congressman, Alderman and Assemblyman from our district by daintily keeping their hands lily white. Both sides engaged in campaign mischief.

In the weeks before Election Day, large crowds gathered as competing Socialist and Democratic orators heckled each other from atop horse-drawn wagons at opposite street corners. Seemingly, the whole neighborhood turned out for the shows. "Grafters," screeched one side. "Utopians," screamed the other.

Mingling into the crowd were campaign workers from both

groups. Occasionally, a Socialist speaker found his wagon being lured from under him. Inevitably, a juicy carrot or lump of sugar waved in front of his horse proved an irresistible attraction. Democratic steeds, made of sterner stuff, rarely yielded to such temptations. At least, not when someone had the foresight to hold the reins or bridle.

Surrounding tenement buildings temporarily took on the appearance of fortified castles. From atop their roofs, water cascaded down on invading speakers at the street corners below. Alien ideas were soaked away. These contests were not one-sided. As I have indicated, the Socialists were no Caspar Milquetoasts themselves. They simply were less adept at paramilitary techniques. An example here should illustrate this lack of skill.

On one occasion, both parties sparred for position at the choice corner of Attorney and Rivington Streets. The Socialist speakers, arriving earlier, enjoyed squatters' rights. From a nearby rooftop, however, their own henchmen peered down and prepared liquid armaments. Not recognizing that the beaming candidate below was their own champion, they set loose a storm of water. It caused general confusion and a hasty evacuation from the target area. When the streets dried, we Democrats had recovered the fumble and moved into the abandoned position.

After the successful 1919 campaign, I received my first political reward. At least, I thought it was a reward—a job at the central post office. I arrived neatly dressed at the appointed hour and was immediately cast into the midst of a mountain of packages.

"You'll throw these down the chute," barked a martinet-type foreman. After ten minutes, my fresh white shirt was yellowed with perspiration. Exhausted, I sat down to rest. Just at that moment, in marched the foreman. "Jew shirker," he shouted, "get up and get back to work!"

Naturally, being so addressed, I picked up the nearest mail bag and clobbered him over the head with it. Prudence would have dictated a less violent response, for he was twice my size. Instead of fighting, however, he ran to his supervisor, a stiff little man, who promptly fired me.

That afternoon, I spoke to Mr. Ahearn. By evening, our Congressman prepared a very official-looking letter. Post office jobs were federally-handled appointments, which accounted for Gold-fogle's role.

The next morning, I was back at the scene of the encounter. Envelope in hand, I walked straight into the office of the super-intendent, whose position was a notch above the supervisor of the foreman who had slurred my religion. "What do you want? I have a note you were fired yesterday," he said curtly.

"That was yesterday," I replied. "Forget the memo. Read this letter instead."

He peeled open the envelope, read Goldfogle's letter, looked up and said, "I wish I had someone looking out after me like that. Please tell the Congressman I'll work things out."

I spent the next two years doing cleaner, less arduous chores than the ones assigned the previous morning. In 1921, when the Republicans reoccupied the White House, post offices all over the land passed into their hands, along with less important matters such as foreign policy and defense. I have no doubt that the man who replaced me was a loyal, reliable Harding supporter.

Like many another good Democrat, Congressman Goldfogle was swept out of office during that 1920 turnover. Of course no Re-publican licked him. Only Socialist London could do that.

Goldfogle had been a colorful neighborhood fixture since the last decades of the nineteenth century. Once, as a judge, he heard a case involving a gentile landlord and his bearded Jewish tenant. The dispute concerned a flimsy, wooden, leave-covered succoth (or shack). The tenant had erected it in the tenement yard as part of the time-honored ritual in observance of the autumn harvest holiday. "It is a fire hazard," charged the landlord, "and I want it removed!"

"You are absolutely right," agreed Judge Goldfogle. Facing the accused, he warned, "If that succoth is not torn down in eight days, I am going to fine you."

The landlord smiled smugly in victory. The tenant meekly accepted the decision. Few saw the judge and the tenant exchange knowing winks, however, as the participants left the courtroom. Both knew the succoth festivities would end within eight days and the shack would be torn down anyway. Justice had been served and everyone was pleased.

His Honor moved on to Congress shortly after this Solomon-like verdict was reached. His biennial up-and-down rivalry with Meyer London provided the Lower East Side with some of its most exciting political episodes. I have no doubt that Goldfogle could have returned to Congress in 1922 if he had wished to do so. But, by that time, he had been appointed to a more responsible city post, President of the Board of Taxes and Assessments.

The close of 1920 marked the end of an era on the Lower East Side as well as in Washington. On December 20, John F. Ahearn died quietly in his home after a long illness. The death of few Hebrew sages could have occasioned more widespread mourning in our overwhelmingly Jewish district than the passing of this Irish politician. Women wept, peddlers turned over their pushcarts, stores closed, black crepe was draped over fire escapes and thousands followed the funeral cortege. Prayers were heard at more than one synagogue for this devout Catholic.

Mr. Ahearn's deeds carved his epitaph. They reflected a political and personal credo that many expressed aloud, but few followed.

"You ask me what makes for success in politics?" he once remarked. "Head and heart, I say. A political leader needs a good supply of both—but the greater need is heart. I have grown up among politicians and I have seen organizations come and go. I have participated in campaigns and I have been the standard bearer for the club that bears my name for about thirty years. I think I am able to give an opinion and it is that no man ever succeeds in politics without a big heart. It does not mean so much in his charities as it does in his humanity. Of course, every leader has to give away money. But the mass of people who follow a district leader prefer employment and fair dealing to charity.

"In our poor section of New York, we see a great deal of want. We do not parade the misfortunes of our neighbors. When we hear of a case in need, we take care of it ourselves and we do not rush off to some charitable institution and report it. We give immediate relief and look for the cause later. If the cause is due to lack of work, we look around and try to help the father or son or whoever may be the wage earner of the family.

"It is all part of our job, for we agree to take care of the people who see fit to make us their district representatives at Tammany Hall."

IV

Ahearn the Younger:
Not by Breadbaskets Alone

THROUGHOUT THE 1920s, NOSTRUMS, NOT NORMALCY, PREVAILED in New York City politics. While Warren G. Harding presided over the dissolution of Washington's integrity during the early part of the decade, James Walker awaited his turn up in the wings at Albany. His turn came in 1925, when he danced onto the City Hall stage.

By that time, the rest of the nation had already cooled off with Coolidge. So Jimmy had the spotlight to himself. He certainly made the most of it. I sometimes wonder, though, whether the hanky-panky under our town's Beau Brummell would have smelled so badly under the shadow of Teapot Dome. Republican sins had been quickly forgotten. Democratic wrongdoing never seems to fade away.

The physique of Tammany Hall, more than the rest of the body politic, suffered near-fatal wounds during those chaotic years. As the ever-witty Walker put it, the Hall's "brains" were buried in Calvary Cemetery after Charles F. Murphy's death in 1924.

Party factionalism, fractionalism and feudalism followed "Boss" Murphy's passing. By the end of the decade, the Democratic organizations in other boroughs would no longer be Tammany fiefs. Even within the island of Manhattan itself, district chiefs would form protective clusters and issue virtual Declarations of Independence from the county leadership.

By 1929, a group centered around our own Edward J. Ahearn would gather strength—but not quite enough—to take control of the Hall. Less than two votes in Tammany's Executive Committee, whose membership consisted of district leaders from throughout the borough, would separate us from victory. Instead, power was destined to pass into the hands of a small, starchy old-timer of narrow gauge mind, who, in the next five years, would lead the party to the wreckage heap.

Eddy Ahearn's political career was meteoric. In 1921, he was just a wiry, sandy-haired, youthful looking thirty-year-old. Yet, within the fourteen years of life left him, he would inherit his father's district leadership, cement his control of the Lower East Side, mold it into the core of Tammany's strongest sub-group, take part in a bitter intra-party scuffle for power, lose it by a hair's breadth, find his club shorn of patronage, hang on, recover, see his opponents tottering over the brink of their own corrupt ineptness, and snatch at almost certain victory just as the shroud of death veiled his eyes.

Like his father, Eddy grew up on the Lower East Side, lived politics and considered the district leadership post as one of awesome responsibility rather than one of grand opportunity. His one private ambition, he never managed to accomplish—that of vindicating his father's memory by election to the Borough Presidency.

Born June 15, 1891, he attended Public School 147 across the street from his home and the clubhouse. He went on to high school, then began his political education. Perhaps more than his father, Eddy enjoyed the give and take of politics.

"It's a game," he said. "It has its rules. Ever since I was knee-high to a grasshopper, I have been familiar with politics. I was associated with dad and learned the ropes from him . . . You see, it's heredity. I've had the help of the boys who went to school and grew up with me. They pitched in and helped.

"There's a lot to politics. It's a science. But it was dad who built up the organization and we're just carrying on."

The fact that Eddy quietly received the scepter and crown of the John F. Ahearn Association with ease was the result of more than heredity. There could have been a bitter squabble for control. Other districts went through such transitions with spasms of malice and long-lasting wounds. This did not happen here, and much credit belongs to Barney Downing, State Senator, confidant of Eddy's father and the man who wielded authority while the elder Ahearn lay dying. The Senator could have made a contest for the district's leadership. But he chose not to, for the sake of the club's unity.

Barney Downing was already of voting age when Eddy was born. In many ways, he was the most influential man in the Fourth Assembly District. Like the elder Ahearn, he demanded and deserved respect. Also like the elder Ahearn, he always kept his word. It was his bond. Downing was a hard liver and a hard drinker. But he was an honest and honorable man.

"Barney Downing is the only Irishman who ever curses in front of me and gets away with it," Father Byrnes, one-time police department chaplain and head of St. Mary's Church, once complained to me.

"So why don't you threaten to get him thrown out of the State Senate?" I asked him. "That would teach him a lesson."

Father Byrnes winked. "Oh, I wouldn't do a thing like that," he said. "Barney's too old to mend his ways. Besides, my Jewish friends would kill me."

Everyone liked the Senator. Around the neighborhood, he was our "Irish-Jewish legislator"—and Father Byrnes was our "Jewish priest." Both lived to ripe old ages and were able servants of the Lower East Side.

Downing became known as a humorist in the State Senate. He introduced quaint conservation measures, such as one to protect bullfrogs. But he was also a competent legislator and a close associate of Governor Alfred E. Smith. On more than one occasion, Smith's chauffeur-driven limousine pulled up in front of the Ahearn club and discharged its sole passenger, the Senator. He climaxed his career in Albany as the Senate's minority leader, replacing Jimmy Walker when Beau James moved on to City Hall.

Together with Henry S. Schimmel and Aaron J. Levy, Downing formed the triumvirate of professors who prepared Eddy for his political diploma. The younger Ahearn did not need much tutoring. He was a born politician.

Downing usually accompanied Eddy on his trips up to Tammany Hall or down to City Hall. During those early months, the aging "Boss" Murphy still held court at Tammany's Fourteenth Street citadel. His austere throne room was no place for a youthful, recently-elevated district leader to venture alone.

Downtown, at City Hall, John Francis Hylan still reigned, and occasionally ruled. A dull, plodding official with a flaming red mustache, "Red Mike" fought bankers, transit companies, reformers, his own Board of Estimate and the whole British Empire with equal ferocity. He was a well-meaning man but he found the tasks of the Mayor's office a bit baffling and drifted aimlessly.

At the Municipal Building, Downing, with Eddy in tow, would march into various departments. Surveying whatever office they were in, the Senator would point to an empty, obviously unused desk and ask, "Who works there?"

"It's . . . ah . . . unoccupied at the moment," was the usual response by an uneasy official.

"Well," Downing would announce, "tomorrow I'm sending down a man from my clubhouse. Put him to work."

Commissioners occasionally winced when they received word that Barney was in the building. They knew he did not come around for social calls. He wanted jobs for his people.

Eddy once told close friends the story of a journey he took with Downing to the inner sanctum of Grover Whalen. Later in his long, flamboyant public career, Whalen would steward the fortunes of the Police Department and milk that semi-military post for all the publicity he could squeeze. In that exalted role, by grace of Jimmy Walker, he would surround himself in a regal aura. His private quarters at 240 Centre Street would be furnished with luxurious mahogany, blue carpet and a bronze equestrian statuette of Napoleon. Pompous glory indeed lay ahead for this splendidly mustached dignitary.

At the moment, however, Whalen was merely Commissioner of Plants and Structures in Hylan's regime. This was far from an exalted position. But it was one garbed in wreaths of patronage.

Downing stopped before the receptionist's desk and asked to see the Commissioner. Whalen sent back word he was busy conferring with colleagues. Barney and Eddy therefore cooled their heels in the anteroom. Minutes passed. They heard no voices in the inner office, so they asked the receptionist to remind Whalen of their presence.

"Is the Commissioner still busy?" Downing inquired.

"Yes, he is," was the reply. "You can't go in."

The pair sat down again. More minutes passed. Finally, as the clock ticked away, Barney lost patience. Ignoring the receptionist, who had buried his head in a stack of papers, the Senator barged in unannounced.

There sat Whalen, alone, flower in his lapel, feet on his desk, carefully manicuring his fingernails.

"Why, Barney, it's good to . . ." said the startled Commissioner.

"Senator to you," interrupted Downing.

"I'm sorry I didn't know it was you," apologized Whalen. "What can I do for you? Do you want something?"

"Nothing!" snapped the Senator, spitting in the Commissioner's face to emphasize his contempt. Downing then turned around and briskly walked out.

Somehow, Whalen never found room to relate this incident in his modestly titled autobiography, *Mr. New York.*

When a district leader in the 'twenties made an odyssey to City Hall, his usual intention was neither to fight it nor exercise his right of petition. Rather, it was to insist on his right to munch on a few minor patronage plums.

The really big appointive jobs, of course, were handled by Murphy uptown on Fourteenth Street. So, too, were the nominations for practically all elective offices, especially those crossing the boundaries of two or more assembly districts. The Tammany leader arbitrated the conflicting claims of his district lieutenants to state court judgeships and seats in Congress. Selections for small constituency posts such as State Assemblyman and Alderman (later City Councilman), which usually fell within the jurisdiction of one district, were the prerogative of its leader.

Murphy made it clear, however, that district chiefs would be held responsible for the men they suggested and for their subsequent behavior in office. The same held true for appointed officials.

Had Murphy lived another decade, crusader Samuel Seabury might have passed through a quiet, legally productive life in relative obscurity.

Downtown, to the quaint masterpiece of colonial architecture that has been the working address of Mayors for a century and a half, leaders made their frequent pilgrimages. They eagerly sought to snap up little jobs for their home districts—jobs that were too small to concern Murphy. Unfortunately, patronage has all too often been considered a dirty word. It was far from an evil term depicting a sinister device. Patronage was a necessary organ of the political body.

Bear in mind that political activity then was no weekend form of recreation, designed to replace gardening when fall set in. For many captains in our teeming district, it was a daytime, nighttime, full-time chore, exhausting no matter how exhilarating. It demanded body and soul and far more than a forty-hour week. A city payroll job did not mean leisure for these workers. It meant a living could be assured while they did their more important job, one that has since been taken over by bureaucratic agencies at perhaps two or three times the expense—and probably with half the efficiency. In an age when the prevailing attitude of government was "hands off" towards social problems, to whom else could the poor turn besides their Tammany captain?

Logically, the district leaders who produced the greatest turnout on every Election Day should have gotten the most jobs. But infighting was always rough. There were 23 Assembly Districts in the 1920s, and, with splits because of state legislative reapportionments, 35 leaders. After Murphy's death, court favorites harvested the juicier fruits, no matter what their political merit. Others were left with the stems.

By all that was politically holy, the Fourth Assembly District should have been granted the largest possible slice of patronage. Year after year, it won recognition as Tammany's "Banner District". The neighborhood our club served, cluttered with tenements, was probably the most crowded in the Western World. It gave way only to the teeming slums of Asian cities. And it would produce an overwhelming majority for almost any candidate on the Democratic ticket.

Eddy Ahearn worked hard for his captains, just as he expected his captains to work hard for their constituents. Once he got word that a note he had scribbled on behalf of a captain had been torn up right before the man's eyes by a bureaucrat at the Municipal Building. Eddy was furious. He dropped everything, dashed down to the city's "capitol", and stormed into the office of the offending bureau chief.

"If you can't make good on a contract, that's one thing," he said. "If you don't want to carry out a contract, you may have your reasons and I'll listen to them. But when you tear up a contract in front of my man's face, that's an insult to him and it's an insult to me!"

On that note, Eddy, who learned well his lesson from Barney Downing, spat at the shaking executive, about-faced and strutted out.

I don't think Eddy ever weighed more than 120 pounds. But he was no political featherweight. Titles meant nothing to him. He did not stand in awe of nameplates or other symbols of civic authority or prestige. (I know of only one other case, however, when he actually spat in a man's face. On the receiving end, that time, was Mayor Jimmy Walker, himself. The gesture soured their relations for many years—to the detriment, as we shall see, of both men.)

After his brief apprenticeship under Downing, Schimmel and Levy, Eddy clearly took command. He quickly earned the respect of old-timers despite his youth. He judged all comers on their individual worth and everyone got a fair shake.

Book learning was no royal road to success in Eddy's domain. Not that he had anything against erudite young lawyers. He just felt they often made poor captains. Too many carried chips on their shoulders. They looked down on the people they served. Ringing doorbells, climbing tenement staircases and mingling with the masses soiled their dignity. Fresh out of law school, their diplomas' ink barely dry, they could probably quote Blackstone from cover to cover. But they lacked common sense and the common touch.

These rarely lasted long at the club. No doubt, some built up fat private practices, relocated on Park Avenue, joined Good Government Leagues and, without leaving their swank surroundings, worked out eleborate schemes to help the slum-dwellers. It is easier to be a pillar of a community than it is to shovel crunched rock.

Counselors around the clubhouse were necessary, nonetheless. Many ordinary constituent problems—dispossesses, landlord-tenant disputes, minor transgressions of local ordinances—had to be settled in court. Legal aid required legal minds.

None should get the impression, however, that the John F. Ahearn Association was a clearing house for criminals. Far from it. If a shattered couple sought aid for their youngster, guilty of a first offence, and it was obvious that hiring a lawyer would make a deep slash in their savings, we would help. But Eddy would never truck the likes of narcotic peddlers, procurers or gunmen. Maybe they found "protection" in other Tammany circles. But they spotted no welcome mat in front of 290 East Broadway.

One notch below these offenders, in Eddy's view, ranked the captain who misused his position of trust. I remember a complaining call Eddy got from a district leader in another section of the city.

"Listen, Eddy," said the voice on the phone, "one of my voters says a captain of yours shook him down for ten dollars last week."

"Who was it and how did it happen?" asked Eddy.

"Here's the story just the way I heard it," the caller said. "Your man's name is ———————— and he works for the buildings department as an inspector . . ."

"Yes, I know," Eddy interrupted. "I put him there a few years back myself."

The leader reeled off the details while Eddy bit his lip. Immediately after the phone had been clicked back in place, the offending captain was summoned. He readily admitted his petty extortion. Confronted with the easily proven details, he had no choice. After a tongue-lashing, he was sent packing.

On another occasion, Eddy similarly blew his top at an erring lieutenant. During the depression, three club members lost their posts and their income. In order to tide them over the lean weeks, collections were made from the area's elected and appointed officials. Each man's dues amounted to a few dollars and the contributions poured in unbegrudgingly.

Eddy turned over the distribution chore to one of his closer lieutenants. "See that the three captains get forty dollars apiece every week till they're back on their feet," he instructed.

Several weeks passed. Their unemployment continued, and so did the dole. In the course of a conversation one afternoon, Eddy asked one of the recipients, who had a large family, whether he could make ends meet on forty dollars a week.

"I'm satisfied with all you've done for me," the man assured him, "but why do you say 'forty' dollars? I've been getting thirty a week all along."

"Thirty?" questioned Eddy.

"Yes," the captain answered. "————has been giving me that amount at the end of each week."

Flushed with anger, Eddy called upon the other two captains. They related the same story. Each thanked him for the aid, then corrected his figure by ten dollars.

The detective work over, Eddy turned on his distributing agent in language that fitted the occasion but not the printed page.

"What do you mean, you ———— pocketing ten dollars off the top for yourself!" scolded Eddy. "You have a $95 a week clerkship and you're not worth half that. Still, you have to go out and take the bread from your neighbor's mouth."

Eddy was concerned with retribution as well as punishment. He made certain that every nickel was redirected along its proper course.

There are bad apples in every crate. These two incidents, thank goodness, were not typical occurrences. But they were typical of Eddy's reaction whenever he suspected something underhanded was going on at his clubhouse. No shakedowns were tolerated. No rake-offs were permitted. No jobs were sold. That was all the more reason why no disgruntled clique ever arose in Eddy's district, as they did in other Tammany corners where leaders winked at such practices—or even blatantly conducted them.

During the soaring height of the Jazz Age, Eddy was offered a $10,000 a year plum to give one of his followers. The plum was a soothing peace offering at a time of intra-party strife. It was the type of job most district chiefs would have gobbled up with relish. And not a few of them would have bartered it rather than have given it away.

But not Eddy. He refused the offer with thanks and a suggestion. "I'd much rather you give me five $2,000 a year jobs, not one $10,000 handout," he said. "My people aren't sharing much in this prosperity and I'd like to make five little fish and their families happy instead of bloating up one big fish."

As for himself, money meant little. I noted earlier that neither Eddy nor his father died rich. Once, $46,000 was raised through advertising in a journal for Eddy's testimonial dinner. Not a penny of it slipped into his own pocket. And neither was the money used for the campaign funds of local Democratic candidates. Every cent was spent on the neighborhood's poor. These were the people who could not afford to buy ads or attend fund-raising affairs. But they were the fibres of Eddy's political muscle, and Eddy knew it.

Somehow, the much publicized prosperity of the 1920s never trickled down to the slums of the Lower East Side. Although federal legislation was bringing an end to the steady stream of immigrants that filled the area, the last waves were still groping their way about. As in the case of their predecessors, only the vicarious thrills of the movies or a streetcar ride up to the bright showcase of Broadway provided a hasty glimpse into the Good Life.

Some of the older residents, however, were making their way into the middle class. Occasionally, we were asked for a favor by a voter not tottering on the brink of poverty. One disadvantage in dealing with the well-to-do, we discovered, was that they often showed less gratitude than the poor. More important, they showed less understanding of our work.

Such constituents, unfortunately, never seemed to realize the effort we put into fulfilling contracts. The case of a young doctor, still unaccustomed to his suffix, "M.D.," is typical. He had just finished medical school with high grades and was no doubt quite bright. Otherwise, he could not have waded through four tough years of training with honors.

But now, diploma in hand, he sought entrance into one of the city's most highly regarded hospitals. His goal was indeed steep. And he tackled his task with abandon. That is, he abandoned the task to us.

Eddy had never personally met the lad. He acted solely on the say-so of a club captain, who had grown up with the boy's father. Over a period of several days, Eddy tried to arrange the appointment by phone call after phone call. It was not easy, and Eddy handled all the details himself.

Finally, when success seemed near, he gave instructions for the young doctor to come to the club. The meeting was set for eight o'clock on a mid-week evening, a night not normally set aside for conferences with constituents. Eddy, another captain and I waited as the minutes ticked by. Twenty minutes. Thirty minutes. An hour. He did not show up all evening.

We called his home. There was no answer. Could he have suffered an accident? What else could keep him away from the club on such an important night? After all, his future was at stake.

The next day, we got the answer. Bright and early—I shall give him credit at least for that much—he called his captain.

"Sorry about last night," he said. "My girl had tickets to a show she's wanted to see all season. Naturally, I couldn't let her go alone. When can we make another appointment with Mr. Ahearn?"

The captain, normally an even-keeled individual, nearly flipped. "What a nerve!" he told me later. "The kid stood Eddy up all night because of a girl friend. Here his bread and butter is at stake and he goes off to the theatre on a date. He didn't even have sense enough to call and let us know what he was up to."

"What do you want to do next?" I asked.

"Well, I'm certainly not going to tell Eddy what happened," said the still seething captain. "He'd blow his top even higher than I did."

My friend's judgment was unchallengeable. So we spent the next fifteen minutes figuring out a serious, but short-lived, malady that we could retroactively inflict upon the young doctor. The acceptable answer was pneumonia. We rescheduled the appointment, and Eddy, I am certain, never did find out the real cause for the postponement.

Midpoint in the seductive decade of the 1920s, Tammany Hall was shaken by the death of Charles Francis Murphy. The summer of 1924 was Tammany's crisis point.

Like the Roman Empire's system of law and order, Murphy's firmness cemented together the whole unwieldy mass of New York City's political life. No sooner was he buried than the Dark Ages descended over Tammany's domain.

This veil of darkness has never lifted. There have been many reformations since Murphy's passing, but, except for the DeSapio era, never anything resembling a renaissance.

As any standard history textbook will remind you, the fall of the Roman Empire led to a disintegration of authority. Across the breadth of Europe, universal order ceased to exist. Local rulers became little Caesars, obeying no one. Alliances formed and faltered. Allegiances were sometimes sworn to overlords in distant castles. But these were mere gestures more often than not.

So, too, did the Tammany Empire fall apart. Fourteenth Street, the traditional seat of power, became just another city thoroughfare. District leaders were on their own. They followed no one and nothing but the dictates of their own consciences. And, in the absence of conscience, some followed the counsel of their pocketbooks, instead.

Across the Harlem and East Rivers, the Bronx and Brooklyn Democratic organizations set out to carve their own paths, just as the lands across the English Channel and Mediterranean Sea had, in ages past, cut themselves off from the affairs of continental Europe. Edward J. Flynn, the Bronx leader, and John H. McCooey, the Brooklyn chief, were not prepared to take orders from the likes of George W. Olvany, who now assumed the reigns, but never the mastery, of the Tammany Tiger.

Immediately after Murphy's death, a committee of seven senior members had formed a caretaker regime. Past experience had shown the inadequacy of government by committee. So Surrogate Judge James A. Foley, a distinguished juror and son-in-law of the late boss, was offered the leadership. He turned it down, preferring to stay on the bench.

General Sessions Judge George W. Olvany entertained no such instinct of restraint. He leaped at the opportunity.

When Olvany first doffed his black robes and tried on Murphy's shoes, he seemed, in size at least, capable of fitting into them. He was 48 years old, six-foot-two and a 200 pounder. The press described him as being "in the prime of life and, judging from outward appearances, the embodiment of physical and mental vigor and alertness."

Well-educated, austere, even distant, Olvany was also acclaimed as the embodiment of a "New Tammany." Over the next five years, he would prove that what is new is not always good. Articulate and academically trained, he seemed disdainful of his less educated associates and frequently dealt with them at arms length.

No one in politics, especially a district leader, would accept this "brighter-than-thou" treatment. It is easily understandable, therefore, why few tears were shed when he suddenly announced his resignation in March, 1929—for reasons of health, he said. District leaders did not drop to bended knees and beg him to remain.

The Judge did well for himself and his law firm. It prospered admirably during his tenure. But he did not do nearly as well for Al Smith in his bid for the Presidency.

One of Olvany's few memorable contributions to municipal affairs took place at the debut of his regime. At that time, he accepted Governor Smith's motion to cast the bland Hylan aside in the 1925 Mayoralty race. James J. Walker, the sparkling State Senate Democratic leader, was substituted in his place.

Hylan, a representative of Brooklyn, and McCooey, his county chief, did not surrender meekly. Instead, Hylan entered the primary, waged a bitter campaign and tried to prove he deserved a second term. But he was beaten severely. In our Fourth Assembly District, 98.5% of enrolled Democrats voted. Of the ballots cast, the Mayor won less than 5%.

This primary contest established the course of New York City's government for the next eight years. In the November general election, Walker was opposed by a Republican fountain pen manufacturer. No burning issues captured the public's attention. Softly, therefore, Frank Waterman did as all good Republicans are supposed to do in normal city elections. He lost.

Perhaps more than any other Democratic Mayor, Walker treated the patronage claims of the Fourth Assembly District shabbily. Especially during his second term, we were left bone dry. Yet none of us ever really hated him. No one could. Certainly not the voters. Despite his obvious shortcomings, it would have been interesting to see how he would have fared against Fiorello La-Guardia in 1933, 1937 or 1941. In their first duel in 1929, Walker won by an even wider margin than that by which he had blotted out Waterman.

Jimmy Walker was no fool, though at times he acted like a court jester rather than a chief executive. He grew up under genteel circumstances in Greenwich Village, spent vacations in the Catskill Mountains and studied law at New York University. His father had been a Tammany Alderman and an associate of the elder Ahearn.

At first, the young Walker preferred song-writing to politics. Only in 1909, when he was already a ripened 28, did he turn to a public career. That year he won election to the State Assembly, where his wit, self-assurance, urbanity and undeniable intelligence attracted the attention of Charles Murphy and the friendship of Al Smith. A vigorous supporter of home-rule and social welfare measures, Walker moved up to the State Senate in 1914 and soon became Democratic minority leader there.

Now, after sixteen years labor as a legislator, he was Mayor of the City of New York. And he set out to enjoy it.

It is not that Beau James did not take to hard work. He merely held a different conception of a chief executive's functions than they teach at schools of public administration. Just try taking in 100 banquets and luncheons across the country in a thirty day period. That is work, all right. A man cannot earn a reputation as his city's "Good Will Ambassador" by sitting still behind a desk all day.

Walker also earned a reputation as New York City's "Nighttime Mayor." In some circles, this was considered a charge rather than an honorable title. Let the record on this matter be set straight.

This, remember, was in the days before air conditioning was installed at City Hall to cool the brain on long, hot summer days. I believe it is widely accepted now that the decision-making process is numbed by heat and high humidity. Walker, though no psychologist, realized this. He rightfully left sunlight chores in his sticky office to subordinates. By evening, he could conduct the city's affairs at more roomy surroundings, cooled by the night air. Anyone who needed him could easily reach the Mayor at the Central Park Casino or Madison Square Garden, where a man could truly breathe more freely and think more clearly.

Walker subscribed to the widely-held belief that the government which governs least governs best. While later investigations proved that his "live and let live" policy had been converted by some subordinates into a program of "steal and let steal," by no means were all of his top-level appointments misfits.

In George V. McLaughlin, New York City was blessed with one of its best Police Commissioners. I say this despite the fact that his raids on Tammany clubhouses cut off an important, painless source of revenue for many welfare activities we conducted outside official channels. This is perhaps as good a point as any to throw a few laurels to a man who was generally considered anathema to the Tammany organization.

McLaughlin, I am told, did not seek the Commissionership and was warned by friends it would bring him little but woe. At the time of his appointment, he was New York State's Superintendent of Banks, a prestigious post which he had ably filled. They said the hot seat on Centre Street could certainly add no luster to his reputation.

Nonetheless, McLaughlin accepted the thankless task. Walker's role in the appointment of his Police Commissioner was probably limited to telling McLaughlin to raise his right hand at the swearing-in ceremony. The two men proved to have little in common during their short association.

For the next fifteen months, New York City was treated to the best policing it had ever experienced. Much incompetency was swept away. Morale in the department soared. Any policeman, down to the rawest rookie, had access to his leader's dark-paneled office. Efficiency at Centre Street replaced pompous ritual.

Most important of all, crime was cut nearly in half during his regime. Shortly before his resignation, the department could report that the number of assaults and robbery cases in the city had dropped 42% from the corresponding period during the preceding year. Arrests rose for these crimes by 10%. Life was made uneasy for "fences," who purchased stolen merchandise. And holdup gangs, prospering when he took office, were broken up.

McLaughlin's eventual undoing resulted from the very independence of spirit that made him a good Commissioner. He enforced the law—all laws. Thus, he annoyed, harassed, plagued and eventually incited to revolt the one force on which the ultimate power of his immediate superior, Mayor Walker, and his sponsor, Governor Smith, rested—the district leaders of Tammany Hall.

Gambling here was illegal. The law said so. But in the very dim back rooms of many Tammany clubhouses, it flourished beneath the portraits of Democratic Mayors. The games, in most districts, were "clean." That is, they were run as legitimately as you could run an illegitimate activity.

Under preceding Commissioners, the games were quietly permitted to continue. What was sometimes described as police "protection" might more aptly have been represented as police "neutrality." The patrolmen on the beat simply did not interfere. The club's percentage from the games often was the adrenalin that invigorated the organization's financial bloodstream.

One of McLaughlin's successors later alluded to "those corrupt politicians whose safe-deposit boxes bulged with profits from gambling." This was an immense exaggeration. As I mentioned before, there are bad apples in every crate. But, for the most part, the club's share went directly into its treasury. From there it was disbursed in services for the area's constituents. The money was often put to far better use than the state's "take" from legalized gambling at local racetracks.

McLaughlin set out on a crusade to end this clubhouse sideline. Half a dozen Tammany buildings were raided. The Harry C. Perry Democratic Club in our neighboring Second Assembly District fell victim. Several nights later, Eddy advised members of the Ahearn club to "expect a visit from Commissioner McLaughlin's boys." No such visit ever materialized however. The Fourth Assembly District remained untouched.

Throughout the city, as the weeks passed, calm gave way to uncertainty, and uncertainty led to apprehension. Then came well-justified fear.

No less a figure than Peter J. McGuinness, venerable sage of Brooklyn's Greenpoint section, was arrested with forty others at his own bailiwick. In a town where this could happen, no one felt safe. McGuinness, who doubled as Alderman, solemnly proclaimed on the floor of the city's legislative chamber, "This man McLaughlin will find he's not bigger than the whole Tammany organization."

District leaders regarded the Police Commissioner as unapproachable politically and Governor Smith, his mentor at far-off Albany, as unapproachable geographically. This left Mayor Walker squarely as the man in the middle.

Protesting Tammany visitors streamed in and out of the Mayor's office, when they could catch him in, and demanded the ouster of McLaughlin. But the Mayor could not or would not anger the Governor by dropping his hand-picked choice for the Commissionership.

The conflict between Tammany Hall and City Hall continued as the weeks skipped by. Finally, under somewhat cloudy circumstances, McLaughlin departed the $10,000-a-year crisis-clad job for a well-paying post in private industry.

It was said at the time that he feared repercussions of his independent tactics would hurt Al Smith when the Governor, his friend, reached for the Presidency in 1928. If true, it was probably the only thing George V. McLaughlin had ever feared. When he left public service, Father Knickerbocker had good cause to groan.

McLaughlin never knew—and could not have cared less if he did—that he sparked a clash which dashed the relations between the Mayor and Eddy Ahearn against the rocks. (The split between the two men would last six years, until 1932. Then, in another little-known incident, the scandal-battered Mayor would call on his adversary to intercede with Governor Franklin D. Roosevelt on his behalf. And Eddy, to Walker's happy astonishment, would consent.)

The eruption occurred shortly before McLaughlin left office. It had been a customary practice of Tammany district leaders to request City Hall to occasionally have a policeman transferred into or out of their districts. The reasons were not always as sinister as some critics have hinted. In our thoroughly Yiddish neighborhood, peddlers and shopkeepers observed Saturday as their Sabbath and conducted business on Sunday. New York, at the time, had long had a Sunday "blue law", now extinct, prohibiting business on the Christian day of rest. Many pious Jews could not afford to keep their small shops closed on both their own holy day and that of the gentile community. So, technically, they became criminals for twenty-four hours each week.

Understanding patrolmen usually looked the other way. Less understanding patrolmen were transferred to other precincts. Because these changes were made through Tammany's intercession, we did not have to ask storeowners twice, at election time, to accept Democratic candidates' placards in their windows. "You can decorate my store with all the posters you want," each would say. "I welcome them. Without your help, I'd have to stay closed on a day when I do 20% of my business."

Unfortunately, the Sunday law was undefendable rather than unenforceable. When George McLaughlin became Police Commissioner, transfers of policemen, be they patrolmen or inspectors, could no longer be obtained by district leaders. The number of tickets and fines soared. Down to the clubhouse trooped complaining shopkeepers. "What can you do?" one spokesman asked Eddy. "If we can't stay open on Sunday, we can't make a profit. And if we can't make a profit, we won't be able to stay open at all. We'll have to close our shutters and go out of business."

So down to Mayor Walker's office trooped Eddy Ahearn. He related the story and asked for action. "These are my people," he said. "I don't want to let them down and I don't intend to let you let them down."

The Mayor, always eager to escape responsibility, feigned helplessness. There was nothing he could do, he said. McLaughlin took no orders from City Hall. And he would tolerate no interference by City Hall.

"You're still the Mayor," Eddy reminded him. But Walker remained unbudged. Eddy then pointed to gripes from other district leaders, some admittedly less noble in motive.

The irritated Mayor, whose characteristic charm now momentarily deserted him, snapped, "Look, Al Smith put McLaughlin here. Let Al Smith pull him out."

With that comment, the Mayor sought to wash his hands of the matter and close the conversation. Eddy boiled over with rage. Rising from his chair, he spat in Walker's face and angrily left the office of the city's flabbergasted chief executive.

This one moment of disgust and contempt cost Eddy dearly during Walker's remaining years in office. The affable Jimmy, by no means the vindictive type, barred Eddy's path to the leadership of Tammany Hall in 1929. He also stopped completely the flow of our district's share of City Hall patronage.

Unwittingly, however, he thereby left Eddy's name free from the long scrolls of scandal in the late 'twenties and early 'thirties. Eddy's name suffered no dishonor during those bleak years. He escaped with nary a scratch, and remained one of the few uncorrupted Tammany chiefs with whom Governor Roosevelt would still sit down and talk.

Except for the McLaughlin period, relations between the police and the clubhouse were usually amiable, or at least amicable. That is, if you discount one night's dragnet as a fiction straight out of the Keystone Cops.

It happened on a Monday or Thursday, the two evenings when large crowds milled around the clubhouse building, standing, sitting on the stoop, talking, listening, socializing. A rookie patrolman, unfamiliar with the neighborhood but well versed in the

departmental rule book, ordered the group to disperse. Some
laughed. Apparently no one pointed out the Ahearn Association
sign in front of the building. Or, perhaps, someone did, and he
did not grasp its significance. In any event, the patrolman warned
he would run several men over to the station house as "examples"
unless they got off the street.

They did not leave—and he was a man of his word. The surprised night sergeant at the Clinton Street Precinct probably never
played host to a more distinguished delegation of lawbreakers than
the one that appeared before him that night. Included were a
Congressman, a State Assemblyman, several judicial figures, club
officers and a sprinkling of some of the best legal minds in the
area. It was something less than an auspicious occasion.

The night sergeant proved himself a diplomat as well as a gentleman. No formal charges, of course, were preferred. But everyone was sentenced to an evening of embarrassment.

Throughout the 1920s, New York City was blessed with not one,
but two, police forces. The second, and smaller of the two, had a
very specific job—to turn the city into an alcoholic desert. This
was no easy task, for, during the era of Prohibition, this metropolis was about as dry as the Amazon rainforest.

The federal Prohibition agents, or "revenuers" as they were
called, had their work clearly cut out for them throughout Tammany's domain. All sorts of hindrances, especially public hostility,
hampered their work. Enforcing the Volstead Act became an art
as well as a police science. Its practitioners certainly grabbed their
share of the headlines.

Few, though, attained the brilliance of performance achieved
by the team of Einstein and Smith, more popularly known as Izzy
and Moe. Izzy Einstein grew up on Ridge Street, barely a block
from my father's store. Some talented Lower East Side youngsters
became comedians. Others became policemen. But Izzy was unique. He combined the two trades in a manner never duplicated
before or since. He became a clown with a badge.

Everyone needs a push, and I believe Izzy got his from John
F. Ahearn, who probably never imagined the heights his young
constituent would one day reach. Izzy liked to call himself "Pro-

hibition Agent Number One." I do not believe he was ever challenged for that title. His partner Moe Smith, might have thought it a bit presumptuous of him. If so, he said nothing—at least to me.

Izzy and Moe went about the business of harassing our city's illegal liquor trade, using clever camouflage in their work. They assumed a multitude of disguises. Few actors had wardrobes as varied. And Lon Chaney, the acknowledged master of make-up, might have learned a trick or two by observing their techniques.

Izzy, for example, posed as a common laborer one day and a bearded fiddler the next. The third day might find him in the role of a grave digger, while the fourth might see him as an iceman or fisherman. Once, he even took on the role of an opera singer. But whatever his disguise, Izzy's purpose was the same—to foil those lawbreakers who sold and drank beverages with a stronger kick than ginger ale.

On occasion, Izzy and Moe sneaked beyond the city limits and took up the cudgel of law enforcement on foreign soil—places such as Michigan, for example. I happened to be in Detroit one day when I heard the fellows were penned up in a hotel there with gunmen watching the exits. Everyone is entitled to an off-day, and I guess this was theirs. Later, I asked Izzy about the incident.

"Why didn't you come over to the hotel, Louis, and see us?" Izzy inquired.

"Do you think I wanted to risk getting killed," I answered.

"Oh, we weren't in any real danger," said Izzy. "At least I don't think we were . . . Then again, they did have real guns. Maybe you're right. It never would happen like that in New York."

Their assailants probably did not know too much about Izzy and Moe out in the Middle West. Putting bullet holes through them would have been downright indecent, if not criminal.

At times, the pair made mistakes in Manhattan, too, and raided the wrong stills. But the penalties they paid were usually mild— such as rolling the beer barrels up a ramp into the warehouse. This caused them a lot of perspiration and a little embarrassment. But not much embarrassment, since no one involved wanted to see an item, complete with addresses, leaked to the press.

For the most part, Izzy placed discretion above valor in his own neighborhood. He let the "Great Experiment" sizzle and fizzle on its own in the Lower East Side.

Not nearly so cautious was another Prohibition agent, named Greenfield. He was an out-of-towner with no roots in this area. Usually, he swooped down on establishments that Izzy and Moe managed to miss. Though he never achieved their fame and lacked their flamboyance, he was a prickly thorn in the side of many a Volstead Act sinner.

One day he raided a restaurant next to my father's store. Its owner, a shifty character, did not intend to remain the victim for long. He was a master at the art of slipping out of tight situations, liquid or otherwise. And he did not particularly care whom he dragged in as a replacement.

It so happened that among the alcoholic loot seized in his basement, under the main floor, were barrels of California wine. The restaurant proprietor eagerly disowned them. He volunteered the information that the barrels belonged to none other than Rabbi David Frankel, patriarch of our Attorney Street synagogue.

It was well-known that rabbis could purchase, by license, limited quantities of wine for use by their congregations on special occasions. With the Passover season approaching this was such an occasion. Unfortunately, the storeowner saw fit to embellish his tale a bit, hoping to thrust the entire illegal cache on the rabbi's broad shoulders. Who would prosecute a rabbi? he figured.

Rabbi Frankel was summoned by federal alcoholic authorities to their office, where his license was revoked. It brought on a crisis. Where would the congregation get its wine for the annual Passover ritual? Rabbi Frankel called my father, and my father called me.

"What can I do, pop?" I said. "This is a federal matter. My connection with Tammany can't help. It might even hurt. I don't know the people handling the matter. They're all Republicans from out-of-town."

At the time, I had not yet met Sam Koenig, New York County's GOP leader. If I had, I am sure it would not have mattered one whit. The chief Prohibition administrator in the city, E. C. Yellowley, was politically unapproachable. Mississippi-reared, with a slow

Southern drawl and tortoise-shell glasses, Yellowley had been a federal agent since 1899. In those days, a revenuer could get shot by mountain folk who regarded their stills as cherished possessions. Yellowley had come a long way since those buckshot-filled days.

At my father's insistence, I accompanied Rabbi Frankel to the federal Prohibition office in the old Marshall Field Building on Broadway. We had no appointment, for had I asked for one, we might have been turned down. It was a risk worth avoiding. So we dropped in unannounced.

As secretaries are trained to do, Yellowley's tried to detour us to an underling's office. This was expected, but we insisted on seeing the chief anyway. So she let us wait. On returning to his office from a conference downstairs, he told her to send us right in, appointment or not.

The rabbi outlined the details leading up to his loss of the permit. Then the Prohibition administrator turned to me. "What's your interest in this matter?" he asked.

I told him of my father's concern for the congregation and their need for wine at this time of the year.

"What did you do during the war?" he asked next.

I told him of my brief career in the United States Navy.

Yellowley then turned again to the rabbi. "Today is Friday. If you don't get the permit in the mail by Monday, tell Mr. Eisenstein. He'll tell me and I'll see that you get it without any further delay."

The matter was thus successfully resolved.

I have often found that the bigger a man is, the more approachable he is. Small bureaucrats hide beneath their secretaries' skirts and bask in solitude behind closed doors. Yellowley was a big man, whatever his politics, a man to be admired.

The ten year spree of the 1920s earned the title, in some quarters, as "The Lawless Decade". On the whole, however, despite prohibition, racketeering, "big name" criminals and constant charges of Tammany meddling in police affairs, the average city street was a much safer place to walk down than it is today. The night certainly held less terror. Criminals may have been better "organized" during that period. But how many of us, old enough to remember, prefer the "unorganized" crime—senseless murders, rapes and muggings—of the 1960s?

Four teeming decades ago, the average patrolman on the beat received far more respectful obedience from the average citizen. And he faced far less personal danger from the average criminal. His shiny badge provided all the authority he needed. The general level of law enforcement was certainly not lowered by Tammany Hall to the extent pictured by reformers and publicists.

Indeed, the Tammany Tiger was far too busy devouring its own reputation. This was not apparent, however, until the grim dawn of the depression cut short the span of its political prosperity. Even while Tammany Hall's foundations were being gnawed away by undisclosed corruption, poor leadership and aimless drifting, the organization appeared outwardly safe, sound and secure. New York County had a Tammany Borough President, New York City had a Tammany Mayor and New York State had a Tammany Governor, whose well-deserved popularity might soon make him the first Tammany President of the United States.

The glowing Tiger, softly purring under its "New Tammany" label, with a college man on its back, seemed anything but what it really was—a sick cat. Even the Fourteenth Street structure, where Charles F. Murphy labored twenty silent years re-establishing the "Old Tammany's" lost respectability, was discarded. Since the laying of its cornerstone on a fair day in 1867, the building had become an historic landmark, where toiled both political wise men and political thieves. Now, at the dizzy height of success, Tammany deserted it for a new, more spacious "wigwam" five blocks away at Union Square and Seventeenth Street. Within two decades, this structure, too, would be vacated. But for a far different reason—financial insolvency. Who could have dreamed at the time, however, that the passing of Murphy would sound the death knell for the Hall?

During the season for candidate selecting, I recall attending a session at the luxurious Union Square quarters with Eddy. District leaders pressed vigorously for their personal choices. It even seemed to me that several with conflicting claims might come to actual blows.

"Aw, don't worry, Louis," whispered Eddy, "this is just window dressing. The men were picked last week. As a matter of fact, the showcards are already printed. Do you want to see them?"

Relations with the Republicans were amicable throughout most of the 1920s. Since 1911, the Republicans had been led by the Honorable Samuel S. Koenig. To both his own party members and Democrats alike, he was addressed respectfully, not fearfully, as "Boss". A neat, trim man with rimless spectacles, he was one of those rare leaders without a trace of ruthlessness. Koenig was blessed with a long, useful life, and it was during his later years that I knew him well and treasured his friendship.

The "Boss" was a Tammany man in the best sense of the word. He did not join the Tammany organization, however, because he was repulsed by some of its less admirable traits during his youth. The stench of Boss Tweed's work still hung low over the city in 1872, the year of Sam's birth in far-off Austria-Hungary. Growing up on New York's Lower East Side, he watched the still youthful Charles F. Murphy, a few blocks north in the Gas House District, doggedly carving out a political empire.

Young Sam found the give-and-take of public life exciting. But he chose to follow an extraordinary course for a Lower East Side boy. He became a Republican. At 18, he stumped from carts in support of J. Sloat Fassett, the Grand Old Party's nominee for Governor in 1891. And shortly after the turn of the century, he founded his own clubhouse.

Miracle of miracles, Sam carried his assembly district, the now outdated Sixteenth, in 1904, sent a Republican to the State Assembly and gave Theodore Roosevelt a majority. One ultimate consequence of this act of blasphemy was his elevation to the leadership of New York County's Republicans several years later. At the time, Sam had not yet passed his fortieth birthday.

Through much of his long reign, Koenig's politics were out of tune with those of the national Republicans. His district could not care less about high tariffs, low tariffs, business government and the capitalistic ethic. The soundness of the dollar interested them, but not nearly as much as the accessibility of the half-dollar, or quarter, for that matter. Sam understood New York, especially his corner of it, and he understood that the principles of McKinley would haul away our problems about as aptly as a thoroughbred would lead a neighborhood milk wagon.

Koenig ran his GOP organization along the familiar lines cut by Tammany, with some of the coarser edges smoothed out. If his successes were less than spectacular, the blame belonged elsewhere than on his doorstep. The conservative, genteel approach of the standard Republican candidates did not fit the mood of the teeming slums. The intelligent, upright partrician might win Fifth Avenue, but never First Avenue—or Second Avenue, or Third Avenue.

Let it also be noted, in passing, that Koenig gave Fiorello LaGuardia his first big chance on the ballot. When LaGuardia ultimately rode the Elephant to victory, though, he campaigned as a maverick—and even, at times, a demagogue— pandering to far baser traits than cool, calm GOP reason and restraint. This was the only way a member of the party of Harding, Coolidge and Hoover could win here.

Most blue-blooded Republicans and Citizens Union stalwarts regarded the Lower East Side as an area for foreign missionary activity. They entered it cautiously, with clothespins pinched to their noses, and with a certain tolerance for the apparently uncivilized nature of its denizens. Not so Sam Koenig. He lived and worked among his people. Eddy Ahearn once breathed a sigh of relief that Sam was not his opposite number in our own Fourth Assembly District.

Sam's clubhouse, a few blocks north of our district's boundary line, was open on the same come-one-come-all basis as Tammany buildings. "Nobody needs appointments. All they have to know is whether I'm in town," he once said.

With the Democrats firmly entrenched in city and state, and the Republicans equally entrenched in Washington, Koenig often worked closely with Tammany leaders on patronage matters. The White House during the 1920s was always open to Koenig. If an occasional post office or federal judiciary job was siphoned off to a deserving Democrat, it was equally true that an otherwise unemployed Republican might find work at one of the numerous Tammany-controlled county offices.

At a political banquet, whose guests crossed party lines, I recall leaning over to Sam, who whispered, "We Republicans and Democrats speak the same language. We fight only one day a year—from 6 a.m. to the hour the polls are closed."

Sam was not being cynical. Anyone who knew him well would realize that. He merely was acknowledging a political fact of life— that New York City is a one party city, a Democratic city, and that only an emergency or an explosive un-partyish candidate could briefly upset the status quo.

Koenig's attitude earned him enmity in some quarters of his party. The wealthy, silk-stocking set considered the annual November defeats as a result of his unroyal hand rather than their party's royal principles. Sam, a gentle man as well as a gentleman, tried to set his Republican critics straight.

"They don't understand that government is of the people and by the people and that the people have to be taken care of," he said. "They carry their heads in the clouds and ignore the trouble at their feet. Issues? How many people know about them or understand them? Only the intellectual minority. But it is the man in the street who has the vote."

Sam pointed out the sole road to success at the polls was to win over the common man: "Recognize his everyday needs, run the party for him and you can win. But that means work, and reformers can't drudge."

In 1933, when Herbert Hoover departed the White House, federal patronage in New York City passed out of Sam's hands. His opponents within the party took full advantage of the national situation. They ousted him from the Republican leadership here. His successors during the 1930s were two socially prominent and wealthy "Juniors", Chase Mellen Jr. and Kenneth Simpson Jr. Neither lasted long, and neither did well for his party workers despite the fact that a Mayor wearing a Republican tag sat in City Hall during their tenures. Koenig had done better for his followers while Democrats from Hylan to "Holy Joe" McKee occupied the Mayor's desk.

Sam held the respect and affection of political allies and foes alike long after his immediate successors were just names in outdated society columns. He was still the "Boss" till the day he died in 1955, at age 82.

It is now necessary to return to the affairs of Tammany Hall as the mad decade reached its climax. In contrast to Koenig's sturdiness throughout the 1920s, the regime of his Democratic opposite number, Judge Olvany, was shaky and short. With the last bricks of Tammany's new Seventeenth Street headquarters scarcely in place, Olvany's fortunes began to wane, then crumbled beneath the Presidential election returns of the year 1928.

The Tiger, of course, did not lose the city to Koenig's awkward Elephant. But Al Smith's plurality here in his bid for the Presidency was small, so small that it was easily overriden by the staunch Republican upstate vote. Smith lost not only the election. He failed to even carry his own New York State.

This political disaster, coupled with Olvany's aloofness from his own lieutenants, fanned the already present undercurrent of dissension among the district leaders. As a result, few tears were shed when Olvany suddenly announced his resignation as Tammany chief in March, 1929. Officially, the reason released to the press was "ill health".

Once out of the job, however, Olvany's physical state improved rapidly. He outlived the administrations of James J. Walker, Joseph V. McKee, John P. O'Brien, Fiorello H. LaGuardia and William O'Dwyer, and died during Vincent R. Impellitteri's term, in 1952, well beyond the biblical quota of three score and ten.

Olvany's political demise was one streak of lightning in a sky full of electricity. That fateful spring of 1929, whose winter would last long into the thirties, ushered in clouds of change. Wall Street entered its giddiest phase. In Washington, Coolidge gave way to Hoover. In Albany, Smith gave way to the second Roosevelt. And in New York City, Tammany's throne, once occupied by William Tweed, Richard Croker and Charles Murphy, now fell vacant.

At this point, onto the stage strode Eddy Ahearn. At age 37, he gathered his political arms and prepared to stage his first assault to win the Seventeenth Street citadel.

V

Days of Grandeur and Grime

ALTHOUGH NO ONE REALIZED IT, THE NINETY MINUTE SESSION OF Tammany Hall's Executive Committee on April 24, 1929, was probably the most pregnant gathering in Tammany history. The meeting did not merely give birth to a new leader. It set the course followed by the organization for the second Walker administration. And it paved the way for a grand spree of loose public dealings that made Tammany's defeat almost inevitable four years later.

Eddy's brisk bid for the leadership failed. Instead, the post was awarded to a middle-aged, rigid, stern district chief who had strength of will, stubbornness of purpose and stupidity of judgment. In retrospect, the accession of John F. Curry to Tammany's throne was the coronation of an undertaker.

Unlike George Olvany, Curry at least had to fight for the post. Eddy was his stiffest opponent. But Martin G. McCue, a former lightweight fighter and strongman of the northern third of the Twelfth Assembly District, also sought the job.

Eddy had the support of most leaders south of the Fourteenth Street boundary line. In McCue's corner stood Surrogate James A. Foley, who had himself turned down the crown five years earlier, in order to stay on the bench. Foley was acknowledged as one of Tammany's "Big Four," the others being Senator Robert F. Wagner, former Governor Smith and, of course, Mayor Walker.

Senator Wagner was cool to Curry's candidacy. And the relationship between Smith and Curry bore marks of clearly undisguised coldness. But Smith, nationally known and respected though he was, held no present public office. He had sacrificed the Governorship in his unsuccessful quest for the Presidency. And political power is rarely based on nostalgia or sentiment.

Mayor Walker's will carried more weight. All City Hall patronage flowed through his hands, and he made full use of his position to destroy Eddy's dreams and McCue's hopes. Curry was his choice. It was an open secret. Many district leaders at the meeting served in well-paying city jobs "at the pleasure of the Mayor" and had no intention of incurring his displeasure.

As the Executive Committee's balloting began, the angered McCue stirred a hornet's nest. He announced his withdrawal and threw his support to Eddy. "I was a candidate but I am not now," he said. "I wouldn't stand for taking jobs from anyone. You can make the most of that."

The seventy startled leaders, some with fractional votes, buzzed in conversation, then resumed their task. When the doors of the council chamber again flung open, John F. Curry was the victor by 12 and one-sixth votes to 10 and one-third votes. Eddy's strength surprised many, for once "the word" of Walker's choice had been quietly circulated Curry was regarded a shoo-in.

The reason for Walker's preference seemed obvious. Eddy's career had been aided by Al Smith's friendship, and Eddy would no doubt seek to repay favor with favor. Besides, Eddy was tough and independent. He would be no rubber stamp for Beau James. The Mayor, facing an uncertain bid for renomination, wanted no part of a man who had the nerve to spit in his face. Curry was much safer.

Naturally, reporters quickly pounced on Curry with the question, "Are you in favor of a second term for Mayor Walker?"

"Unqualifiedly so!" he replied.

The anointed chief reclined in his newly-won throne, behind which had been placed a floral horseshoe, relaxed comfortably and remarked, "It feels pretty good sitting in this chair."

Later, leaving his host of well-wishers, he went to the Polo Grounds, enjoyed the Phillies-Giants baseball game, dined quietly with his family and received evening tributes at his Fifty-seventh Street clubhouse.

I do not know what dreams rolled through Curry's brain on that fateful night. Perhaps he envisioned grandiose plans for Tammany and himself. In any event, he went to bed amidst the fanfare of victory while the presses of the morning newspapers hummed with banner headlines announcing his triumph. No one, especially Curry, could have imagined that the day marked the beginning of Tammany's dizzy descent to disaster and its long, unbroken procession to the cemetery.

Fifty-five years old, white-capped, conservative in dress and a good family man, Curry was also a grim and cold species of politician. He had battled his way up in the "old school" tradition.

Born in Ireland, Curry was brought here as an infant. The New York City of his youth was politically dominated by still earlier emigrants from the Emerald Isle. After brief tours of duty as a Western Union messenger and telegraph operator, he turned towards Tammany. Curry could run the 100 yard dash in ten and two-fifths seconds, as fine a recommendation for a public career as could be found outside of prominence in the fight ring.

The young man became a trusted lieutenant of Daniel McMahon, leader of the Fifth Assembly District, and was pushed by his mentor into the state legislature. At Albany, Curry kept his ears open, his lips buttoned and his eyes on the fences back home.

McMahon unlike his contemporary, John F. Ahearn, had used his position of district leadership to amass a personal fortune. He spent long periods away from his neighborhood, vacationing in distant states and enjoying the fruits of his ample wealth. In time, he lost contact with his constituents.

This record of absenteeism fueled Curry's own ambition. In 1904, he challenged McMahon for district control and nearly succeeded in his bid. Only 78 votes out of nearly 3000 cast separated him from victory. The closeness of the contest shocked the old leader. He saw the handwriting indelibly imprinted on the wall. The next year, McMahon abdicated his crown and Curry became leader.

As a district chief, Curry ably served his people. By 1929, he had a well-established and well-deserved reputation for rewarding his capable captains and finding jobs for his club's membership. Even his detractors admitted as much.

As a county leader, however, he did not broaden his perspective. Loyalty to himself rather than performance on Election Day for the party became the basis for political reward throughout Manhattan. Within Tammany, two groups crystallized—Curry men and anti-Curry men. He willed it so.

Eddy Ahearn's district, the Democratic "Banner District," the district that piled up the largest Democratic pluralities year in and year out, did not get a whit of patronage. Curry, a vindictive man, with the unswerving collaboration of Mayor Walker, set out to destroy Eddy politically. If the John F. Ahearn Association were wrecked in the process, so be it.

The strategy was simple. By cutting off job opportunities and denying favors for the district, Curry and Walker hoped to stir disgruntlement among club members. Ultimately, they hoped, a revolt against Eddy's leadership could be provoked. Next, the blossoming insurgent rebellion would gain the blessing of the county leader. When it flared into the open, the conspirators would be welcomed back into the Tammany fold. Following success, the new district leaders would pledge their unyielding loyalty to Curry, and previously withheld bounties would be restored.

This method had worked in the past and would work again in the future. But it did not work this time. Though all the machinery of Tammany and party government was turned against our district, Eddy held out for four hard, long, lean years.

One judicial helping hand tendered emergency aid. James A. Foley, secure in his Surrogate's robes and lord over his court's patronage, provided a steady trickle of jobs and receiverships. And in far-away Albany, Eddy found Governor Roosevelt, no lover of Tammany or its new chief, a friendly figure. The most important factor in Eddy's survival was Eddy himself. His feet were firmly planted in the sidewalks around 290 East Broadway and it would take a far mightier force than the Walker-Curry axis to tear them loose.

A weak leader, or one lacking the sincere loyalty of his captains, could not have survived. Perhaps the best tribute ever paid Eddy by his club members lay in the fact that this critical period passed without a single undercover effort to overthrow him. The depression, it should be remembered, advanced side by side with the second Walker administration. Jobs in private industry as well as municipal jobs were scarce. Like many other captains, I was un-employed part of the grim time. Yet I never entertained the thought of turning against Eddy. How could I? He had always played squarely with me. In the Fourth Assembly District, politi-cal loyalty was a two-way street in those days. Today, I am afraid it is an item open for barter.

Curry's relentlessness could not destroy Eddy Ahearn. But the county leader's implacability stymied Eddy's sole political am-bition—to vindicate his father's reputation by his own election to the Borough Presidency.

In 1930, Nathan Miller, the incumbent, moved up to the State Supreme Court. All over the Lower East Side, we circulated peti-tions. Ten thousand signatures were collected urging Eddy's nomi-nation for the vacant Borough President's office. But Curry, who controlled the nominating machinery, said no. He chose Samuel Levy for the post instead.

The county chief's vendetta was not limited to holding Eddy down. He also struck—but less successfully—at one of his lieuten-ants. In contrast with far too many present district leaders, Eddy staunchly backed his captains.

Sam Weintraub, long a club member, had served as an assistant to the Borough President under Miller. Curry now ordered the new Borough President, Levy, to fire him. Eddy accepted this slap in the face far less gracefully than he had his own disappointment. As soon as Weintraub reported the news, he rushed to Tammany Hall headquarters for an audience with Curry.

"What's between you and me has nothing to do with my people," Eddy angrily protested to the county leader. "You don't like me and I don't like you. But my people work hard and they get out the votes that let you sleep easy. I want you to pick up that phone on your desk and tell Levy to reinstate Sam Weintraub."

Curry at first flatly refused. Then, seeing the fire in Eddy's eyes, he hemmed and hawed. "Well, I'll think about it," he said, and suggested a delay of a day or two.

"There's no need to wait," responded Eddy. He realized a delay would give the nervous Curry time to slip out of the net. "Do it now while I'm in your office," he insisted as he handed Curry the phone. By tonight I want Sam Weintraub to tell me he's back on the job."

By nightfall, he was. Weintraub was fired and rehired on the same day. The speed of his downs and ups precluded any public announcement of what was going on in the Borough President's office.

The Ahearn name was clearly still one to be reckoned with. Even at low tide in the district's political fortunes, it was strong enough to rescue Christopher D. Sullivan, last survivor of the colorful Sullivan clan, from losing both his district and his seat in Congress. Sullivan's crisis was rooted in the borough's changing population patterns.

Before outlining his plight, some background on people and neighborhoods might be useful at this point. Lower Manhattan had undergone a startling transformation by the end of the 1920s. As I noted earlier, our own compact district, once as Irish as Dublin, was now virtually a Jewish ghetto. Successive waves of persecution in East Europe had sparked successive waves of immigration here, assuring this.

In 1931, before subsequent reapportionments, the Fourth Assembly District ran from Corlears Hook and the East River west along Stanton Street and Houston Street to the corner of Ludlow Street, where once stood the jail in which Boss Tweed withered away after his downfall. Then it turned back along Grand Street and swung diagonally toward the river following Gouverneur Street.

Within these boundaries, Yiddish was spoken as often as English, and the *Jewish Daily Forward* and the *Jewish Day* rivaled their sister daily newspapers, published in English. Yet for 56 years, our Irish chief, be it John F. Ahearn, or his elder son, Edward, or his younger son, William, never had cause to worry about his status as leader. No religious rebellion took place. Our leader never let us down and we judged him by his worth. Whether his name began with a Gaelic lilt made no difference. The name "Ahearn" was good enough for everyone.

So much for our own secure bailiwick. It stood in striking contrast with several other Tammany strongholds. Pressing against us at the western and southwestern extremes was the accordion-shaped Second Assembly District, politically shared by Christopher Sullivan and his half-brother, Harry Perry. The Second Assembly District had undergone an even greater population turnover than our own area.

By the opening guns of World War One, it too had become predominantly Jewish. There were scarcely 200 Irish voters left in the section. Sullivan's chief lieutenant, Max Levine, was given a slice of control. Levine later became a city Magistrate and drifted out of district politics. Sullivan remained.

But the Jews, like the Irish before them, departed. Into the western half of the district—Perry's half—poured a new immigrant tide, this time from Italy. The newcomers quickly became dissatisfied with their Irish chiefs. Many Italians felt they were getting the short end of job opportunities. They said they wanted equality in the Second Assembly District's political councils and could not attain it under the old leadership. It was a far different story from that prevailing in our own district.

In Albert Marinelli, they found an energetic and forceful, though somewhat tarnished, champion. Marinelli's father had been an interpreter at Ellis Island for fellow Italians. He was a respected neighborhood figure, and his son drew on a wealth of friends in bidding for political influence.

During the 1929 fight for Tammany's control, Sullivan—with Perry tagging along—had supported Eddy Ahearn. Curry did not forget or forgive this. He put Sullivan and Perry on a skimpy job diet and hinted that a Marinelli triumph might set the patronage mill grinding again. This was the same strategy that had failed to unseat Eddy. But now it proved successful, at least in part.

One Italian captain after another in Perry's populous western half drifted into the Marinelli camp. There was no need even for a primary contest. Perry was through and he knew it.

Marinelli's sights now turned eastward. He trained his vision on the whole Second Assembly District, not just part. And he nearly got it. Only Eddy's intervention, repayment for his 1929 political debt, saved Sullivan.

A fog of apprehension choked the political atmosphere of the Lower East Side during those tense days. Finally, Eddy called for a "summit" meeting at his clubhouse. Marinelli, with little to gain, preferred to stay away. But, in the end, he came. The neighborhood buzzed. Marinelli brought along several "bodyguards". And Eddy, as host, was not exactly naked to his potential enemies.

For hours, behind closed doors, the complexion of lower Manhattan's political future was hammered out. Marinelli's justifiable claims were not questioned. But, when the meeting broke up, Christopher Sullivan could breathe easier. He would both stay in the House of Representatives and, more importantly, on Tammany Hall's Executive Committee.

A few years later, after Eddy's death, Marinelli again attained power in widening Democratic circles. Then, following disclosure of his underworld connections, he faded away. Sullivan—surprisingly—outlasted him and became an aging figurehead as Democratic county leader. But that story belongs to a later chapter.

During the early thirties, the Fourth Assembly District remained overwhelmingly Jewish. At the fringe areas, though, Italians were being absorbed. In 1931, I sponsored the first Italian lawyer as an Ahearn captain, a step, I regret to say, that was not cheerfully welcomed by some old-timers. Later, the lawyer became quite prominent in city affairs.

The cold depression winters of the early 1930s were winters of watchful waiting for Eddy. The city leadership of Walker and Curry floundered through one exposure after another. Despite the dark mood that pervaded Tammany Hall, though, Eddy managed to find time for macabre humor. On one particularly frigid Monday night, our Congressman, Samuel Dickstein, knocked on the door of Eddy's office in the back of the clubhouse.

"Sorry, I can't see you right now, Sam. But hang around," said Eddy mysteriously, "There's something I want to talk over with you. Not in here though. Wait in front of the building. I'll be out in a few minutes."

Sam waited on the sidewalk in snow several inches deep as flurries whirled around his face. Several minutes passed. Must be pretty important, he figured, if the chief wanted to see him alone out here. A half hour passed. Then almost an hour. Sam still waited. He shook the snow from his shoulders and rubbed his hands to keep them warm. At last the door creaked open and Eddy appeared—with several of us.

"Sam," he said, "what on earth are you doing out here shivering in the snow? I thought you left."

"But you told me to wait. . . ." replied the chattering Congressman.

"Wait?" Eddy responded with a look of mock astonishment. "Why should I have you wait in the middle of a blizzard? Do you think I'm crazy? Go home and warm up!"

Sam Dickstein spent more than twenty years in Congress. Today, less than fifty feet from where the clubhouse once stood, rises a tall post signifying "SAMUEL DICKSTEIN PLAZA." It is no doubt a fitting memorial for his long, lonely vigil that terrible night.

Eddy dominated all the Fourth Assembly District's elected officials. He held only one public position himself, though any within the Lower East Side, from Alderman to Congressman, could have been his for the asking. Political responsibility, the father of governmental responsibility, was his full-time concern.

During the summer of 1931, State Senator Barney Downing, his mentor, died. District sentiment—Eddy's father had once served in that post—coupled with the desire to avoid bickering within the club for the job led him to fill in temporarily. He ran for the State Senate in November, served out the term, but impatiently yearned to return to Manhattan's battles. The political skirmishes centering on Curry's Seventeenth Street Citadel were far more important than anything Eddy could accomplish at Albany.

Nonetheless, Eddy's brief upstate interlude was quite significant. There, his "cards-on-the-table" frankness earned the respect of Governor Franklin D. Roosevelt. In future months, Eddy would prove a useful agent in honestly setting forth Roosevelt's views to the embattled Mayor Walker. And he would be instrumental in Roosevelt's plans, following his elevation to the Presidency, in toppling Curry's corrupt and stumbling regime.

Samuel Mandelbaum, our Assemblyman in Albany, also won Roosevelt's confidence during this period. Sam was a respected figure throughout the Lower East Side, a man easily capable of gaining anyone's trust. He replaced Eddy in the State Senate when

Eddy gave up the post, and remained in the upper legislative chamber until President Roosevelt made him a federal judge in 1936.

Born in Poland, Mandelbaum was an able legislator whose conscientiousness impressed even the Citizen's Union, no small feat for a Tammany man. He was also a devout Jew, strictly Orthodox, who imported wine from Palestine during the Passover holy days. Whenever Sam visited Albany's Executive Mansion, his host made certain his meals were always completely kosher.

As Roosevelt's star waxed, Jimmy Walker's suddenly waned. The Mayor's popularity reached its dizziest height in the 1929 city-wide election, when he swamped LaGuardia, the blustering Republican nominee, by 856,000 to 368,000 votes. Beau James was 48, seven months older than Roosevelt, and in the prime of life. A future as sparkling as his wit seemed ahead of him. Yet Walker's career crashed with the suddenness and inevitability of the stock market. I believe Walker's personal disaster was fueled by the national catastrophe. He was a luxury and the city could no longer afford luxuries.

Details of the successive waves of investigations and exposures have been spelled out in countless reports, books, pamphlets, studies and articles. They will therefore be mentioned only in passing here, as they led up to Judgement Day at Albany. There, Eddy played his secret, but historical, role as the paths of Walker's and Roosevelt's careers met, one skidding downward to exile, the other ascending to the Presidency of the United States.

The opening salvo was directed at the Magistrates' Courts. One judge was quickly removed, another left the bench following his indictment. The target expanded with further indictments. By early 1931, the Republican-controlled state legislature ordered a broadened investigation of city affairs. The icy, puritanical Samuel Seabury served as counsel—that is, as chief prosecutor. Machine-gun fire was sprinkled by the legislative committee over a wide range of public officials and politicians. When County Sheriff Thomas M. Farley said his huge bank deposits came from a "wonderful tin box," the term caught on as a symbol of Tammany's corruption.

Seabury confidently trained his major artillery barrage on the

Mayor himself. Careful investigation showed that Walker had indulged in some rather unusual business activities. His financial transactions led to embarrassing questions. He could not satisfactorily explain away nearly a million dollars deposited for him by his accountant, who conveniently vanished into Mexico.

Ultimately, fifteen specific points comprised Seabury's charges against the Mayor. Not the least important of these stated that Walker's conduct had rendered him unfit to continue as Mayor.

Seabury submitted the charges to Roosevelt shortly before the 1932 Democratic National Convention convened in Chicago. The timing was designed to embarrass the Governor as well as destroy the Mayor. Roosevelt faced a terrible political dilemma. Dragging his feet in the Walker case would oil the charge that Tammany could lead him by the nose. The Governor's opponents for the Democratic nomination would certainly capitalize on that at Chicago. The art of twisting the Tammany Tiger's Tail was a respectable practice in "holier" Democratic circles west of the Hudson River and extending to the Pacific. And, if Roosevelt captured the nomination despite this intra-party criticism, he would still not face clear sailing ahead. The Republicans surely would make a campaign issue of Roosevelt's bow to Tammany's Beau James. The Tiger, with Roosevelt in its belly, might be fried along with a chicken in every pot. Such were the potentially dismal consequences if the Governor hesitated to act.

On the other hand, the Governor did not control his own state's delegation. Though certainly not fond of Tammany's leaders, he could not afford to completely alienate the city's Democrats. They, not his supporters, were topheavy in convention votes assigned to the Empire State. Walker, whatever his real and imagined sins, was still a very popular man south of the Westchester county line.

Roosevelt could not therefore make a politically "good" decision. His choice was limited to the lesser of the two evils. Which would prove less damaging to his cause? He decided to put aside the Walker case until after the Convention.

The scene now shifted to Chicago. New York's delegation buzzed as the leaders and the led took their seats. Many wondered in what direction Tammany would throw its weight. The answer came as the balloting began.

Though there was little love lost between John Curry and Al Smith, Curry tossed the county organization's votes to the popular former governor, a past antagonist, rather than Albany's current occupant, a present political foe. On the first futile ballot, Smith polled 65 and one-half votes and Roosevelt 28 and one-half in the New York State delegation.

Among the Smith votes was Eddy Ahearn's. This was an act of sentiment, not one of obedience to Curry. Eddy certainly took no orders from the county chief. But Smith and Eddy's father had been close. So had Smith and Barney Downing. Smith had given Eddy guidance and encouragement during his political apprenticeship. Now an old debt was being acknowledged.

But as surely as "The Sidewalks of New York" gave way to "Happy Days Are Here Again", Roosevelt gathered (and Garnered) strength. Curry and Walker had good cause to sulk. The Governor was moving closer to the nomination. Vote by vote he inched toward the magic number. Then a wave of despair rolled over the Tammany delegation. Roosevelt was over the top.

Back in Albany, a few days later, Walker's "trial" resumed. This time, however, his interrogator was no longer a mere committee counsel. As Governor, Roosevelt had the power of judge and jury. He could remove the Mayor from office.

Day after day, beginning August 11, the Executive Chamber of the State House was the scene of public hearings that grasped national attention. Again Walker recited the story that impressed few but the faithful. Again he squirmed, dodged, then was forced to answer biting questions. And again his answers were transparent veils that could not conceal his obvious misdeeds.

Roosevelt, now a Presidential candidate, faced an awesome decision. A judgement based purely on fact and principle might lead to political suicide. A triumph over Hoover in November was not yet a certainty. Walker's conviction could lead to Roosevelt's mortal loss of the city vote. Four years earlier, a small city plurality, far too small, had cost Al Smith New York's hefty total of

electoral votes. The 1932 Democratic candidate did not wish to
see history repeated.

At the other end of the spectrum, a judgement based solely on
political expediency would be interpreted as an act of cowardice.
A whitewash meant moral suicide. Besides, it might backfire, in
terms of votes on Election Day. Though it might assure victory
in New York State, the backlash throughout the more puritanical
hinterland could really prove disastrous.

Clearly, only the kind hand of fate could remove the unwanted
sword from the Governor's hands.

As the long, hot days of late summer ticked away, the eyes of
city, state and nation turned in the direction of Albany. No one
waited more apprehensively than Walker. For no one, including
Roosevelt, had as large a personal stake in the Governor's decision.

At seven o'clock on a late August morning, Eddy's phone rang.
On the wire was the Mayor. Would he, asked the embattled Walker,
be willing to go to Albany and speak to Roosevelt about the chances
of removal?

The request was startling. Here was the Mayor of the City of
New York asking a Tammany district leader to intervene on his
behalf with the chief executive of a great state. But, if the request
was strange, so were the circumstances. The Democratic county
leader, John Curry, had no access to the Governor—they despised
each other. Neither did any other member of Tammany's ruling
circle.

Eddy, of course, had ample reason to refuse the role. In the
last three years, the Mayor had tried to destroy him. Walker had
kept him from the Tammany leadership in April, 1929. He had
shorn him of patronage. In collaboration with Curry, he had
denied him his sole political ambition, the Manhattan Borough
Presidency.

Because of these very acts, however, Ahearn had been saved
from the tidal waves of corruption that swept over other Tammany
leaders and their clubhouses. While many drowned, Eddy's personal integrity remained unquestioned. Eddy thus appeared one
of the few conceivable agents of communication open between City

Hall and the state capital. Eddy agreed to listen to whatever the Governor had to say and report back to the Mayor.

Ahearn boarded a train for Albany, accompanied by William Wagner, a friend of both Walker and the late Barney Downing. Upon their arrival, they parted company. At the Executive Mansion, Eddy sat down alone with the Governor. No advisers were present. For more than an hour, they discussed the crisis in which the stakes were not merely a Mayor's fate but perhaps the future occupancy of the White House. The Governor willingly let the Tammany district leader pick his brain. Roosevelt outlined his position and put his cards on the table.

He said he had the Presidency in the palm of his hand. He could not allow the Mayor to escape the penalty for his conduct. He said his mind was made up. He would have to remove him— if not for intended wrong doing, then at least for neglect of duty.

Eddy listened attentively as Roosevelt weighed possible courses of action. There could be no doubt that Walker would have to go. But the matter of timing and the method of leaving were crucial. If Walker were to resign before being removed, the Governor concluded, unnecessary embarrassment all around might be avoided.

Ahearn thanked the Governor for the interview. Now he had to break the news to the Mayor. He arranged a meeting with Walker at Albany's Ten Eyck Hotel to pass on the Governor's decision. Associates of Walker were present, but apparently knew nothing of the Roosevelt-Ahearn discussion. For his part, Eddy held to a confidence and did not disclose the source of his "inside" information. Walker alone knew, and his interests did not include advertising the preliminaries. The source's identity remained unrevealed. In fact, to disguise his own initiative, Walker feigned hesitancy about seeing Eddy at all!

Eddy related to Walker and his allies the unwelcome details of the Governor's thinking. He suggested that Walker resign, then seek vindication by running for Mayor again. He added that Walker did not have to resign immediately. He should make out a letter, but could delay any announcement for two or three days. For Walker, who never liked to live by the clock, time had indeed run out. On September 1, 1932, he sent a terse message to City Clerk Michael J. Cruise. It read: "I hereby resign as Mayor of the City of New York, the same to take effect immediately."

In announcing his resignation, Walker charged that the proceedings in Albany had become "a travesty, a mock trial, a proceeding in comparison to which even the practice of a drumhead court-martial seemed liberal."

The use of this strong language was understandable, though, of course, not justifiable. A man who, in a short time, would seek the very office he had just surrendered under pressure could not be expected to praise the hearings that interrupted his career.

Later, at a conference with Curry and Curry's Brooklyn counterpart, aging John H. McCooey, Walker secured support from the two borough leaders. Since Democratic nominations for the citywide ticket would be made by county committee members controlled by the borough chiefs, he had good cause for optimism.

Unfortunately for the Mayor, two roadblocks developed. First, Bronx leader Edward J. Flynn flatly refused to go along. He favored the acting Mayor, Joseph V. McKee, President of the Board of Aldermen. Flynn was prepared to run his man as an independent candidate if necessary. This would rip party unity asunder.

Second, and more important, there were indications that Walker's well-known indiscretions had made him unacceptable to his church. A respected clergyman, Msgr. John P. Chadwick, noted as chaplain of "The Maine", had been a guest at Curry's home during the period of behind-the-scenes activity.

Shortly thereafter, Msgr. Chadwick spoke at the funeral of Tammany district leader Martin G. McCue. McCue, it may be remembered, had supported Eddy against Curry back in 1929. "He was faithful to his wife, true to the interests of his home and his children," said Msgr. Chadwick of the departed McCue. "Would to God that every man in public life would understand that he is an example, a model, a guide to young people who are apt to be drawn to him. Not only in official life, but in private life should a man be clean and pure."

These pregnant comments not only accompanied McCue to the grave. They also helped seal the political coffin of the loose-living

Beau James. They stirred a hornet's nest above the head of New York's Democratic leadership.

Walker, vacationing in Europe after his withering ordeal, cabled home that he was no longer interested in running again for Mayor. Instead, he embarked on a long European exile.

Back in New York City, clouds of uncertainty again shrouded the future of Tammany Hall.

VI

Changing of the Guard:
The White House,
City Hall, Tammany Hall

NINETEEN-THIRTY-TWO WAS A PIVOTAL YEAR FOR CURRY AND EDDY as well as for Roosevelt and Walker. In the past three years, Tammany's aging leader had made one error after another on his way to the grand blunder. Yet he was far too stuffy and stubborn to backtrack when faced with unassailable realities.

Following defeat at the national convention in Chicago, Curry refused to strike any chord of party unity. While others sought to smooth out the friction and restore Democratic harmony in New York, he sat glumly through Roosevelt's victory celebration.

Later that summer, at New York State's own Democratic convention in Albany, Curry sought to withhold the principal prize, the Gubernatorial nomination, from Lieutenant Governor Herbert H. Lehman. This was purely an act of political vendetta. Lehman, able and competent, was Roosevelt's personal choice. He became a convenient substitute target for blind, unreasoning revenge against the Presidential candidate.

Al Smith intervened. He put Curry on notice that he would take the city's control out of the county chief's hands by running for Mayor himself if Curry persisted in his tactics of obstruction. When the Tammany leader asked on what ticket, Smith reportedly answered he could beat him "on a Chinese laundry ticket". This was more than a jest. Curry finally backed down.

(In the subsequent election, Lehman handily beat Republican William J. Donovan, who later won fame as OSS chief during World War II. Lehman polled 15,248 votes in our district. When an evening newspaper credited Donovan with a 1,750 total, Eddy

Ahearn quickly protested the tabulation. Donovan's actual figure
was 978. Few Republicans scored 1000 votes in the Banner Democratic District in those days, and Eddy wanted the record set
straight.)

Curry found room for yet another tragic mistake before Novem-
ber's day of judgement. Having backed the wrong horse for
President, and nearly tripped the right one for Governor, he dug
deep into Tammany's treasury of manpower for a successor to
Walker. He plucked out an obscure justice of Surrogate's Court,
John P. O'Brien, and decided to make him Mayor.

It was not difficult. His Republican opponent, Lewis H. Pounds,
was a closely guarded secret throughout the special Mayoralty
campaign. But O'Brien, a well-meaning fellow, stepped into the
nation's second toughest job totally unequipped for his unpleasant
tasks. He was honest, honorable, dignified, but not very bright.
He was hardly the shining knight capable of slaying municipal
dragons.

O'Brien was forthright in his pledge of allegiance to Curry. If
he did not love or cherish, he at least promised to obey. When
asked by reporters to name his choice for Police Commissioner,
the Mayor politely declined on the grounds that he had not yet
been told! The penalty for backing O'Brien, however, would not
be keenly felt by Tammany Hall for a full year, until November,
1933. The moment of reckoning was still months off.

The year 1933 dawned with deceiving brightness. For the first
time in twelve years, Democrats occupied all three major sources
of power and patronage—City Hall, the Executive Mansion and the
White House. But under the gleaming mantle, darkness gathered.

Roosevelt had won despite Tammany's Tiger, not because of
it. And Lehman had done the same. True, O'Brien was distinctly
Curry's creature. But his term would run out in twelve months. A
new battle would loom against a well-organized, well-financed
Fusion movement.

On January 19, 1933, almost 1,200 of Tammany's faithful
gathered to celebrate November's "victories" at the Hotel Commodore. I guess the festivities might be compared with a Roman
orgy shortly before the Huns arrived. Or maybe with a Vienna

ball shortly before the Archduke waved farewell and headed off
on a pleasant journey to Sarajevo. There were music, good conversation and song.

Mayor O'Brien announced that "all citizens of New York will
have just cause for rejoicing." He was cheered. The noisiest applause of the evening, however, greeted a rendition of "Will You
Love Me in December As You Did in May." That tune's composer
was Jimmy Walker. There were other melodies with less successful
lyrics. One, dedicated to Curry, followed the melody of "Shanty
Town".

I doubt that anyone present at the Commodore believed it would
become a popular favorite. It went:

> So here's to John Curry,
>   The Chief of the Clan;
> We won't have to worry
>   While he's our head man.
> All his loyalty fine
>   In our hearts we enshrine;
> He's the life of the Party
>   That gave us O'Brien.
> The Tiger is strongest
>   When John's in his den,
> A Man among leaders,
>   A Prince among men.
> So let's all raise a toast
>   To the heavens above
> For John Curry, the man we all love.

Mind you, this was meant as tribute, not satire. And a similar
accolade in song was bestowed upon Mayor O'Brien:

> In East or South, or North or West,
> There's no denyin' John O'Brien is the best
> We give you a hearty welcome
> And know that you will pass the test
> New York is more than overjoyed
> For it is you who will relieve the unemployed

And when the year is through
We'll cheer for you then
And you'll be elected again!
We'll never have to change our plan,
John P. O'Brien's our man.

In addition to its obvious poetical faults, this musical tribute contained several erroneous assumptions. For one thing, when the year was through, so would be O'Brien. He would, in the language of the song, flunk the test. He would fail to relieve unemployment, fail in his bid for re-election and be cheered only by his county leader, John Curry. And no one at all would be cheering Curry.

On the dais with other celebrants were such luminaries as Elmer E. Strudley, Richard P. Lydon, David S. Rendt and Raymond J. O'Sullivan. But other faces were missing. For example, President-elect Roosevelt could not make it. Governor Lehman sent a wire saying he was busy at Albany. Senator Robert F. Wagner was absent. And other invited "guests of honor", such as Bronx county leader Edward J. Flynn, stayed away. It was something less than Tammany Hall's Finest Hour.

Following Roosevelt's inauguration, the Presidency became a cockpit for national resurgence and, at our local level, for political intrigue. The weapon he used here was federal patronage. Just as former Mayor Walker and Curry had set out to destroy Ahearn four years earlier, Roosevelt turned this potent tool against the county leader of Manhattan island, Tammany's chief.

Unseating Curry was not easy. During the first hundred days—even the first two hundred days—it was impossible.

O'Brien still inhabited City Hall and municipal government was still the main spring that spurted bursts of jobs. But, at least, a beginning was made.

Once Roosevelt was installed in Washington, patronage in the post offices, Internal Revenue offices, Customs offices and federal agency branches throughout the city came under Democratic control. Under normal circumstances, local Democratic leaders would have made their selections as jobs opened and the national administration would have approved them as a matter of course, without much ado.

President Roosevelt and Postmaster General James A. Farley, whose triple responsibilities included those of National Democratic Chairman and State Democratic Chairman, could not have cared less about who Curry wanted to fill any job. They worked around Curry, not through him. In the process, they hoped to spawn a local purge.

Eddy Ahearn willingly joined forces with the national administration and became the President's agent. After four years' starvation in patronage during the Walker-Curry regime, he now become a patronage dispenser in his own right. Eddy was no longer an ostracized district leader, disowned by his organization's leadership. The Tiger's tail had turned. Through Eddy, federal vacancies were being filled. And around Eddy began to gather many of the county's anti-Curry forces.

I was one of the first beneficiaries. One day, Bert Stand, whose name will appear again and again on later pages, cheerfully greeted me. Bert, stout and smiling, was secretary of the John F. Ahearn Association and the bearer of good news.

"We've just been given three spots at Internal Revenue," he said. "Eddy asked me to recommend three people and, of course, I suggested you."

I thanked Stand, then sought out Ahearn. I did not get hold of him until evening.

"Eddy, I saw Bert this morning and he . . ." I began.

"Good!" Eddy interrupted. "Did he tell you about the three jobs? You were the first one I thought of. Don't thank me. You've earned it."

Nonetheless, thank him I did. Later, when I ran into Bert again, I mentioned my conversation with Eddy.

"Gee, Louis . . . er . . . I hope you didn't say anything to him about my recommending you for the job," Bert said haltingly. "I was only kidding, you know. It was just a joke."

"Of course I didn't say anything," I assured him.

Bert and I had worked closely for twenty years. We had been boyhood friends. We would work closely for the next twenty years.

I genuinely liked him. He had charm, intelligence and many admirable traits. But he had also developed certain personality failings alien to Eddy's nature. This incident represented one of them.

Thus began my career as a federal employee. I served under James J. Hoey, Collector of Internal Revenue in the Second District. It was not a soft, cushy, part-time job. I worked hard. The Hatch Act, barring political activity by federal workers, still lay in the future. So, come Monday, come Thursday and come election time, my working hours extended far into the night. As a captain, I never brushed aside the requests of my precinct's many constituents. Nor did I beg off after a long day's labor.

Some other captains were less content and less ardent. Politics, like all trades, has its ingrates.

While walking with Eddy one day, he suddenly stopped short.

"Louis, quickly, let's turn east at this corner," he said.

Two blocks ahead, coming in our direction, was a fellow who had also received an Internal Revenue position. Eddy wanted to avoid him.

"I get sick every time I see him," Eddy complained. "I can't pass down the street without having him stop me to gripe about something. I gave him the job because he's a good captain. But he's never satisfied no matter what kind of job he's holding down. There are ten people I could find who would jump to fill his spot. And from him all I get are heartaches and aggravation."

The man Eddy spoke of had once held a county post—and did not like it. He had next been placed in a good spot in private industry. He did not care for that either. Perhaps the League of Nations held something he considered worthy of his talents. But I doubt it. Besides, Eddy had little pull at Geneva, almost as little as he had with City Hall's current occupant.

Mayor O'Brien pushed and plodded on as his year in office progressed. He worked hard. He did his best. But everything was against him—entrenched corruption, tangled inefficiency, the deepening depression, the almost Rasputin-like influence of Curry and his own mental awkwardness.

In public, he suffered from foot-in-mouth disease, a political affliction aggravated by its treatment in the daily press. Reporters quoted his comments sentence by sentence, word for word. To understand the devastating impact of such coverage, read an account of a typical Presidential news conference. Then read the actual transcript of what was said. Multiply the difference in grammatical comprehensibility tenfold. Then allow for O'Brien's pontifical style. (William Jennings Bryan, who had augustly set the pattern followed by the Mayor, died less than five years earlier.) At this point, your calculations will have given you a fairly good idea of the impression O'Brien left on his listeners and readers.

An uninspiring figure, the Mayor was even occasionally booed at sports events—an ill omen for any politician, especially one who intended to run for re-election. A disgruntled public would not settle for O'Brien's pleas that "Rome was not built in a day."

Clearly, with November approaching, the search for a more bold, dashing, daring, imaginative candidate should have kept Tammany's ruler busy round the clock. Curry never bothered to look twice. He enlisted O'Brien once more at the head of the Democratic ticket—this time, though, with disastrous results.

Across the Harlem River, the perceptive Bronx leader, Edward Flynn, saw defeat looming ahead in the 1933 general elections. To save his county's elective offices for his party, Flynn spawned the Recovery Party, which, in turn, gave birth to the candidacy of Joseph V. McKee. McKee, who once temporarily filled in for the resigned Walker, had pulled 242,026 write-in votes during the O'Brien-Pounds contest the preceding year. He was able and attractive. He was indeed to prove a worthy sacrificial lamb.

As a going concern, the Recovery Party was a sham. Flynn could not expect to turn his creature into a city-wide machine. But it was destined to accomplish one prime objective. It would keep the Bronx partially secure from the tornado which was to sweep Democratic officeholders out of power in the wake of O'Brien's defeat. While many Tammany "ins" were tossed out, their counterparts north of the Harlem River remained at their posts.

The national administration in Washington did not stridently voice disapproval of O'Brien. The Mayor was still a Democrat— no matter how still a Democrat. But Roosevelt's circle made no secret of the fact that Fusionist candidate Fiorello H. LaGuardia, a nominal Republican and devout maverick, was its preferred candidate. Roosevelt made no effort to stem the anti-Tammany tide. Instead, the White House prepared to wipe the blood from the ground after the slaughter and develop a new, more vigorous breed of Tiger.

Shortly before the election, many captains, including myself, received instructions: "Don't push too hard for the head of the ticket. Get the rest of the candidates of our party in, but tell your people to vote their consciences for Mayor."

Translated, this meant "A vote for O'Brien is a vote for Curry and against Roosevelt." Eddy had far more confidence in the Governor he had known, now President, than in the Tammany leader he knew far too well.

La Guardia won, McKee placed second, saving many Bronx posts for the Flynn organization, while O'Brien, in show position, received a severe drubbing.

On January 1, 1934, the bewildered Mayor left office. Curry still hung on as Tammany leader. But regimes come and go, and his was tottering. The final crash was merely weeks ahead.

On assuming Tammany Hall's helm nearly five years earlier, Curry had explained, "There is nothing mysterious in wise political action, for it is simply composed of applying common sense to the situations as they arrived."

His first months in office glittered with wisdom. Walker's 1929 re-election over LaGuardia approached landslide proportions. Even Alderman McKee, his later foe, had praised Curry's devotion to the interests of the people and lauded Walker as "one of the greatest Chief Executives the city has ever had." McKee was not alone in fulsome accolades. If McKee's crystal ball failed him, he may be excused.

Franklin Roosevelt, at the time serving his first term as Governor, had also found easy words of praise for Tammany and its leader. (More realistically, he acknowledged his debt to Walker for teaching him the art of going to six dinners in one evening.) Curry's apparent acumen had also earned him an honorary L.L.D.

for "philanthropy, knowledge of governmental affairs and executive ability."

All this was history. More recently, he had displayed phenomenally poor judgment—Smith over Roosevelt, parties unknown over Lehman, O'Brien over anyone, stand-patism over dynamism.

Still, Curry arrived smiling for his daily chores at Tammany Hall. But the White House was unfriendly. Albany was in unaccommodating hands. City Hall, now ruled for at least the next four years by a Fusionist coalition, would happily join the entourage of political pallbearers. For Curry's supporters, the patronage cupboard was bare. While Eddy Ahearn journeyed to Washington with other Tammany anti-Curry leaders, such as Nathan Burkan and William J. Solomon of the Seventeenth Assembly District, their nominal chief passed his impotent last hours at the Hall's Union Square headquarters.

The end came on April 20, 1934, at a special session of Tammany's Executive Committee. The meeting was called two days after a petition had been signed by a majority of the members. Though slated for five o'clock in the evening, the Hall was crowded by early afternoon with both "pro" and "anti" Curry factions. Hundreds gathered at the Seventeenth Street entrance, held back by police. By way of comparison, the present-day comings-and-goings of Democratic New York County leaders stir about as much deserved interest as the selection of a dogcatcher.

Curry arrived at 4:50 p.m., cheered by his friends, and waited in his second floor office. Fifteen minutes later, the conference was officially called to order at the assembly hall.

Former Sheriff Charles W. Culkin, leader of the Third Assembly District South, pleaded with Curry to resign rather than be ousted. "John Curry," he said emotionally, "every man and woman in this room holds you in the highest personal esteem and is 100% for you socially. They don't want you to do anything that might humiliate you. Their prayer to you is to resign."

The atmosphere was tense as a pallid Curry rose to defend his record. "If mistakes were made," he said, "they were mistakes any leader could have made. There has been no leader in the past but has made some mistakes."

Even now, the Tammany chief could not understand the gravity of his blunders. He continued, "I have been your leader for five years. There are no charges against me. No one can say I have not been an honest man. Therefore, why this proceeding?"

Curry pointed to Tammany's history. No leader had ever been forcibly removed from his post. "I challenge the right of the Executive Committee to do this," he declared. "I was elected for a term of office and can only be removed under charges."

Another leader arose to outline the grievances against his stewardship. Friends again urged him to avoid putting the matter to a vote. Curry refused to give heed. "Let them count me out," he persisted. To the very end, he maintained the stubborn posture that decision by decision had led inevitably to this day.

The resolution formally ending his reign was adopted by a vote of fourteen and one-third to ten and one-sixth. Ironically, in defeat, Curry polled nearly the same number of votes that Eddy Ahearn received back in 1929.

The defeated chief returned to his former office, remarked "It's just another day in our lives," then departed the building by limousine. Curry's days of power were over.

Back in the Hall, cheers rang in Eddy's ears. He was the most likely successor to the throne that had earlier eluded him. Who knows what altered course might have been followed by Tammany these past five crisis-filled years with Eddy in the saddle? Now, at least, he hoped the task of remolding the organization would be his.

There was some talk, at first, of a leader being "brought in" from outside the ranks of the corps of district leaders. But the memory of "Judge" Olvany's unlamented reign was all too fresh. One influential Democrat scoffed at the idea and commented: "These men who are leaders have to bear responsibility 365 days in the year. Why give the honors to wax work figures? They are the ones who reap the benefit of the labors of the leaders. The organization is no stronger than its leaders and if they're not strong enough to lead, they ought to be thrown out!"

None could doubt that Eddy Ahearn was well-qualified to lead. He had the backing of almost the entire section of Manhattan south of the Fourteenth Street line. But there were other cliques. These associations, though less cohesive, were still potent. In combination, they commanded the majority of votes on the Executive Committee. One group drew together Curry's closest aides. They feared an Ahearn victory would be capped by a display of political vengeance with themselves as the target. Another group formed around Jimmy Hines, overlord of the Harlem area, and swayed to his tune. By the end of the thirties, Hines would be safely deposited in jail. But, at the moment, he controlled a large bloc of votes that could be swung heavily in any direction he chose.

There were several leaders, opportunists with few convictions, who envisioned the fumbled crown of Tammany rolling in their directions. Running in front of this pack, Eddy naturally became the principal target for their sniping and rumors. Conspiracies formed behind his back, as they always do behind the probable victor.

Though a bond of respect existed between Eddy and the national administration in Washington, Roosevelt and Farley were wary. Word eventually circulated that Eddy did not have their support for Tammany's top prize, even though they had been closely allied in matters of patronage and opposition to Curry.

Speculation centered on Eddy's relationship with Al Smith. Loyal as he was to Roosevelt, Eddy was even closer to Smith. They both came from the Lower East Side, and both grew up in the old neighborhood political tradition. Eddy's father, as I noted earlier, knew Smith well. Barney Downing, Eddy's teacher, was a Smith confidant. Eddy had learned much from Smith, admired him, and respected him dutifully as a youth for an elder statesman.

Smith had always dealt fairly and generously with Eddy, and the Fourth Assembly District leader was not one to forget. In fact, it was at Governor Smith's direction some years earlier that Eddy was permitted to place Bert Stand in the post of secretary to the New York State Athletic Commission, then headed by James A. Farley.

Farley, now the President's shrewd political adviser, carefully scanned local developments. It was no secret that Smith and

Roosevelt had parted ways over the past few years. The cigar-smoking graduate of machine politics and the patrician of Hyde Park no longer saw eye to eye on policies and issues. Smith, though still a sentimental favorite of many New Yorkers, held no present office. The administration probably anticipated that an Ahearn coronation would no doubt lead to a Smith comeback.

Eddy was definitely a "front man" for no one. But, by circumstance and background, saying "Sorry!" to a Smith request would demand much soul-searching for him. And ignoring Smith's advice would be even more difficult. Eddy could not easily cast aside past loyalties. For better or worse, the national administration feared that Eddy was firmly knotted to Smith and an Ahearn victory would mean Smith's triumph.

There was still a slight chance that Washington would stand aside—or even help. The newspapers carried a report that financier Bernard M. Baruch, "adviser to Presidents," pressed for the approval of Eddy. But fate's long arm, extending a far, far greater distance than the 230 miles to Washington, intervened.

Eddy was taken suddenly and seriously ill with an attack of appendicitis. For more than a week, the gravity of his condition was hidden. But word then leaked out and spread quickly through Tammany's ranks. His absence from Executive Committee meetings gave his opponents here speedily-grasped opportunities to loosen his footing. His condition also resulted in Farley's casting bait for other potential leaders.

Eddy lingered for weeks at Post-Graduate Hospital, just blocks from the northern boundary of his assembly district. For many days, he wrestled with the problem of both his and Tammany's future. In the afternoon of July 11, 1934, Eddy announced his decision at a dismal bedside conference.

At 6:00 p.m., a formal statement was issued to the press on his behalf by Bert's brother, Alderman Murray W. Stand. It read: "I desire to announce the withdrawal of my candidacy for the leadership of Tammany Hall. As a life-long Democrat, I place the interests of my party above mere personal ambition. I earnestly desire harmony to the end that there might be a united democracy and the present dissension ended."

Eddy's statement outlined the attributes of a good leader and also thanked his friends for their support and loyalty. He threw his decisive strength behind a young West Side district leader, with little political background, but acceptable to all factions of the party.

"As to my own personal choice for the candidate for leader," he said, "I shall take pleasure in casting my vote for James J. Dooling, who in my opinion fully measures up to the ideals of our party and who is deserving of the fullest confidence of all supporters of true progressive democracy."

A proxy was arranged for Eddy, since it was not expected he would be well enough to attend the Executive Committee meeting at which the ballots would be cast. Thus, illness dashed Eddy's second opportunity to lead Tammany Hall, just as surely as Walker had blocked the first. Death would cheat him of any third try.

Eddy sought to protect the interests of our own district under Dooling's reign by placing Bert Stand in the pivotal post of Tammany Secretary. It was not difficult. After all, it had been Eddy's influence that assured Dooling's election. This crucial appointment marked Stand's rise as a behind-the-scenes political force.

In the aftermath of his attack, Eddy's life slowly ebbed away. At one point, death appeared imminent. But he fought back tenaciously. He even seemed on the verge of reaching the path to recovery when, again, he suffered a relapse.

One day Jimmy Hines went to the hospital—and nearly got into a scrape. The two leaders disliked each other, one difference between them being that Eddy admitted as much. At the end of the long fight for Tammany's control, Hines had offered to throw his votes to Eddy if Eddy re-entered the race as Dooling's foe. Eddy had rejected the bid, recognizing it as a gesture to block Dooling, deadlock the Executive Committee and put the Harlem leader in the position of kingmaker. Hines was no friend of Eddy.

Nevertheless, he came around to pay a courtesy call. By a coincidence, Dooling had picked the same hour for a visit. The

Tammany Tiger's new chief and Hines were out-and-out enemies and made no bones about it. Fortunately, Bert Stand spotted Dooling in the lobby and alertly ran interference. He realized that if Dooling marched into Eddy's room while Hines was there, the two might trade blows—and Eddy might get off his deathbed to referee. A quick thinker, Bert grabbed Dooling by the arm, ushered him out of the building and took him to a Fourteenth Street cafeteria for a bagel and lox. By the time they returned to the hospital, Hines had finished his call and left.

Death was to overtake Eddy soon enough without being pushed along by the excitement of a bedside quarrel. Shortly after the appendicitis attack, peritonitis, a general infection of the abdominal cavity had set in. As the summer days slipped by, it worked its evil. Eddy passed away at 5:00 a.m. on the morning of August 23, 1934. He was 43.

Word of his death circulated swiftly through the Lower East Side. Shopkeepers put their flags at half-mast and clusters of Jews gathered to express in Yiddish their sorrow at the passing of their Irish district leader.

Many of us gathered at the club or at his home, three doorsteps away. Bert Stand took messages of condolence. Al Smith expressed his "deep regret." Farley, in Chicago, announced he would fly East to attend the funeral. Governor Lehman sent a telegram to Eddy's mother saying, "I had known Senator Ahearn for a great number of years. During the period that he served in the Senate while I was Lieutenant Governor, we had formed a fine friendship. He was loyal and devoted to his friends, who held him in respect and affection."

By midnight, more than 2,000 persons had filed in and out of the Ahearn brownstone home on East Broadway. The continuous stream mounted the stone steps and passed through the parlor where Eddy lay. Five patrolmen and a sergeant from the Clinton Street precinct were dispatched to control the crowd.

As the new Tammany chief, James Dooling, left the Ahearn home, he remarked to reporters, "I am at a loss what to say.

But if you will just go around the neighborhood, you will find out what kind of man he was without my trying to tell you."

For 100 years, Eddy's family, on both his father's side and his mother's side, had lived on the Lower East Side within a three block radius. He was born a stone's throw from his home and went to school across the street. Like his father's, Eddy's life centered around the clubhouse. He never married. Following his father's death, Eddy lived with his widowed mother.

Eddy loved politics for itself, not as a steppingstone to wealth or glory. During his last years, however, as the depression widened, clubhouse responsibilities were no longer a "game" but a wearying ordeal. They took a lot out of him, perhaps too much.

"This institution has been here more than fifty years and the people here depend on it," he remarked some time before his death. "A few years ago there was a kick to it. A man came in and wanted something and you got it for him. Now they all want jobs and money and there are no jobs and money is scarce. You can't say no—that's a slap in the face, but you can't do much either. It's depressing."

For the neighbors he served, few events could have been more depressing than Eddy's death. His funeral was described as the largest ever held on the Lower East Side. Nearly 10,000 residents and 200 police lined the sidewalks as the cortege proceeded from the Ahearn home to the century-old St. Mary's Roman Catholic Church at Grand and Ridge Streets. Governor Lehman, former Governor Smith, Postmaster General Farley and Tammany leader Dooling followed the rose and orchid-covered coffin as it slowly passed through the narrow streets between the tenement buildings.

Hundreds jammed into the church, whose doors were finally closed by police. After the services, silent crowds watched along Grand, Norfolk and Delancey Streets as 200 cars rolled by on their way to the Williamsburg Bridge and beyond to the cemetery.

Scores of local politicians and public officials were present. Of these I shall say nothing, for many of them attended Eddy's funeral as they would attend any major public event—because they were expected to. But this obligation did not fall upon the common laborer, the small shopkeeper, the tenement dweller, the pushcart peddler or the pants presser. They came because they wanted to come, because they felt they owed it to Eddy.

In their service, Eddy had represented Tammany at its best. No reformist pamphlets on the evils of machine politics and machine politicians could erase one tear of their grief.

VII

The Little Flower: Scent and Odor

FOR NEARLY HALF A CENTURY, TAMMANY HALL'S BANNER IN the Fourth Assembly District had been folded around the Ahearn name. Sentiment decreed that it should continue to do so.

Eddy had a younger brother, William. Though only three years in age separated them, Willie had never become a familiar figure in the political affairs of the neighborhood. Indeed, he has not even been mentioned in this narrative until now.

Early in life, Willie suffered a serious head injury. I believe, at one time, he carried a metal plate on his skull as enduring evidence of this disability. His health was fragile and his mind often became unbalanced as a result of his tragic accident. Clearly Willie, a good kind soul with a heart of gold, could not be expected to command the respect given his father or exert the forceful leadership exhibited by his brother.

Nonetheless, we intended to continue the "Ahearn tradition" despite the inevitable superficiality of the arrangement. Willie did not ask for the job. The district leadership was thrust upon him. He accepted it as a family obligation.

The succession was not automatic, however. The final decision was left to Mrs. John F. Ahearn. She could exercise her veto. Eddy had lived with his mother, and it was apparent that she had witnessed his health, never rugged or robust, wither away under his heavy burden. A million friends seemed to cluster around her elder son and it was always "Eddy, let's go here" or "Eddy, let's go there" or "Eddy, I need to see you right away." Irregular hours, a gobbled meal on the run, worry over his constituents' problems— all these helped cut short his life and lead him to an early grave.

If anything, Willie's health was far more precarious. Mrs. Ahearn might not wish to see her sole remaining son assume the burden of leadership. Only with her consent was Willie installed.

The meeting of county committeemen, who formally elected Willie, was held at the clubhouse one month after Eddy's death. Aaron J. Levy went through all the motions, as only he could. He outlined the duties of leader and exhorted Willie to follow in his brother's footsteps.

"I will try to serve you as Eddy did," replied poor Willie simply. He meant it.

But everyone present knew the Ahearn era was over. Nothing would be the same again.

Actual control of the district passed into the hands of the Stand brothers—Bert and Murray. In future years, Bert was to become a power in Tammany circles, sometimes *the* power. To paraphrase the description tendered Andrew Mellon, "three Tammany leaders —Christopher D. Sullivan, Michael J. Kennedy and Edward V. Loughlin—served under him."

Bert would prove himself Eddy's equal in shrewdness, but not in loyalty or humanity. In the end, he would be ousted by a captains' revolt, partly fostered by an injustice done me.

Before his death, Eddy attempted to safeguard the Ahearn club's position by two acts—each of which was designed to do so through the Stands. First, he pushed Murray Stand for vice-chairman, or floor leader, of the 65-member Board of Aldermen. As such, he would be third in line behind the Mayor and the President of the Board, in the exercise of city executive authority. Although it seemed unlikely that Mayor LaGuardia would vanish along with his number two man, Murray could nevertheless gain valuable prestige in this post.

Second, and far more important, Bert Stand was named confidential Secretary of Tammany Hall. Intelligent, witty and ever crafty, he would eventually convert this job into an undercover Premiership and almost reduce the Hall's nominal leader to a ceremonial role.

Bert was just 33 years old when he became the Tiger's right-hand man. We had grown up together and our fathers had been good friends. Bert had entered politics earlier than I did. His dad, Leon, was John F. Ahearn's first Jewish lieutenant back in the days when a Jewish politician was a curiosity. "I inherited the captaincy from my father," Bert used to say.

A big, round man with an easy smile and a quick handshake, Bert was a live wire at the club. His girth and prematurely balding mane seemed to add years to his appearance, perhaps an asset in his dealings with political elders.

In the old Ahearn days, we shared an election district as co-captains and made the rounds together. We remained close friends down through the years. Despite his personal frailties, despite his acknowledged association with Frank Costello in the early 1940s, I believe he could have retained the leadership and respect of the Fourth Assembly District till the day he died had he listened to his conscience instead of his brother Murray. The decline and fall of the Stands, however, properly belong to a future chapter.

Bert first achieved a measure of fame when Governor Al Smith let Eddy Ahearn pick a secretary for the State Athletic Commission. The job was blown Bert's way. Soon, boxing writers were tagging him "Bashful Berty." This was an affectionate title, which he well earned. On the day of a big fight, he would fling his face in front of the cameramen's lens at the weigh-in ceremonies. His became a familiar figure, if not name.

"Berty" made himself indispensable at the Athletic Commission, a talent he later transferred to Tammany Hall headquarters. He was here, there, everywhere. Among his less pleasant chores was the announcement of fighter suspensions. Nobody likes to see his favorite boxer barred from the ring.

"Berty" harvested popularity, though, by his artful handling of free passes. A ringside seat could work wonders in winning friends and influencing people. And Stand bestowed his favors upon all the right people, and then some. He once remarked, "The biggest headache in the world is giving out China tickets . . . we call them China tickets because they have holes in them . . . once you give a guy one, you gotta keep giving."

"Berty" gave away plenty, and so did his boss, Commissioner James A. Farley. On one occasion, Bert and I were chatting alone in the Commissioner's office. Making myself at home, I rested my feet atop Farley's desk. I offered to surrender this comfort when Farley entered, but he waved me down. "Don't bother getting up," he said, "I just came for my tickets." Bert handed him a batch, and off he went.

Farley received much undeserved criticism for bestowing these gifts on personal and political friends. But almost anyone in his position would have done the same. If, in some small way, it even helped foster the career of Farley's chief political client, Franklin D. Roosevelt, who could complain?

Farley and Stand, who himself was named a Deputy Commissioner when the Athletic Commission was reorganized, became good friends. This relationship perhaps helped Bert years later, when Farley's fortunes advanced. Following Eddy Ahearn's death in the summer of 1934, there were fears that our corner of Tammany would now be placed alongside other districts on a jobless diet. After all, Eddy had known Roosevelt, and Bert did not. Nevertheless, a thin trickle of patronage still came out to the Lower East Side. This manna from Washington's heaven did nothing to diminish Bert's stature either in the Fourth Assembly District or in wider Tammany circles. Remember, City Hall was in hostile Fusionist hands during this period. And the depression gripped the city.

Nominally, Willie Ahearn was our leader from 1934 to 1950. He cast the Fourth Assembly District's vote at Tammany Executive Committee meetings. Certain papers required his signature. But Willie, as well as everyone else, knew his limitations. At times, though the nature of his ailment affected his memory, Willie was quite aware of Bert's role.

During the mid-thirties, I ran into Willie after a hard day's work at the Custom House, then the location of lower Manhattan Internal Revenue offices.

"Louis," he said, "I feel sorry for you. Really I do. It must be awful to be out of work. You deserve something after all you've done for the club. I'm going to see that you get something. Yes, I'll talk to Bert. He'll find some place to put you on."

I nodded as Willie spoke and expressed my gratitude. Naturally,

I wanted to reach Bert before Willie did. I called him immediately and related the incident.

"Did you tell him about your job as an investigator?" Bert asked when I finished.

"Of course not!" I replied.

"Good," said Bert. "When Willie sees me, I'll tell him that you'll get the next vacancy at Internal Revenue."

We always made every effort to safeguard Willie Ahearn's feelings and ignore the mental lapses traceable to his accident. If the situation were reversed, poor Willie would have done no less for us.

Like other elected district chiefs, Willie trekked to Tammany's Seventeenth Street headquarters whenever conferences were called or important matters concerning our district were to be transacted. Bert, by contrast, kept his hand at Tammany's pulse day-in and day-out. This was his duty as Secretary. Few contracts and even fewer job requests filtered through the Hall without first crossing Bert's desk. He heard all, saw all and discharged his tasks capably.

The position carried no salary, but had compensating advantages for a rising young politician. The post fitted Bert exceptionally well, since he preferred behind-the-scenes activity to policy-making. Anyhow, he still drew $5,000 a year from the State Athletic Commission and retained his "Bashful Berty" image in the press.

His first "boss" at the Hall's general headquarters was James J. Dooling. Dooling was something of a question mark when he succeeded John F. Curry, and Bert's presence at his side was supposed to be our district's insurance policy. That is why Eddy put him there.

Barely 41 years old, Dooling was the youngest leader in Tammany's history. Undeniably intelligent, he simply did not know his way around the Hall when he took over. Without much experience in district rule, he lacked the type of background necessary to quickly rehabilitate the decaying structure. Nor did he ever really get the chance to develop his abilities. Dooling's health failed him, and vigor was well-nigh essential in a job where rebellious district leaders constantly had to be held in check.

Dooling, a former college athlete, was a student of psychology and philosophy, and the best-dressed Tammany boss in recollection. He was above average in height, slim, a dedicated bachelor and an avid golfer. He not only went to college—he also taught at Fordham University. His vocabulary was huge. He could translate the symbols of higher mathematics and speak fluent Latin and Greek. His knowledge of the Greek language helped him communicate with some voters in his native Fifth Assembly District, a feat that few Irish politicians could accomplish. Dooling also learned French while on duty with the 351st Field Artillery in France during World War I. In many ways, he was a remarkable choice for the leadership of an organization many people regarded as wicked.

Like Eddy Ahearn, Dooling learned about politics at his father's knee. The elder Dooling, Peter J., had controlled his district for about forty years. When he died in 1931, young Jimmy inherited it. Though active around his dad's club for years, Dooling had less than three years' actual leadership of his district behind him when he was handed the crown of sovereignty over all Tammany.

A lawyer, a gentleman, a devotee of good music and a master of table etiquette, Dooling set upon his tasks diligently with the best of intentions. But he hesitated to combine soft speech, which came naturally, with a big stick, which was a totally foreign characteristic. He never battered the heads of dissident lieutenants together. Nor could he reassert Tammany's domination over the Democratic machines in other boroughs, lost since the days of Charles F. Murphy.

Murphy never had boasted that he controlled New York City. But he did, and only a fool—or an occasional Mayor—could have had the temerity to doubt it. His successor, Judge Olvany, was too busy wrangling business for his law office to bother about maintaining the Hall's authority over its across-the-river-vassals. John Curry did believe he controlled the city, but really did not.

Dooling neither exercised city-wide power nor made exaggerated or empty boasts. He patiently carried on in his limited role as caretaker for the sickly Manhattan Democratic organization, waiting for something to happen. It never did.

The three year period of Dooling's reign, from the summer

of 1934 to the summer of 1937, was a grim one for Tammany. The Tiger's fortunes continued their downward plunge.

From his desk at Tammany Hall, James Dooling was master of nothing his eyes could survey. Downtown, at City Hall, Mayor Fiorello H. LaGuardia could laugh at Seventeenth Street's impotence while, at the same time and with a straight face, damning it as evil incarnate.

La Guardia dominated New York's political life during the depression years. No story of Tammany could ignore his role as the Thirties unfolded. For more than a decade, this fiery, ambitious, ornery, roly-poly little man wore civic virtue on his sleeve and mouthed profanities at his associates. He ruled as a dictator—no matter how benevolent. He worked outside normal party channels to achieve his ends, noble or otherwise.

The Mayor breathed publicity and knew how to draw it in. If New York were surrounded by Pontine Marshes, he would no doubt have drained them. But not before an audience of photographers could be assembled to record the scene as he shoveled the first lump of mud. The Little Flower left for posterity an image larger than life.

LaGuardia married the New Deal, certainly no sin. But it was a union of convenience. Almost any "Deal" that poured millions of dollars into programs that, in effect, cemented him to the Mayorship would have held similar appeal. LaGuardia was scrupulously honest with money, but not with people. He engaged in ties, never loyalties. He needed Roosevelt far more than Roosevelt needed him. So he gleefully accepted federal funds and clung to the President year-in and year-out.

It is plain that when the national administration's attentions were diverted from social programs to foreign affairs, LaGuardia's local star faded. He could no longer pluck leaves from the money tree. Had he run for re-election in 1945, there were many indications he would have been badly licked.

Far too many historians have viewed LaGuardia through rose-colored glasses. But the Little Flower exuded an odor as well as an aroma. It was harder to detect, and few have bothered to close in for a good sniff. His biographers, ranging from intimate associates to distant college professors have long pointed out his virtues. This is only natural. LaGuardia was a master of propaganda and his admirable public virtues are part of the public record.

In his three terms, LaGuardia not only did much *for* the *city,* however. He also did much *to* the city. Before he took office, charity was a sometime thing. People did not want it. People did not expect it. They accepted it only when they needed it. Always, they sought the means to better themselves and earn their own way. At our clubhouse, people rarely came for direct handouts. They wanted opportunity, not alms.

The Mayor removed charity from the realm of an unwanted necessity and rechristened it as a way of life. At a time of mass unemployment, drastic measures were needed. All over the country, drastic measures were taken. However, when the immediate economic crisis waned, most urban areas strove to clear the slate of these emergency measures. Not New York City. Welfare activities were expanded, like Topsy, beyond the limits of desirability, propriety or control. Many recipients here even formed an alliance to protect their interests!

In our own Fourth Assembly District, poverty had always been present. But poverty was something your family sought to pull itself out of. It was never considered a permanent occupation until the Little Flower promoted it as such. His motives may have been primarily humanitarian. But by no means were they solely based on lofty ideals.

Tammany had often been criticized for buying votes with relief. It is true that a basket of food was often converted into a vote for the stars on Election Day. But the money that paid for the food did not come from public funds. It came from neighborhood merchants and fund-raising activities held by the club. Distribution was handled by a captain who knew the recipient and knew he needed the handout. There was no "chiseling" on a grand scale. How many of LaGuardia's welfare workers were similarly familiar with their charges?

The Fusionist Mayor depersonalized charity and transformed it from a neighborhood necessity into a city-wide institution on a come-one, come-all basis. LaGuardia's propaganda pamphlets boasted that relief was handed out without "a taint of favoritism or politics." But he did not divorce the two. He merely reshaped them. Indeed, his dispensing power helped purchase his second and third terms in office.

The fact that help was given at an office instead of a Tammany clubhouse did not veil the samaritan's identity. Nor was it intended to. The name "LaGuardia" was indelibly impressed in the mind of every recipient. It could have been no more effective a weapon had he chosen to personally distribute each check at the doorstep of City Hall.

Talk about eliminating "favoritism" in welfare was mostly nonsense. A vote "the right way" on Election Day was the result, not the cause, of Tammany's favors. At the Ahearn club, we did not ask a man for his party allegiance before supplying his needs. There were no advance commitments. Behind the closed curtains of the voting booth, gratitude played its role. This, too, was La-Guardia's tactic.

At one point, close to 1,500,000 persons, one out of every five New Yorkers, were direct or indirect beneficiaries of the public welfare program. Discounting children, it still added up to an awesome number, and LaGuardia was certainly alive to their voting potential.

Eighteen thousand employees were involved in relief work and their expenses sucked in 10% to 12% of the welfare budget. This was no menial overhead. Surely, the economic chaos wrought by the depression cried for massive action. Much of the welfare funds came from Washington and would have been applied to good works by any progressive City Hall occupant. LaGuardia happened to be lucky enough to reap the federal harvest. He may be rightfully applauded for acting decisively in those hours of crisis. But not for piling brick upon brick in the towering relief structure while other urban areas had begun to dismantle theirs.

Roosevelt's working relationship with LaGuardia dimmed any chance for Tammany's speedy recovery. This not-so-grand alliance might have been broken, however, had it not been for Tammany's stubbornness and the administration's vindictiveness. Let us now turn to the roots of this continuing Democratic family squabble.

When James Dooling succeeded John Curry during LaGuardia's first year in office, happy days seemed here again. The corner leading to party harmony seemed at first to have been turned. Unlike Curry, an implacable foe, and Eddy Ahearn, a protege of Al Smith, young Dooling appeared "safely" in the New Deal's pocket. From Iowa, National Chairman Farley wired his congratulations: "Pleased to learn it was unanimous."

Dooling, college-bred, clean-cut and progressive, seemed just the fellow to lift Tammany out of its tarnished past and line it up with the national administration. His right-hand man, Bert Stand, even younger than Dooling and a former associate of Farley, also had no strings tied to the Old Guard of the party.

Yet, within months, Washington and the Tiger were again glaring at each other bitterly and Democrats within New York hung together only by the name they still retained in common. Why did the chasm remain unfilled?

People tend to forget that the sinews of a local political machine stem from its bottom, the individual districts. The man at the top, the county leader, may push, he may press, he may cajole—but he cannot dictate. Even Charles F. Murphy, the strongest of leaders, backed off on rare occasions when persistence might have incited his lieutenants to revolt.

Dooling was certainly no Charles F. Murphy. He did not enjoy one-tenth of that political giant's control of his party. No one should be astonished, therefore, about his inability to bring Old Guard district chiefs into the new world of the New Deal. When the head cat realized that he could not lead the pack in the direction he wanted, he turned back and joined the scratching felines in opposition to the leonine-like President.

Many Tammany leaders at the district level had prospered under John Curry's regime. They had been the "ins" during the scandal-filled 'twenties. They stayed loyal to the memory of James J. Walker. They bitterly resented Washington's attitude during the 1933 LaGuardia-O'Brien-McKee Mayoralty race, and they neither forgot nor forgave Roosevelt for his role.

Other leaders were willing to discard the past and permit Curry, Walker and O'Brien to mold away quietly in obscurity. But they

were sore about the national administration's love affair with the
Fusionist Mayor. Their reasoning was simple and could not be
dismissed as simple-minded—"My enemy's friend must be my
enemy."

The dissatisfaction of other district leaders could be traced to
neither nostalgia for the "good old days" nor discontent with the
White House-City Hall axis.

These leaders resented the manner in which federal patronage
was being distributed. Roosevelt and Farley were highly selective
in their political appointments, rewarding staunch friends and
ignoring all others. Curry and Walker had carried out this practice
far more ruthlessly at the local level. But district chiefs, callous
to the treatment accorded the Fourth Assembly District several
years earlier, reacted far differently now that their own ox was
being gored. It was their turn to get along on a skimpy diet of jobs.

Some Tammany strongholds, on the other hand, did well indeed.
While Eddy Ahearn lived, our own patronage flowed freely. In
another section of the city, Jimmy Hines, ex-blacksmith, confidant
of "Dutch" Schultz, leader of the Eleventh Assembly District and
lord over half-a-dozen others, did even better. Hines had deserted
Al Smith during the 1932 Democratic National Convention at
Chicago. His action was not based on principle, for Hines lacked
both principles and scruples. He was an opportunist, pure and
simple. He made his weight known and threw it in whatever
direction suited his private ends.

Charles Murphy never liked Hines, and Eddy Ahearn could
not stand him. Both showed good judgment. Roosevelt and Farley
apparently did not know him as well as they did.

The Harlem leader flexed his newly-sprouted political muscles.
He grew accustomed to a superbly furnished Central Park West
apartment and Long Beach summer home. His well-publicized
affluence and his even more widely-publicized underworld associates invited close scrutiny, however. Hines eventually wound up
in an austerely-decorated cell. His last political "appointment"
was to a penal institution.

I can understand why some diligent district leaders were dis-
turbed about federal patronage practices. I have always felt that

political rewards should be based on party service and Election Day achievements, not on participation in any clique or faction. Curry's forces had set out to destroy the John F. Ahearn Association during Mayor Walker's administration solely because of his personal quarrel with Eddy. This policy had been wrong then and it was wrong now. Only a desire to see vengeance done could have justified our sideline support for the punishment being meted out to Curry's allies.

It is equally understandable why Roosevelt's cooperation with LaGuardia galled some leaders. The Mayor was clearly no friend of the local Democratic organization. He designed plans for our destruction. He called our party workers "bums" and "clubhouse loafers," titles as false as they were malicious. He put an army of thousands to work manning newly-created city offices, yet threw hundreds of Tammany jobholders on the streets for reasons of "economy."

Tammany Hall had easily survived Fusion regimes in the past. Like bees, they stung once and then died. Mayor LaGuardia, though, was unique. He was no one-term phenomena, garbed in a robe of unstained ethics. He was no John Purroy Mitchel, who ruled competently and courageously, compromised no moral principles, campaigned cleanly and faded away after four years. By contrast, LaGuardia employed all the demagogic techniques he accused his opponents of, and lasted for twelve years. His supporters justified these on the grounds that his goals were pure, no matter how foul his methods. Anyway, they rationalized, he acted frankly, forthrightly and in the open.

LaGuardia was engaging in insidious dealings, however, of which his stiffly-upright backers were unaware. Although several potent district chiefs were involved, these dealings were even screened from rank-and-file Tammany Hall workers until the end of LaGuardia's first administration. Any hint of an alliance between the Fusionist Mayor and elements of the Tammany organization would have been scoffed at as a cross between an orchid and poison ivy. Nonetheless, such an alliance existed. And it worked.

In the public's eye, LaGuardia retained the image of a crusader, alternately slashing and hacking away at the Tammany Tiger with bold, ferocious swipes. These were damaging, all right, but not lethal. When the photographers' flashbulbs were exhausted, the reporters gone and city desk switchboards quiet, however, the Mayor silently stole into the sleeping Tiger's cage and nudged the beast. Where he found a weak spot, a vain district leader, an avaricious district leader, an ambitious district leader, he opened his little black bag of soothing medicines and set to work. A job here, a favor there, a promise for post-election time—these were the salves he offered. And some muscles of the Tiger responded to the treatment. They were made well while the rest of the cat languished. The salve had its price. Each November, when Tammany needed every last ounce of strength to lunge against its restraining bars, these muscles were to remain dormant. They were to doze through the annual campaign struggle. Agreed? The pact was made and "Doctor" LaGuardia snuck back out of the cage.

The Mayor had dealt only with the blackest muscles of the creature, for only the blackest would participate in such conspiracies, the kind that would flex themselves in unscrupulous ways in other days. As I indicated, these undercover arrangements were screened from both the integrity-clad reformers backing the Mayor and from most Tammany precinct workers.

When morning dawned and the glare of publicity returned, LaGuardia was again busy smashing at the Tiger through the bars of its cage. He did it with nary a wink nor a pang of conscience. Somehow, I feel there is something more to honesty than not stealing a dollar.

Besides demagogic appeal and a loose set of political ethics, La Guardia also had an unwitting ally which his Fusionist predecessors had lacked. It was called the Great Depression. This ally had a sharp cutting edge that tore at the vitals of the Tammany organization.

Any political machine that contains thousands of workers needs a steady stream of jobs. They are not necessarily city payroll jobs. Private utilities and firms engaged in contracting work with the city have been steady suppliers of such work. These business organizations occasionally need favors, get them, and are not likely to turn down a district leader's request to put a man to work. This favor for favor transaction still takes place today. But it was far more prevalent in times past. Private firms often provided the fuel that kept district clubhouses securely warm during the four-year-winters of reformism that occasionally gripped City Hall.

Admittedly, not everyone employed under these conditions put in a full day's labor for a full day's pay. For example, one captain I knew was hired as a "surveyor." He carried a tape measure in his back pocket and scurried about the construction site. He could not tell a plumb line from a yo-yo. He needed $40 a week, however, to keep his head financially above water and did work worth twice that amount for the constituents of his election precinct. All the company asked of him was that he stay out of the way.

In prosperous times, business firms did not hesitate to comply with reasonable requests. But the decade of the 1930s was far from prosperous. As the Great Depression deepened, business sought to curtail expenses. Retrenchment became the dismal theme and companies fired rather than hired help. Economy measures were certainly justified. But the results were disastrous for the hard-pressed Tammany organization.

Reeling under such heavy blows coming, as they were, from many directions, the Democratic Party in New York County looked vainly for a savior. It found none.

New York's regular Democratic clubs felt cheated by the scant attention their patronage claims received at the nation's capital. The last two Democratic Presidents, Grover Cleveland and Woodrow Wilson, had sanctimoniously snubbed Tammany, too. The situation was nothing new. But now it was more serious. With LaGuardia pulling its whiskers and the depression tugging at its tail, the Tiger was in greater agony than ever before. Throughout the Mayor's first term in office, which coincided with Dooling's Tammany overlordship, the Tiger's condition worsened.

There had been an ever-so-brief glimmer of hope in 1934, during the first months of Dooling's reign. As the year ended, he even emerged smiling one day from a White House conference. "Tammany Hall is 1,000,000 per cent behind Roosevelt," he announced cheerfully.

But Dooling was not Tammany. True, he still remained loyal to the national organization. After all, was it not Farley, as well as Eddy Ahearn, who had insured his elevation to the county leadership? As I have described at some length, however, the district leaders were princes in their own right, and a rebellious lot they could be. Dooling was merely first among equals. He could be neutralized and overwhelmed. And that he was.

Tammany was to be rent asunder by a bill born in far-off Albany. Governor Lehman had raised a proposal to remap the state's assembly and senate districts. Farley, in his role as state chairman, backed the measure. Dooling did not like it, grumbled, but went along.

In effect, the measure would have cost Tammany seven seats in the state assembly and would have cut three Senators out of Manhattan's share in Albany. This redistricting plan, approved by upstate Democratic leaders, was intended to safeguard the party's representation in Rochester and Buffalo. Dooling, no fool, knew this would be small consolation to his own organization's district chiefs. He looked for a face-saving, job-saving formula.

Legislative action calling for the direct election of city magistrates would handsomely serve this purpose. This would take the appointive power out of LaGuardia's hands and give it to the voters instead. It was far easier to elect Democratic magistrates than to get the Mayor to appoint them.

Governor Lehman refused to agree to Dooling's plan. Back to his lieutenants trekked the sullen county leader, grim and empty-handed. He still backed Lehman's remapping plan—but from way, way back.

The district chiefs, on the other hand, waved no white flags. They controlled the votes of their district's State Senators and Assemblymen. And they had no intention of letting their people politically die for the sake of dear old Buffalo and Rochester. This was too great a sacrifice for distant relatives. New York City's Tammany delegation ignored Dooling, rebuffed Lehman, revolted in Albany and relegated the remapping plan to the legislative junkyard.

This rebellion left a bad taste all around and split Democrats even wider apart. Tammany men considered their action, contrary as it was to the will of the party's leadership, a deed of self-preservation. They were angered by Dooling's support of the suicidal measure.

Lehman and Farley—and perhaps Roosevelt, who kept in touch with local affairs—regarded the rebellion as an act of treason. They were furious that Dooling did not give the plan *enough* support and hammer down opposition within the local organization. From their lofty perches of statescraft, they ignored the fact that tiger cubs are not demure lambs. They growl, scratch, bite and are not easily led to the slaughterhouse.

Dooling, caught in the middle, could not satisfy both the district leaders and the party's overlords. Sooner or later, he had to choose sides. It was no easy decision. He aligned himself with the majority of the organization he nominally led rather than with the Roosevelt camp.

This decision helped preserve Dooling's job for the moment, but it did not add to his stature. Federal patronage, already just a trickle, was reduced to an occasional drip. The year 1935 progressed glumly for most of Tammany Hall. Only Hines and his crew fattened. As they always do in times of trial, conspiracies formed in several quarters to wrest "control" from Dooling. Ousting him would not have been difficult. He lacked the solid core of allies that buttressed Curry's position long after he had become an albatross on the back of the Democratic Party. Efforts to dump Dooling petered out, though, over the problem of succession. The rebels had a cause, but no leader.

In our corner of Manhattan, Albert Marinelli, leader of the western part of the Second Assembly District, took advantage of the disunity. He made another strong bid for control. Five years earlier, Eddy Ahearn had stifled his ambitions. Now, in 1935, with the Hall in turmoil, and Eddy dead, the path seemed clearer. As his first move, he inspired revolts against Alderman David A. Mahoney and Dan Finn, leaders of the neighboring First Assembly District, on the tip of Manhattan island. Both men were quite capable of holding on against all comers, Marinelli included. So he withdrew with a politically bloody nose.

Following this rebuff, he turned toward an easier target, his old adversary, Christopher D. Sullivan. Christy's spot in the eastern half of the Second Assembly District had not been secure for years. With Eddy gone, it seemed ripe for seizure. Marinelli had long enjoyed undercover control without the external trappings. Now he wanted both the power *and* the title.

Once more, he was stopped short. This time, it took the combined opposition of James Dooling and Bert Stand (acting through Willie Ahearn) and Jimmy Hines to convince the Italian leader of his unwisdom. Marinelli again halted his neighborhood aggression, hauled in his colors and resumed a posture of watchful waiting. The setback was only temporary.

Following Dooling's death, Marinelli's star would rise high in Tammany's sky thanks to his own persistence and the blackjacks of his somewhat less dainty associates. Then, swiftly, it would pummel downward with the fury of a meteor. Marinelli was to be undone, like Hines, by a mustached young investigator named Thomas E. Dewey.

The Presidential election campaign of 1936 saw no soft reconciliation within the Democratic family. In a sense, Tammany "took its fight to court." In June of that year, Roosevelt appointed two federal judges to New York's Southern District without asking for the advice or consent of local Democrats. As is customary, when the appointments went before the United States Senate for consideration, the New York members voiced their opinions.

Senator Robert F. Wagner, a Murphy protege and stalwart New Dealer, ably defended them. Senator Royal Copeland, who was closer to the Tammany organization than his colleague, sharply assailed the nominees. His attempts to obstruct the appointments failed, however. The Senate voted confirmation of Roosevelt's choices.

The battle over the courts next shifted to New York. Governor Lehman had appointed Jonah J. Goldstein to temporarily fill a vacancy in the Court of General Sessions here. As fall approached, Dooling refused to give Goldstein Tammany's nod for a full term. This was a direct slap at the Governor's face.

Goldstein was considered a competent judge. In his behalf, Al

Smith approached the bar of Tammany justice. But he received a deaf ear. Dooling even refused to see Goldstein, as courtesy demanded, and explain why the nomination had been denied him. The castaway judge ran in the primary as an insurgent, which was his right, and was beaten.

Three years later, Goldstein again ran in the primary. This time he won. He received regular party support in the general election that followed and resumed his judicial career. Unfortunately, he had higher ambitions. He later sought the Democratic nomination for Mayor, failed to get it, turned party turncoat and ran for the city's highest office as a Republican! Naturally, he lost.

Another aspect of the link between politics and the judiciary might be noted here. Throughout the previous Fusion administrations, elective local courts largely remained in Tammany hands. Crusaders rarely paraded to win judicial robes. Anyway, few voters judged potential judges as individuals. They were usually unfamiliar names. Their fates were spelled out for them by the star or eagle that appeared beside their names. Stars won and eagles lost. As a result, Democratic judges held sway and court workers were the party faithful.

LaGuardia did not capture the courts as readily as he captured the city's administrative offices. Nonetheless, he found a way of striking at Tammany through the courts. He used a fiscal axe. Economy waves swept away some jobs and assured constant pocketbook tension for holders of others. Only the more fortunate had little cause for worry.

In a category by himself fell William Wagner, an old-timer from the Fourth Assembly District. As a court officer, he was utterly unique. During the long duel between John Curry and Eddy Ahearn, he had remained outside the field of battle, for he was a confidant of Mayor James Walker. In fact, it may be recalled that he was the man whom Eddy took along to Albany for his pregnant meeting with Governor Roosevelt, the meeting that shaped Walker's future.

Willie had entered public service as a $2-a-day cleaner in the Borough President's office in 1897. Within seven years, aided by John F. Ahearn, Willie rocketed to the level of janitor. Next, he got an appointment as a court attendant in 1908. Then ambition overtook Willie. In 1917, he sought, but did not get, a clerkship. This setback shook Willie to the core. But Senator Barney Downing came to the rescue. As Democratic leader of the upper chamber in Albany, Downing put through a specially tailored bill allowing Willie to hold down two judicial posts. The second, as attendant to the Board of Justices, paid $700 a year, approximately the amount the clerkship would have provided above his previous salary. By 1933, the $700 had been hiked to $2,025.

Then came poor Willie's darkest hour. An evening newspaper pointed out his dual jobholding to LaGuardia's Commissioner of Accounts. The enterprising periodical was not afraid that Willie was working too hard. Quite the contrary. Since the Board of Justices majestically sat for about fifteen hours a year, Willie was far from weighted down by responsibility. In fact, he was making $135 an hour by simple computation. Not bad for an attendant in the midst of a depression.

Willie Wagner was not precisely filled with righteous indignation, therefore, when the city's next budget request carried a substantial salary cut for him.

At times, Tammany chief Dooling must have wished he had Willie's troubles. By late 1936, his political foes included President Roosevelt, Governor Lehman, Postmaster General James A. Farley, Democratic National Chairman J. Aloysius Farley and State Chairman Jim Farley. This was a formidable group of gladiators. Dooling had even alienated Al Smith over the Goldstein judgeship. Was it any wonder that Dooling fell into ill health?

There have been many fights—verbal scuffles, that is—at Executive Committee meetings of Tammany's leaders. But I have rarely heard of the other kind—with fists—shattering the Hall's dignity. Yet Dooling's illness provoked such a fight. The combatants were both pushing 70, certainly the wrong age for such an encounter. It happened in Bert Stand's office. To pinpoint the location more accurately, it happened at and on his desk.

While incapacitated, Dooling had desired a committee of three leaders—Christopher Sullivan, Charles Hussey and Stephen Ruddy —to function in his stead. Their job would be to keep the Tiger moving straight ahead, without veering off in one direction or another. Most district leaders were agreeable. But some, led by Jimmy Hines and William P. Kenneally, 66-year-old Chairman of Tammany's Executive Committee, were not so compliant. They wanted a powerfully propelled "steering committee," with Kenneally as chief steerer.

On the day the matter was to come to a vote, the district chiefs gathered in the Tammany Hall lobby, chatted, moved slowly through the corridors and then began to file through Bert's office to the conference room. Kenneally was walking side-by-side with Christy Sullivan, also 66, when open warfare broke out.

"Bill, why don't you quit your stalling?" asked Christy.

"What do you mean stalling?" snapped Kenneally, adding a choice phrase usually confined to less austere circles.

Christy, whose normally red nose and cheeks were now absorbed into a completely red face, retorted, "I have been accustomed to dealing with gentlemen!"

Then fists began to fly. Kenneally reeled backward, landing on Bert's desk. He recoiled, then burst forth as he uttered his battle cry. With lowered head, he slammed into Christy, who went down but not out.

The peacemakers, Jimmy Hines, Dan Finn and others, now stepped in. The bout ended as Kenneally shouted, "I'll get even with you!" The meek may inherit the Earth, but ruling Tammany Hall was quite a different matter in those days.

As an anti-climax, the meeting was called to order. After an hour-long debate, Dooling's triumvirate received calm approval. Bert Stand came out from behind the closed doors of the conference room to make the formal announcement to the press. "The Executive Committee unanimously agreed to respect Mr. Dooling's wishes as regards the appointment of the committee named by him," Bert said.

Sullivan and Kenneally, contestants in the over-the-age match, also came out to pose for photographers and explain what great friends they were. This was one occasion when the fighters stole the show from "Bashful Berty."

Both elder statesmen brushed off the affair. "We were talking," said Christy, "and I may have pushed him. We didn't mean anything by it. We have known each other for forty years and we are like brothers—yes, you can say brothers."

Kenneally had represented the Roosevelt-Farley forces in the dispute, with Hines' close support. Apparently, Washington feared that Dooling, or any regency created by him, would attempt to hurt Roosevelt in the coming national election. A low plurality here could cost him New York State's electoral votes since upstate counties traditionally went Republican by heavy majorities. Roosevelt's strategists no doubt recalled Smith's sad fate in the 1928 campaign's climax, when the then leader, George Olvany, failed to push hard enough to pile up local votes for his man. They also remembered that in 1932 the Democratic Presidential nominee ran behind Lehman, running for Governor, by 42,000 votes on Manhattan Island.

But their anxiety was unwarranted. The Tammany Hall organization, though openly at odds with the administration, plunged no dagger into the back of its Hyde Park neighbor. When the returns were in, Roosevelt was master of Manhattan by more than 332,000 votes.

In our own Fourth Assembly District, the name "Landon" might have been mistaken for some new brand of soap or cleaning detergent. Most voters had never heard of him. The rest quickly forgot him. He polled 990 votes to 11,700 for Roosevelt. Bert boasted that only 20 voters pulled the Republican lever in his precinct,and I did just as well in mine. He was a bit more bloodthirsty, though. "I'll find those 20 Landon voters in the morning and I'll shoot them!" he stormed.

The newspapers attributed Roosevelt's beaming success here to his personal appeal rather than Tammany's effort. This was an oversimplification. Without detracting one iota from the President's popularity, I might say that in our assembly district, at least, the people voted for their captains, not the candidates. Even a Calvin Coolidge could have carried this district if he had exchanged the Elephant for the Mule, placed a Tiger on its back and harvested the crop of votes we had sown by our legwork and bellringing.

Nevertheless, the election outcome was translated by many as a personal triumph rather than a party victory. Again efforts were renewed to oust the ailing Dooling and cage the Tiger in the name of the administration. Hines, hardly the image of a clean and spotless reformer, helped spearhead the drive.

While its leader slowly recuperated in Florida, Tammany Hall was virtually headless. The rest of its body, already broken into fragments, now shattered into splinters. Again it would have been easy to drop Dooling. But agreement on a successor would still have been impossible. So Dooling stayed on.

External pressure combined with internal chaos to disable Tammany Hall still further. If Washington could not tame the striped cat, and make it "meow" to the administration's tune, the Roosevelt forces could at least twist its tail a bit and maybe turn the Bronx and Brooklyn Democratic machines into raging lions. After that, it would be up to the king of beasts to slay the ailing Tiger.

In the early part of the century, Manhattan contained about 40% of the city's population. Now it was down to barely half that much. Our island's loss had been the other boroughs' gain. The political machines of Frank V. Kelly, in Brooklyn, and Edward J. Flynn, in the Bronx, now assumed far greater prominence and potency than ever before. No longer were the lands across the East and Harlem Rivers mere colonies and political outposts. They had grown up since Charles Murphy's days. And they would show how well they could flex their political muscles, under Farley's astute tutelage, before the coming Mayoralty campaign, just around the corner.

One well-traveled bridge between Roosevelt's 1936 allies and LaGuardia's 1937 axis was a rather strange conglomeration called the American Labor Party. This outfit, inspired by the President and created by labor union officials, was designed to permit union members to vote for Roosevelt without voting the Democratic Party line.

LaGuardia, who was elected as a Republican, reportedly used the ALP line to cast his ballot for Roosevelt and against Landon. So did many other anti-Democrats.

I have heard that some of the President's advisers disapproved of his blessings for the new party. They prophesied it would eventually turn into a monster. Indeed, they were to be proved right. It took less than a year for the transformation to be performed.

In 1937, Mayor LaGuardia turned the ALP into his own personal creature. He used it to throttle both Democrats and his own nominal party alike. In later years, the monster would be leashed to a new master, Vito Marcantonio, who would use it even less scrupulously for private ends.

The strength of the ALP originally came from the rank-and-file power of trades-union members. It was not a regular party, operating on a day-in-day-out basis. In our district, I cannot remember ever having seen a clubhouse bearing its label.

LaGuardia dealt with its key officials, who then preached their political gospel to the membership through union, not party, channels. In a sense, the ALP was a political operation rather than a political party. No doubt, LaGuardia liked it that way, for he was never a party man. He preferred to rely on wheeling and dealing and disciples such as Vito Marcantonio, who was destined to steer the American Labor Party to the left.

Unlike the unorthodox ALP, the two traditional parties assumed an entangling rather than temporary alliance on the part of its members. This was a duty that LaGuardia refused to acknowledge. Sam Koenig, who spawned the Mayor's political career, later had good cause to wish it had been stillborn.

Back in 1929, the yet pure GOP candidate, warring then on Jimmy Walker, promised Republican workers he would reward their support. Four years later, again as GOP nominee, LaGuardia disowned that pledge on the eve of victory. "I don't owe you a thing and you're not going to get a thing," he said. This time he honored his word. Having supped at the house of Republicanism, he discarded its clubhouse workers and cursed them, along with those of Tammany, as "political punks."

LaGuardia's shabby treatment of the GOP cost its New York County chairman his job. Normally, Chase Mellen Jr., who had succeeded Koenig, would have been hailed as a party hero for installing a Republican Mayor. But City Hall ignored him, patronage eluded him and his followers saw fit to unseat him.

His successor was another blue-blooded "Junior," Kenneth Farrand Simpson Jr. This short, keen-eyed, red-mustached graduate of Yale and Harvard Law School had all the credentials a respectable Republican chief could hope to have. At New Haven, he won a Phi Beta Kappa key, and held membership in Zeta Psi and the senior society Skull and Bones. An extra-curricular activist, he also chairmanned the *Yale Daily News*. In that post, he scooped experienced reporters with his audacious story that Charles Evans Hughes had licked Woodrow Wilson for the Presidency in 1916.

Simpson outlived his journalistic boner, went on to serve in World War I and joined the elegant law firm of Cadwalader, Wickersham and Taft. It was the type of practice in which a young man of his background, upbringing and social caste was supposed to engage. He apparently did splendidly and in no way betrayed his breeding.

Ten years after leaving the university's ivy-covered towers, he wrote his school class secretary: "I am enjoying the general practice of law and especially the court work. I have been active locally in politics . . . I expect to continue an active interest in politics as my principal sideline or hobby outside of practicing law. My other hobbies, I should say, are music (attending most of the good concerts) and sailing (principally on borrowed boats in the Sound) and if I should ever have the money to engage in an expensive hobby, it would probably be collecting etchings or modern paintings . . . also travel."

Simpson did make the money, joined the *Social Register*, put together a collection of modernistic and surrealistic art and continued his "principal sideline" of politics.

Politics was no "hobby," though, for most of his party's workers. They had no law firm to furnish their livelihoods. They sought patronage. Instead, they received lectures. The Republican leader in the Fourth Assembly District, an old friend, sat glumly in front of his clubhouse one day when I passed by. He pointed gloomily at the sign fastened to the building, bearing in huge painted letters the names of Republican leading lights. The Mayor's, naturally, was at the top.

"I'm an organization man," said the GOP district chief, "and I'm going to work for the whole ticket. But, believe me, LaGuardia wouldn't be running again with Republican endorsement if the rank-and-file of the party had its say. He's never kept faith with us."

I do not know, of course, how harmonious the Little Flower's relations were with the top caste of the GOP. Simpson named his sad-eyed Bedlington terrier "Alf," and we know where La-Guardia's sympathies lay in the 1936 Roosevelt-Landon contest. The Mayor's undeniable popularity was largely based on his use of federal funds, generously provided by the Democratic President.

Nonetheless, with a straight face, the Mayor poured on the pressure for Republican endorsement as he made his bid for a second term. And he had no hesitancy about using his ALP instrument as a blackmail weapon to assure GOP renomination. The monster did its work well.

Simpson meekly surrendered GOP support to the Fusion hero, a man who had proved himself totally out of sympathy with the two party system. The 1937 Mayoralty campaign was about to gather full steam.

VIII

Tiger? What Tiger?
Do You See a Tiger?

THE MISFORTUNES HEAPED UPON THE REPUBLICANS BY THEIR little, round cherub turned Frankenstein paled before the chronic agony that plagued Tammany Hall. It no longer ruled the city. It no longer ruled the Democratic Party of the city. Now it prepared for even greater embarrassments.

As the summer of 1937 approached, the search for a Democratic Mayoralty candidate helped shatter the party still further—as if that were possible. Before the year was out, the Tiger would be a toothless pussycat, gaping with hollowed-out eyes at the catnip beyond its reach. The cemetery would be a long step closer.

In May, James Dooling returned from his long stay in Florida's warmth. Although not fully recuperated, he attempted to regrip the reins of the Tiger. He set upon the task of selecting a candidate for Mayor. The choice, however, was not his alone to make.

Leaders in the other counties swayed to the immaculately groomed Grover Whalen, who had quietly survived the indignity of being spat upon by Senator Barney Downing. Whalen's voting appeal remained a question mark. But his nomination surely would have boosted the stature of the Flynn-Kelly axis and, in the process, would have reduced Tammany to just one of the five Democratic organizations in the city.

It is therefore not surprising that Dooling said "no" to Whalen and looked elsewhere for a candidate. His gaze fastened on Washington. The United States Senate provided a talent pool of two. Dooling preferred our Junior Senator, Robert F. Wagner, a proven vote-getter. He knew Wagner was well thought of by the other

117

county chairmen, too. But the Wagner Act author and New Deal crusader preferred Washington's climate to City Hall's. He said "no" to Dooling.

An affirmative response, though, came from Senior Senator Royal Copeland, not so awesome a vote-catcher. Copeland was a loyal Tammany man, an anti-New Deal legislator and eminently unappealing to four of the five county chiefs. Only Dooling championed him and, at this point, Dooling scarcely controlled his own organization. In far-off Washington, President Roosevelt reportedly responded to Copeland's potential candidacy with the comment, "Ha, ha, ha."

The embattled Tammany leader now faced his district chiefs and plugged away for the Senator. The forces of the national administration, led by Hines, pushed for Whalen. Other factions walked a tightrope and adopted an attitude of watchful waiting. Some district chiefs seemed more interested in finding a successor for Dooling than a successor for LaGuardia.

In this crazy-quilt atmosphere, Dooling pulled off one of his few triumphs. It was also to be his last.

A day before the decisive Executive and County Committee meetings were scheduled to be held, he played host at his Belle Harbor summer home to Albert Marinelli and Christopher Sullivan. Both the puppeteer and his puppet agreed to support Copeland. In return, Dooling promised that Borough President Sam Levy's name would appear on the city-wide ticket. Levy sought elevation to the Presidency of the City Council, the newly-hatched, streamlined form of the old Board of Aldermen. That was the bargain.

Aided by the votes these men controlled, Dooling finally gained the mastery of his own county's Executive Committee. Copeland's candidacy under the Tammany Banner was thus launched, much to Hines' dismay.

Dooling did not live to enjoy his victory. Within a week of that fateful meeting, he passed away. The Tammany leader had sapped his energy preparing for the upcoming primary contest struggle. On the evening of July 25, 1937, he sent word to his chauffeur to pick him up at his Long Island home the next morning for the long journey to Tammany Hall headquarters. But by dawn, he was dead.

Dooling had outlived Eddy Ahearn by three years, and, like him, died in the middle of a bitter political fight. His three-year reign held few bright spots. The Tiger's back would have been too slippery for most men, and Dooling was no exception. In all fairness to Dooling, he inherited an impossible situation and left it the same way.

The district leaders took time off for Dooling's funeral, then resumed their fraternal squabbling. Three factions, with little in common but their membership in Tammany's ruling body, maintained Copeland's hopes. One group was led by Marinelli, the second consisted of Dooling's intimates, including Bert Stand, and the third, oddly, contained the remaining cluster of John F. Curry's friends. Al Smith, now an ardent anti-New Dealer, also supported Copeland.

Handling of the routine affairs of Tammany Hall fell temporarily to Bert and William Kenneally. Kenneally, Christy's fistfight opponent of the previous summer, was a staunch supporter of Whalen. From their desks at opposite corners of the Hall's second floor, Bert and Kenneally could keep tabs on each other.

This interim period was brief. Tammany needed a leader, at least a nominal leader, and almost anybody seemed better than no one at all. That is probably why Christy Sullivan was handed the job.

Though, technically, his election was unanimous, there was opposition. Not that anyone could possibly fear Christy. He was too old and too tame to become a roaring wildcat. But Hines and his followers knew that Sullivan up front meant Marinelli in the rear and Al Smith in the background. "No comment," Hines told reporters who asked his opinion of the election. "They wanted it. I have nothing to say."

Christy made it clear he would not confer with the other county leaders to break the impasse between the Senator and Whalen. This knocked the foundation from under one solution, pressed in some circles, that would have resulted in the ditching of both candidates in favor of a third man.

More than a thousand persons crammed the reception room and corridor to cheer the new leader. He posed for many photos, shook many hands, including Kenneally's, and declared he would "get right on with the job." His first official act was to ask Bert Stand to remain as Secretary of Tammany Hall.

The four other county leaders were beginning to have their doubts about the vote-drawing ability of their man, Grover Whalen. Copeland, in their eyes, was of course beyond the pale. So they cast about for a new standard bearer. Surprise of surprises, they found him within Tammany's own councils. Their magic wand touched on one Jeremiah Titus Mahoney, a Manhattan district leader.

At age 60, Mahoney could look back over a long, productive and honorable career. Beginning as a $2-a-week machine operator, he had worked his way up to a $25,000-a-year State Supreme Court judgeship, then resigned it when he found it dull. At college, he had been a brilliant student and a superb athlete. He won high-jump championships in both the United States and Canada.

Mahoney held charter membership in the F.R.B.C. (For Roosevelt Before Chicago) Club, one of the few Tammany leaders in that illustrious society. He was therefore on good terms with the President. In short, he was the antithesis of Copeland.

The ensuing primary contest drew less public interest than the fascinating preliminaries. About half the city's enrolled Democrats bothered to vote. Copeland won Manhattan Island, as he was expected to do. But he could not breach the riverfront walls of Brooklyn and the Bronx. Mahoney's victory was clear-cut, if not inspiring.

Tammany Hall swallowed its pride, accepted its ultimate humiliation and strode off to congratulate the winner. The Democrats of New York County now threw their support behind the choice of the rest of the city's Democrats.

The energy of the party was just about spent, however, by the time the bell sounded for the main event. The LaGuardia-Mahoney match proved to be no contest. This was true for several obvious reasons and at least one major hidden explanation.

As consumed by the public, the fight revolved around such typical issues as the administration's luxurious budget, rising tax rates and the alleged demoralization of the police force. LaGuardia's association with leftist-tinged organizations was aired side-by-side with other dirty linen.

The Hitler menace, a future LaGuardia ace-in-the-hole, had not yet become a major New York City campaign theme. But if LaGuardia had raised it, Mahoney could certainly have held his' own in any shouting brawl over who hated Der Führer the most. While president of the Amateur Athletic Union, the Democratic candidate had actively fought against American participation in the 1936 Berlin Olympic Games. His charges that Hitler would use the games for a propaganda platform were amply demonstrated.

The campaign dragged on as November approached. It created hardly a stir in the surface of the city's life. Apathy was King and the incumbent was its beneficiary. This was a shame. For Mahoney, no doubt, would have made a very progressive, competent and honest Mayor had he been given the chance between 1938 and 1942.

Behind the scenes, and beyond the public's view, LaGuardia worked carefully to guarantee his re-election. The massive relief program, for which he assumed full credit, assured him a large chunk of votes. But this was not enough. He knew he was greatly unloved by the rank-and-file of the Republican organization. He had done nothing to deserve their allegiance and needed further job insurance.

So LaGuardia sought a break-proof chain to bind him to the Mayor's desk. He purchased it in a debasing manner—both for the seller as well as the buyer.

LaGuardia traded on the human frailties of several Tammany figures. As the man behind the imposing desk at City Hall, he was capable of extending or withholding many gifts. He dangled them in front of those who would find them most tempting. La-Guardia did not ask for direct support from Tiger district chiefs. That would have been far too obvious. Besides, it would have incurred the wrath of the righteous, whose support he courted publicly. Instead, he merely asked that these leaders issue "Go Slow" orders to their captains and subordinates. A vote that was not cast for Mahoney was saved for the Mayor.

I will say this of Bert Stand. He never approached me, or any other captain I knew, with orders that we "take it easy" in our canvassing. But I cannot say the same of his elder brother, Murray.

"Don't work so hard, Louis," he advised. "Why knock yourself out climbing staircases. If you want to go someplace, maybe take off for the weekend, go right ahead. Don't worry about this election."

I had always liked Bert and felt wary of Murray. This conversation did nothing to increase his stature in my eyes. Nor did the bounties heaped upon him by the Mayor during his second and third terms in office. Murray was lifted by his Fusionist friend to pedestals of influence and, in times to come, would receive glowing press notices for his civic services. But a man's personal character is not masked by his governmental deeds. It is stamped by his private acts, performed beyond the glare of the public spotlight. It is not something that comes to light in the columns of a newspaper. Nor can it.

I believe that Murray Stand's request that late fall day, doubtlessly made of other captains as well, dissolved his integrity and crippled that of the Ahearn club. Murray deeply influenced Bert's decisions in both district affairs and wider Tammany circles. But Murray acted as his brother's cager rather than his keeper. Eventually, his insidious manner would cost Bert the leadership of the Democratic Banner District, a fate that never befell the Ahearns.

Aided and abetted by Murray Stands within the Tammany organization, the Mayor naturally did far better in Tiger strongholds than had previous Fusionists. He probably would have won anyway. But a healthy amount of insurance lets a man sleep comfortably even when success seems assured. This is especially true of politicians.

The atmosphere smothering Tammany Hall headquarters on Election night, November 2, 1937, was one of premeditated gloom. Not even a spark of expectancy illuminated the large auditorium. Only a handful of the faithful peeked in when the doors opened at 6 p.m. About 100, in all, took seats as the dismal hours slipped by. I heard that even Al Smith did not bother to show up. At times, reporters outnumbered political figures. It was never like this in the days of Charles F. Murphy. But neither were the returns.

Upstairs, Christy Sullivan and his lieutenants sulked. Tammany's general staff unofficially admitted Mahoney's defeat as the first results came in. Only respect for precedent prevented an even earlier concession.

By 8 p.m., Bert received news from the First Assembly District. It showed LaGuardia running ahead. A few minutes later, returns from Christy's own bailiwick had Mahoney leading by only a scant margin. Unconfirmed reports from our own Fourth Assembly District offered an even bleaker picture.

For years, we had been the Democratic Banner District. Rarely had the opposition pulled as much as 10% of the vote. A local revolution was in the making. Bert tried to explain away the apparent catastrophe for public consumption. "What the hell!" he said. "They pay off on one vote. That's what spoiled us around here, winning by half a million. We'll be satisfied to win by one."

Christy, as customary, was less talkative. "Just say I have no comment," he told reporters, pointing to the bulletins. "What's the use?"

Tammany was taking an unparalleled licking. We had lost before, but never like this. The Borough Presidency, with its sparkling gems of patronage, was swept away. So was the District Attorney's office. It fell to young, ambitious Thomas E. Dewey. Few anticipated the deluge he would soon pour down upon some factions of the Tammany organization.

Hundreds of appointive county and city posts vanished as Fusion triumphed. Most attention centered, though, on the dazed candidates for elective office. Clarence Neal, leader of the Twentieth Assembly District, and his Albany representative, Michael J. Keenan, dropped in on Sullivan. When Christy greeted Keenan as "Assemblyman," Neal corrected him. Make that "ex-Assemblyman," said Clarence.

Bert pointed out a pair of winning candidates, almost an oddity that grim evening. "There are the only survivors," he told photographers. "Now give us a nickel to get into the movies, will you?"

Former Assistant District Attorney Alexander I. Rorke announced somewhat more lyrically, "Our heads are bloody but they are unbowed. We'll be ready for the next campaign."

Christy called it a night at 10 p.m. He donned his overcoat, and quietly slipped out the back door.

"When's he coming back," someone asked Bert.

"He's not coming back," Stand replied. "He's gone home for the night."

Bert stuck around for another hour. Reasonably cheerful till the end, he explained, "I'm not a candidate!" By 11 p.m., the slaughter was over.

For me there were two rays of consolation. Henry Schimmel, a dear friend, had been elected a City Court Justice. Henry was one of the best known and respected figures on the Lower East Side. His victory came as no surprise. By contrast, Aaron J. Levy's bid for re-election to the State Supreme Court was the cause of much anxiety.

Aaron, as I mentioned earlier, had been forced to wage an uphill fight to get the judgeship back in 1923, because of his role in the Sulzer impeachment. My father's helping hand on that occasion had soothed the neighborhood's Jewish community. Now, fourteen years later, he faced an even stiffer campaign.

No question of Aaron's legal brilliance was involved. Lawyers used to step into his courtroom, sit down as spectators and absorb wisdom they did not pick up at law school. Lack of intelligence was certainly not one of Aaron's failings. He had others.

Unfortunately, Levy had developed some powerful foes. It seems he once failed to disqualify himself in a case involving a bank to which he owed money. This set many a tongue wagging. The New York City Bar Association also charged that he had interceded with insurance departments of New York and Massachusetts to advance the interests of friends. The Association therefore denied him its endorsement for re-election.

The Citizens Union refused to back him. Mayor LaGuardia, of course, also opposed him. Even the Republican Party, which traditionally did not contest the re-election of a sitting State Supreme Court Justice, under a tit-for-tat arrangement with the Democrats, broke precedent. Poor Aaron had gathered a formidable array of ill-wishers. He was worried. And he had good cause to be.

For two hours that November evening, Aaron sat beside Christy at the Hall, watching the returns come in. "If this were a normal election, I'd have no doubt," said the candidate. "But it's an insane election."

As the clock ticked away, Levy sweated under the tension. Maybe the ordeal made a better man out of him. In any event, by midnight, it was clear he had slipped through as one of the few survivors.

The next morning, newspapers carried complete statistics of the bloody battle's outcome. Soberly, Christy made one of his rare public statements. "The work of building and strengthening the organization has already begun," he said, "and preparations and plans are being perfected to bring the organization to a higher degree of efficiency and to win success at the polls next year . . . the Democratic Party has met defeat, but we face the future cheerfully and look forward to glorious victories in 1938 and in the years to come."

Among the casualties, the name of Murray Stand was missing. Murray, an Alderman for sixteen years, had not sought re-election to the Board's offspring, the City Council.

The old Board of Aldermen, on which he had so long endured, had been scathingly described as a municipal lodginghouse, a place for a weekly nap at the city's expense. Its usual Tuesday meeting usually broke up after half an hour and dealt with such earth-shaking topics as digging up a city street or naming a public playground. On days when important ball games were played, meetings lasted half that time.

The new, more effective City Council, from which he was absent, was to be based on proportional representation.

"It's a tougher job to run from a borough than from a district," Murray reminded reporters. "And more expensive. A district campaign costs at least $2,000, and, by the time your term ends, you have contributed as much to church affairs, civic affairs, block parties, souvenir programs and all that. Under the new system, a Manhattan Councilman will have everybody from the Harlem

River to the Battery after him. His salary will not mean a thing to him."

As an Alderman, Murray had always handled contracts and other minor problems begrudgingly. Neighborhood affairs sometimes slipped out of his focus.

"What's the matter?" Eddy Ahearn once chided him. "Is the job getting too big for you? Don't you think that working for your constituents is worth your time anymore?"

Murray knew he was no neighborhood idol. He freely admitted the cause of his longevity on the Board. "While I was running for Alderman," he said, "I never got less than 87% of the votes in my district. Once I got up to 92%. But a lot of people that voted for me didn't vote for Murray Stand. They voted for an emblem. A lot of them couldn't read—couldn't even read my name. But they knew what the emblem stood for. There will not be any emblems on the ballot with proportional representation."

Murray did not have to worry long about unemployment. Two months after the election, this Tammany leader was awarded a job by the Tammany-hating Mayor. He became "Director of the New York City World's Fair Commission."

At the swearing-in ceremony, LaGuardia said, "In appointing you, I know I am naming a man who has long and seriously studied the city's legislative and administrative procedures. You understand them as well as any person I know."

Stand got $6,000 a year, a healthy salary in those hard times. But I never did figure out what he did to earn the money. Robert Moses, the Commission's executive officer, did all the work. Murray just signed papers and busied himself at his more important chore as delegate to the state's Constitutional Convention.

When some unemployed members of our club approached him for jobs at the Fair, Murray just shrugged his shoulders. "What can I do?" he said. "Grover Whalen and Moses are the bosses. Go see them."

Many Tammany workers did not do nearly as well as Murray in the months following the election. The annual gift of 1,000 post office jobs during the Christmas season rush offered only temporary consolation. The long stretch following November, 1937, was indeed a difficult one.

This snowy winter of Tammany's discontent led to talk of a monumental shake-up in the organization. Suggestions were sprayed over a wide range of topics. One plan called for "new faces" in the district leaderships. Another pressed for new methods of selecting candidates. Some people advised burial of the very name "Tammany Hall." Its proposed replacement was to be something fresh, such as "The Old City Democracy." There was even talk of making a prominent business leader or professional man leader of the Hall. This would bring respectability to the organization, at least, even though it offered no guarantee of success at the polls.

Nevertheless, Christy Sullivan, who feared replacement following Copeland's defeat in the primary, survived not only that disaster but the Mahoney debacle as well. Christy's durability was in part due to luck. But, mainly, it stemmed from the fact that no one could justifiably hold him responsible for Tammany's defeats, since he really never ran Tammany's affairs to begin with.

Just as Mayor John O'Brien had made few public decisions before receiving "the word" from John Curry, Christy rendered no political decisions without hearing "the word" from background powers in the Hall. He dutifully awaited orders as well as advice and consent.

The crown that had been placed on Sullivan's balding head when he succeeded James Dooling was devoid of jewels. Nobody hated Christy and nobody greatly respected him. He was a nostalgic figure, a relic of sorts. He was a link to the dear, dead days of Tammany's past when the Sullivan clan ruled the Bowery and much of lower Manhattan.

Christy, 67 years old despite his baby-blue eyes, was well-liked. But he was far from a mental giant. He barely hung on to his half of the Second Assembly District through much of his reign. Eddy Ahearn had saved it for him in 1931, and a cartel of district leaders had joined to pull the same feat in 1935. On both occasions, Albert Marinelli nearly gobbled him up.

Christy looked like the public's conception of a machine-type politician, complete with derby hat and long black cigar. He oc-

casionally ate kosher food such as gefuelte fish, a desirable menu
for any Irish politician on the Lower East Side. But he made his
home at 1192 Park Avenue, far removed from the neighborhood
scene.

Sullivan's record of public employment was at least long, whatever its lack of other virtues. He served several terms in the state
legislature following the turn of the century. The Citizens Union
declared him an "undesirable and valueless member" there. He
left Albany and moved on to Washington in 1917.

In the United States Congress, Christy warily kept his political
positions a mystery. Few members of the House of Representatives
have matched his performance. Following his 1937 elevation to
Tammany's leadership, a New York press service, according to
columnist Drew Pearson, wired its Washington correspondent:
"Rush 250 words on Sullivan's Congressional record." The jour-
nalist reportedly responded: "Impossible. Sullivan has no Congressional record."

This was an injustice to Christy. Let it be said in his defense
that he did rise—twice—in the House. First, to eulogize the late
Congressman Anthony J. Griffin. Second to eulogize the late
Congressman Stephen A. Rudd.

Christy himself was once honored on the floor of that august
chamber. A Kentucky Congressman conferred the title of "Colonel"
on him "by reason of his devotion to duty and to the industry that
made Kentucky famous—the development of thoroughbred
horses."

Many Tammany leaders have considered themselves improvers
of the breed. Few, however, have been as devoted to the sport as
Christy. He loved to go to the races here or in Florida. He found
the aroma of the track irresistible. One winter day, while assigned
to the airport by my Internal Revenue office, I ran into Christy.
"Bet I know where you're going, Chief," I said.

"You guessed it all right," he laughingly replied. "I'll put an
extra pair on the nose for you."

Christy reigned over the Hall for five years. Not for one minute
did he actually rule. Though he eventually wound up as the scapegoat for Tammany's continuing slide, the blasts of critics were

unwarranted. He did not contribute to the organization's downhill journey. He was merely a high-placed witness.

Albert Marinelli's will carried the weight of law during Christy's first months in "power." Marinelli was the holder of the $15,000 a year County Clerkship as well as the leadership of the western half of Christy's district. From that post, the ambitious leader had launched his neighborhood aggressions.

A heavy, large-faced, energetic barrel of aspirations, Marinelli appeared, at 57, to be headed for bigger things. But his fall was as meteoric as his rise. During the 1937 campaign, Dewey had said some nasty things about his gangster associates. Rather than face removal charges, the district chief decided to remove himself from the County Clerkship. Though he did not realize it at the time, he also removed himself from a position of any future political influence. Within two years, he completely dropped out of the political scene by losing his district leadership.

His conqueror, John DeSalvio, was better known as "Jimmy Kelly," the name he had adopted thirty years earlier as a middle-weight fighter. In those days, it had been advisable for boxers of Italian or Jewish extraction to transform themselves into descendants of the Emerald Isle. In fact, sometimes it had been downright necessary in order for them to advance in their fistic careers.

DeSalvio owned a Greenwich Village nightclub and developed a large following. This became his base in his bid to topple the discredited former County Clerk.

"Since Marinelli had his trouble with the court and quit his job, he can't do anything for anybody," said DeSalvio. He was right. Marinelli realized the game was up and surrendered quietly without much of a struggle.

In the Fourth Assembly District, we watched this transfer of authority with interest. The Second Assembly District bordered our own, and developments there often affected the whole Lower East Side.

John DeSalvio became a forthright and faithful leader, one who ably served the constituents of his district. So did his son, Louis DeSalvio, who followed him.

Not only Marinelli but Hines, too, was politically demolished by District Attorney Dewey after the 1937 election. Thus, the New Deal lost its most agile ally in high Tammany circles.

The departure of both Marinelli and Hines from positions of power created a vacuum at Seventeenth Street. Tammany Hall's scepter was left temporarily ownerless. However, it did not remain so for long. The long regency of our district's Bert Stand and Clarence Neal, leader of the Twentieth Assembly District, now began.

Bert's "inside" post as Secretary of the Hall provided a built-in advantage. Clarence, though, was no "junior" partner. In many ways he was more potent a figure than Bert. The two men were complementary rather than competing regents. Clarence supplied the political muscle and Bert furnished the organizational mind.

Occasional thrusts were directed at Neal by newspaper correspondents and insurgents familiar with his rough ways and rugged exterior. He engaged in some odd dealings and formed some shady associations. But few critics knew him as a person rather than a personality. Let me therefore emphasize that I never saw Clarence back away from a promise, betray a trust or commit a political double-cross. Of how many current, less tarnished public figures can the same be said?

Neal had worked closely with Eddy Ahearn while Eddy was a weighty Tammany influence. He had thrown his uptown strength behind our Lower East Side leader during the gruelling struggle against John F. Curry. When Eddy died, Clarence, in a sense, inherited Bert.

They held their own during the regime of James J. Dooling. But they did not approach either the status or importance of the two independent operators, Hines and Marinelli. With Dooling's death, Christy's promotion and Dewey's gang-busting, Clarence and Bert jointly rose to the summit of Tammany Hall. For the next decade virtually every decision made by the Tiger's nominal leaders was to bear their stamp.

Behind heavy glasses, Neal, or "Commissioner" as he was sometimes called, looked more like a college professor than a Tammany powerhouse. He was born on the East Side, about fifty blocks north of the Lower East Side. As a teenager at the turn of the century, he peddled newspapers in Harlem. Later, he spent some time as an electrical apprentice, then joined the structural engineering department of the New York Central Railroad. Finally, he turned to his true calling, politics.

Clarence began as a precinct captain, then advanced to the post of secretary to his district chief, Sheriff Percival Nagel. When Nagel died, Clarence succeeded him as leader. (Bert's rise followed the same pattern, though titular leadership of the Fourth Assembly District remained in the Ahearn family.)

Clarence acquired the title "Commissioner" for service rendered as deputy Commissioner of Markets under Mayors Walker and O'Brien. The coming of LaGuardia's administration freed him, of course, from public office and permitted him to fully concentrate on politics. LaGuardia's re-election in 1937 continued his freedom from official responsibilities.

The Tammany Tiger awaited its chance to strike back at its cagers as the year 1938 progressed. When November came, so did the opportunity. Thomas E. Dewey, the icily-composed prosecutor, sought the Governorship on the Republican ticket. Dewey had singed several Tammany leaders, many not without cause, and they eagerly greeted the campaign in which they could defrost him.

On the Democratic side, Governor Lehman was thinking of retirement and James Farley was thinking of himself as a replacement. Farley had certainly been fair to our district. But many within the county organization were embittered toward him. They remembered his opposition to O'Brien in 1933, his backseat support of the Recovery Party, his aid and comfort for Tammany's enemies and his lackluster efforts in recent campaigns.

Most of all, they still smarted under his smothering patronage practices. Farley was certainly no hero to Tammany Hall. His rceception in Manhattan as Democratic candidate would hve been less than enthusiastic. Fortunately, Lehman decided to run again, thereby saving Albany's Executive Mansion for the party.

Farley's unpopularity on our island also sprang from his attempt to realign the power set-up of the five Democratic organizations in the city. Here, criticisms of Farley were far from justified. Brooklyn and Queens were filling up with people. Their Democratic county chiefs, along with Edward J. Flynn of the Bronx, had every right to demand more weight in party councils. Their combined vote-getting power exceeded Manhattan's.

Our own neighborhood offered an excellent example of the island's population exodus. In 1910, some 531,615 residents made the Lower East Side a tightly packed corner of humanity. By the mid-1930s, the gradual shift had dwindled this figure to slightly more than 240,000. Where had the others gone? Across the river to Brooklyn and Queens, and northward to the Bronx and beyond.

Despite the outward flow, our part of the area, the Fourth Assembly District, retained its basic Jewish composition. It also retained its Democratic political texture—except on those perfidious occasions when precinct workers were ordered to slow down in their canvassing.

Whenever insurgency reared its head, the district's voters clung to the "regular" ballot line on Primary Day. Aspirations based on the similarity in religious background between a rebel candidate and the area's voters simply fell flat.

During the thirties, a fellow named Berger (I have long since forgotten his first name) tried to wrest William J. "Bud" Murray's place as our State Senator. He found that the only religion that counted at the polls in our district was a man's political religion. He was soundly trounced. My all-Jewish constituency cast every single vote for Irishman Murray. In another precinct, we nearly demanded a recount. Berger had been credited there with getting one vote!

Unfortunately, some minor officeholders after the Ahearn era ceased to accept the fact that they owed their Election Day triumphs to the district's precinct captains. To admit as much might have been ego-deflating.

A classic example involved our State Assemblyman some years after Eddy's passing. The iron law that "an elected official's first duty is to his constituents" was beginning to get rusty. Eddy was not around to enforce it.

One Monday evening. I approached the Assemblyman with a tenant's plea to have a dispossess case postponed. It was a normal request, one usually requiring little time or effort. Nonetheless, he balked.

"Oh, I don't want to bother," he protested. "Get one of those young lawyers to handle it." He pointed to a corner of the club where several youngsters stood.

"Don't push me off," I replied. "Who do you think put you in office? You're not here to kill time. Even if you were busy, which you're not, you should still make time for constituents. If you think I'll let you carry my precinct in the next election, guess again."

The following Friday night, I was called at my apartment and told to report to the Ahearn home. When I arrived, Willie was sitting with a group that included the Assemblyman, Senator Murray, city officials, a future assistant Borough President and a future Municipal Court Justice. All were key people from our club. Bert Stand was conspicuous by his absence and poor Willie, of course, did not know what the meeting was about.

It soon became clear that I was being "tried" on a charge of insulting the Assemblyman in the crowded clubhouse. Senator "Bud" Murray, the Assemblyman's colleague at Albany, acted as "prosecutor." In oratory that perhaps better suited the august chamber up in the state capital, he outlined my alleged misdeeds. I was then invited to speak in my own behalf.

"I wouldn't waste time defending myself," I said. Instead, I directed my comments to the startled Senator, not the Assemblyman's charges:

"Bud, what makes you think you were elected by the people on your own? They don't even know you. The captain is the backbone of this club, as Eddy used to say. The constituent votes for his captain, not a meaningless name on the ballot. And the voter expects service, not rebuffs, when he needs help. If Eddy were alive, an officeholder would know what his duties were."

Everyone sat stunned for a moment. Then the Senator exchanged the robes of prosecutor for those of a mild conciliator. "Let's make peace," he said.

"Agreed, but on one condition," I answered. "When the Assemblyman is told to handle an honest contract, he should do it. That's why people voted for him. That's what they expect of him."

I was in the right and saw no reason to retreat from my stand. In those days, a precinct captain was every bit as important as I indicated. When an elected official shirked his duty, the voter lost confidence in his captain for letting him do so. I had no intention of casting aside the legitimate interests of my constituents.

The Assemblyman and I shook hands. His future actions showed he was capable of "growing" in office. He moved on to higher offices and, today, I count him as a friend. The lesson he learned was certainly not wasted.

The day after the incident, I saw Bert and asked why he was missing from the meeting. "Gee, Louis, I didn't even know about it," he said.

This at first seemed inconceivable to me. After all, Bert ruled the club. How could he *not* know what was going on under his nose? He asked who was there. I began to reel off the names of those who had been present. When I reached that of Arthur Greeninger, Bert stopped me.

"Greeninger?" Bert said quizzically. "I was with him all day and he didn't say a word to me. Believe me, if I knew what they were planning, I would have stopped it short."

Bert rarely failed to stay on top of a situation. On this occasion I had no doubts about his good intentions. Nonetheless, the incident points out the change that had overtaken politics in the Fourth Assembly District since Eddy Ahearn's death.

IX

Years of the Meek "me-ow"

BY THE FALL OF 1939, TAMMANY HALL HAD BEEN SUBJECTED TO a period of upheaval, if not reformation. Hines was exchanging Tiger stripes for convict stripes. Marinelli vanished from the political scene. William Kenneally, Christy Sullivan's sparring mate of former days, lost his district leadership and his post as chairman of Tammany's Executive Committee. Sheriff Daniel Finn, scion of an old established political family, narrowly squeezed in as leader of part of the First Assembly District. His election was being disputed, however, by an energetic insurgent named Carmine G. DeSapio.

This young rebel had formed his own Tamawa Club and drew strength from the corner of Greenwich Village with a large and still growing Italian population. His early ambitions were temporarily checked. Tammany refused to admit him to its Executive Committee despite his claim—and many considered it a just claim —of victory over Finn. Carmine again petitioned for admittance to the Hall's inner circle in 1941 and again was to be ignored. Finally, he would make it through Bert Stand's intervention, an irony that helped spell disaster for Bert in the years ahead.

No major offices were up for bids in 1939. Attention therefore gravitated in the September primaries to the Democratic contest for nomination to General Sessions Court. Jonah J. Goldstein, who had been rebuffed by Tammany back in 1936 when he ran for the judicial post, was making a second try. Tammany once more opposed him.

The Tiger supported Jacob Gould Schurman, the Republican Chief City Magistrate, who, with Democrat John A. Mullen, had

135

won bi-partisan endorsement. Both Governor Lehman and Mayor LaGuardia supported Schurman, too. Nonetheless, Goldstein defeated the Magistrate. His victory in the primaries was not final, though, since he would have to stage a repeat performance in November.

In our assembly district, Goldstein had been soundly trounced, 2,115 to 912. In my precinct, he picked up no more than three or four votes. Goldstein was naturally eager to bolster his strength, pick up support and mend fences between Primary Day and Election Day.

As his day of judgement approached, he dropped in at the Ahearn club. Bert welcomed him, pointed to me and said, "Judge, there's the fellow that beat your brains out here last time."

Goldstein strolled over and laughed as he said, "I don't mind what happened last time. You'll be getting other orders for November."

"Whatever Bert says," I replied.

When the next returns came in from my precinct, the tally was almost exactly reversed. This time, his opponent pulled no more than three or four votes—probably the same spoilsports who kept me from a perfect score two months earlier.

Goldstein wondered how it was done. I do not think he realized then—as he certainly did not six years later when he sought the Mayorship—that Lower East Side Democrats voted for their captains, not the candidates. A good captain who kept faith with his people was never betrayed at the polls. When he reversed direction, so did they.

The off-year elections brought smiles to the face of the Tammany Tiger for the first time since LaGuardia's appearance on the political scene. It was a quiet November Tuesday. No national issues stirred the electorate, so the turnover was small. Democratic judicial candidates came home winners throughout the city. Over in Brooklyn, upcoming County Judge William O'Dwyer easily defeated a Fusion candidate for District Attorney. Some people might have wondered why he had taken a step down to run for the office. But O'Dwyer had his gaze fastened on City Hall, and the prosecutor's job was the logical steppingstone.

Christy Sullivan, suddenly alive with exuberation, broke tradition—at least his own silent tradition—and issued a ringing victory statement.

"The candidates of the Democratic Party appear to have been elected by overwhelming pluralities," he said. "The Tammany organization, as always, has done its part to bring about the splendid results. I feel confident that the result indicates a returning confidence on the part of the people in the Democratic Party of this city."

There was even a temporary thaw in Tammany's relations with Washington. Christy made a pilgrimage to the White House to assure Roosevelt of Tammany's support at the forthcoming Democratic National Convention. Consequently, the national administration halted, for a while, its campaign against the Hall's leadership.

With Europe already at war and the smell of conflict crossing the Atlantic Ocean, Tammany adopted a resolution praising the President's "constructive statesmanship in every crisis." It specifically pledged support to Roosevelt's effort to repeal the embargo that hurt the British cause and helped Germany.

Throughout this critical period, Samuel Dickstein continued to represent our district in Congress. Sam had grown wiser as each passing year drifted into history. He no longer succumbed to practical jokes, such as the one Eddy had pulled on that cold, snowy day outside the clubhouse. Moreover, Sam was playing a major role in the struggle against Nazi infiltration and other "Fifth Column" maneuvers.

The son of a rabbi, Sam was born on a frigid February day in Lithuania in 1885. Brought here as a child, he attended New York City Law School, picked up a degree, then steadily advanced up the political ladder from neighborhood Alderman all the way to the United States Congress.

Sam dressed snappily, even to the extent of wearing stiffly starched collars on his summer suits. He occasionally showed up at the club with spats, cane and gloves. He certainly had no worries about, or knew nothing of, the "plain folks image" that seems popular among today's political psychologists.

Dickstein was aware that his Jewish constituency was alive to
the Nazi threat long before the rest of the country. As early as
1937, he insisted Hitler "was trying to create a world war" and
urged a break in diplomatic relations. He kept lists of Nazi and
Fascist agents, occasionally inserting them in the Congressional
Record. He boasted of a large, private file of individuals engaged
in subversive activities. At one point, he accused the German-
American Bund of staging military drills and said members joined
the state militia to get weaponry training at United States expense
for use in Hitler's service. Some one actually wrote a biography
of Sam, modestly titled "American Defender".

Sam could always expect the applause of his district whenever
he hammered at fascism. For the stench of Hitler's policies had
already filtered through every tenement window on the Lower East
Side. But the same enthusiastic response could not be expected
to greet his vigorous quarrel with another lethal "ism"—communism. The impoverished residents here had no vested interest
in capitalism to protect. Besides, Soviet anti-semitism was still
cloaked in the Kremlin's Brave New World. Thus the spectre of
creeping Bolshevism held little terror for Sam's voters.

Nonetheless, he plugged away at this latent foe. "To make my
own stand clear, I am opposed to communism, fascism, and nazi-
ism and all other subversive movements in the United States," he
said. "I consider communism just as dangerous a menace to our
Republic as any other undemocratic movements."

The biennial award bestowed upon Sam was re-election to Congress. A less kindly reaction came from groups he denounced. At
times, Sam needed a bodyguard or received police protection. His
safety was threatened during a Congressional investigation, which
he fathered, of Nazi propaganda in this country. Sam served both
his country and his constituency well.

In the prevailing war climate of 1940, Roosevelt had no difficulty carrying the city at the November election. Some Irish districts harbored anti-British sentiment, a legacy of the late "troubles"
in Ireland. But no one cherished the cause of the Nazis, especially
the residents of the Fourth Assembly District. Despite the fact
that political canvassing by many precinct workers in the years

following 1940 was severely hampered, our district continued along its well-cut Democratic groove.

More than a few captains, including myself, were affected by the Hatch Act. This law prohibited federal employees from engaging in political activities. It struck at everyone from district leader to captain to the lowliest campaign leaflet distributor. It meant that anyone holding down a United States Marshal's post or an Internal Revenue position or even a Works Progress Administration relief job had to drop either his livelihood or his electioneering. Penalties included a $1,000 fine and a year in jail.

The choice was not difficult. Resignations quickly poured into Tammany Hall headquarters from County Committee members. Other Democratic organizations were similarly decimated. I did not have to quit the John F. Ahearn Association. But if my own brother had run for political office, I would have had to stay out of the race.

My position in the Internal Revenue office of the Second District was no sinecure. True, I was a political appointee. But so was the Secretary of State. Neither of us carried our party affairs into our government offices. Both our jobs required our full concentration.

My first boss was James J. Hoey, a Tammany district leader who staunchly supported the President. Jim handled his job as Collector for the Second District impartially, though with a tinge of humanity frequently absent from the makeup of today's typical bureaucrat.

I vividly recall the time Sam Levy, then Borough President, approached Jim in behalf of a new employee. The fellow had worked for Levy and was a devoutly orthodox Jew.

"Listen, Jim," said Levy. "You've got a boy on your staff who's very religious. His grandfather's a rabbi. He needs Saturdays off and he's willing to come in all year round without taking a vacation to make up for it. Is it okay?"

Jim agreed. The young fellow worked well and the compromise remained in effect for more than a year.

One day, Hoey ran into the boy in the Custom House lobby and said, "You're way overdue for a vacation. When would you like to be penciled in for one?"

"Oh, I can't take a vacation, Mr. Hoey," he replied. "I don't come in any Saturdays, you know."

"Well, don't you get sick?" Jim asked.

"No, sir," the boy answered.

"Not even a little bit sick?" Jim hinted.

"No, hardly ever, sir," the youngster repeated.

Jim gave up. Frustrated, he bit the bottom of his lip, bade the fellow goodbye and called Joseph Ryan, his chief field deputy, to his office. The two Irishmen put their heads together briefly.

"Joe," directed the boss, "there's a youngster in your department. You know the one I mean. I just can't seem to get through to him. Tell him to put his papers away, clean off the top of his desk and get sick for a couple of weeks."

This kind of humaneness has largely disappeared from the executive ranks of government bureaus today. The computer-trained mind has replaced the politically-trained heart. Bland impersonality has been lifted to an unwarranted pedestal.

No doubt, the altar of civil service has received deserved prayers. But a civil service statute does not guarantee the caliber of men in governmental service. Both Jim Hoey and his successor, William J. Pedrick, were honest, honorable, capable men. Both came from the ranks of the county Democratic organization.

Pedrick, a dynamo with flaming red hair, had been an Army captain and President of the Fifth Avenue Association, a fashionable business group. He won Christy Sullivan's Seal of Approval for the revenue post shortly after we entered World War II.

Going ahead of our story a bit, he became the first Collector to administer a $1,000,000,000 income tax district. From his Customs House office, he conveyed this fact in a very unbureaucratically phrased communique. It said: "The private taxpayer's spring offensive has given the Axis hell to the tune of more than a billion dollars."

Into the office one day marched a distinguished-looking, mustached gentleman, complete with homburg, striped pants and spats. He asked a clerk, "Who is this Louis Eis . . . Eisenberg . . . Eisen . . . oh, I can't pronounce *those* names." He produced a paper from his pocket, pointed to my name and added, "He sent me this subpena to come down."

His stentorian tone resounded throughout the office, so I waved him over to my desk. Others in the room glanced in our direction.

"Did you send me this?" he said, dropping the subpena on my desk. "Don't you know who I am?"

Ignoring the theatrics, I said, "I pronounce my name EIS-EN-STEIN. And don't you think you should take your hat off in a federal building?"

A trifle embarrassed, he complied with the request, then repeated lordly and loudly, "Don't you know who I am?"

"All I know is that you owe tax money to Uncle Sam," I replied. "It was due five months ago. Are you going to pay it or aren't you?"

"Now, listen," he said impressively, "I'm in the stock exchange and I know your boss. He's a friend of mine and I insist on seeing him."

"Oh, is he going to pay your bill?" I asked. Since he still wanted to see the head man, I took him to Pedrick's assistant, Raymond F. Ryan.

"So you want to see Mr. Pedrick?" said Ray. "Let's check the background of this case first. According to the records, Mr. Eisenstein waited to see you several times at your office. But you said you were too busy and chased him away."

"Well, I'm a very important man on Wall Street and I didn't have much time," the man answered. "Anyway, he had no business sending me a subpena."

Ray called Pedrick, summarized the case and mentioned that the man claimed to be a friend of his.

"So what's he want me to do, cancel his taxes for him?" replied the Captain. "I'll talk to him. But first, get the names of the banks he keeps his money in, ask what stocks he carries and what other assets he possesses. If necessary, we'll put a lien on whatever we can."

"Okay, you win," said Ray mockingly to the visitor as he put down the receiver. "You can see him. All you have to do first is give me the following financial data. Also, list any real estate you own. Then the chief will be glad to discuss things with you."

The man hemmed, hawed, then backed off. He decided "not to take up Mr. Pedrick's valuable time." The next day, a check arrived covering the full amount of that important gentleman's tax bill.

There were times when the taxpayer, like the customer, was not always right. Pedrick, whom we often addressed as "Captain" because of his military service, called a conference of some 200 deputy collectors one day. A citizen had sent him a note, he reported, complaining about the dress of some employees.

"Men," he announced in soldierly fashion, "from now on I want you to make certain you wear starched collars and ties when you make field calls. After all, these people are taxpayers. Are there any questions?"

I had always dressed appropriately and knew his lecture was not addressed to me. A bow tie was my trademark. Therefore, I felt no compulsion to withhold my views on the basis of personal involvement.

"Now, Captain," I said, "did it ever occur to you that we're taxpayers too. And we're more honest. *Our* taxes are deducted now even before we see our paychecks. If *they* paid their taxes on time, they wouldn't have to see us in the first place. They lounge about comfortably in their carpeted offices, then have their secretaries tell us they're out whenever we call. I've had to go back three or four times to some offices and threaten to leave a summons before I was admitted. Why should we give them more respect than they show us?"

"Okay, Tammany Louis," said Pedrick. "I'm not giving any orders. I'm just making a speech. Use your own judgement."

Inflexibility is no virtue and changeability is no vice. Pedrick, like Jim Hoey, was not immovable when he saw a degree of justice in both sides of a question.

Occasionally, a bad apple slipped into the basket of political appointees at Internal Revenue. This was not frequent. A bad apple still slips into the basket of civil service appointees just as often, but stirs less resentment among its peers.

One day, Clarence Neal phoned Bert Stand at Tammany Hall headquarters. "Bert," he said, "there's a fellow in Internal Revenue who's been shaking down storekeepers in my district . . . no . . . I don't know his name . . . that's why I called you. See if you can find out who he is."

Bert listened, took notes, then called me. "Can you come up to the Hall?" he asked. "There's something important I want to discuss that I don't want to talk about over the phone."

I hopped up to Seventeenth Street later that day. Bert outlined Clarence's story and asked who was working his district. "I don't know offhand, but in two phone calls, I can find out," I replied. I made the calls and got the answer swiftly.

"I guessed it was him all along," I said. "He's just the type who would steal from his own relatives. But it always pays to be sure."

Bert took the matter from there, and the shakedowns immediately ceased. The system was far more effective than a long, drawn-out departmental investigation, complete with accusation and denials.

As 1941 approached, the city's political life revived. Although the Hatch Act prohibited election canvassing by employees drawing federal paychecks, LaGuardia's political workers, on the city payroll, labored under no similar restrictions. No matter how he boasted of non-partisan government, thousands of jobholders knew on whose plate their bread was buttered. They realized where their Election Day gratitude should be directed.

Murray Stand missed, then scored a hit, in the spring of 1941. The Mayoralty race was still several months off when LaGuardia pushed Murray for the $10,000 a year post as United States Marshal of New York's Southern District. LaGuardia was far more influential than Tammany in the White House, from which the appointment was to be made. This time, however, the Little Flower did not get his way and Murray did not get the job.

Bert's brother did not have to brood very long. In late July, as the election neared, the Mayor threw a consolation prize to Murray. He was named "Inspector General of the Office of Civil Defense in the Second Corps Area," whatever that meant. Murray's duties were not immediately outlined, but the pay was good.

LaGuardia was wise to play his ace-in-the-hole. The Democratic candidate for his job, William O'Dwyer, had tackled Brooklyn's crime syndicate as District Attorney and had established an enviable reputation as a gang-buster. This had been the same glory road to political success that Thomas Dewey had taken. In many ways, O'Dwyer appeared a far more formidable candidate than had his predecessor, Jeremiah Mahoney, four years earlier.

On the other side of the ledger, LaGuardia's wild tactics got him into trouble. His unprovoked slurs at Governor Lehman infuriated a large segment of New York City's Jewish population, including our district's voters. The Mayor's undercover aides, therefore, had their work cut out for them.

By 8 p.m. on the night of the election, November 5, 1941, some 250 persons were gathered at Tammany Hall headquarters. Christy Sullivan and a few associates sat around a table in his inner office. Bert took calls from leaders reporting the results in their districts.

Enthusiasm waxed and waned. At first, O'Dwyer was running neck and neck with the Mayor. Then he slipped slightly behind. Within an hour, the tide was against him. By 9:30 p.m., gloom pervaded the Hall. With occasional interruptions for news from European battle fronts, the monotonously grim election statistics were recited over the radio at the Seventeenth Street citadel. By 11:30 p.m., the New York political war was over.

Reporters sought Christy. But he had already vanished into the night, just as he had done four years earlier. Bert issued a statement in his stead. It read, "The vote speaks for itself. Judge O'Dwyer and his associates on the Democratic ticket made a fine and decent campaign and deserved a better fate."

LaGuardia easily captured the Fourth Assembly District on his assorted party tickets—Republican, American Labor Party, Fusion and United City. The Mayor pulled in 8,000 votes in our "Banner District," where Eddy Ahearn used to boast that no opponent could win 1,000 ballots.

At his cushy Civil Defense post, Bert's brother, Murray, offered no wailing whistle of the city's still primitive sirens. But the rest of Tammany prepared to dig in for another four lean years.

During its long history, Tammany Hall had periodically grunted under charges of moral bankruptcy. These accusations pierced the organization's ego, but rarely its pocketbook. Now, bankruptcy of a more biting stripe loomed. As Tammany's political fortunes cascaded, so did its treasury receipts.

Back in the glory days of Mayor James Walker, "Judge" Olvany, the Tiger's steward, had acquired a home worthy of the Hall's prosperity. The handsome, four-story tall structure, of colonial design, stood at the northeast corner of Union Square and cost $950,000. Only one floor was devoted totally to political business. A bank occupied the ground floor, a fact that led to many a sly wink by the organization's opponents. The annual maintenance expenses ranged to $35,000, including taxes and mortgage interest.

Tammany's extravagance was justified by its wealth in former days. By 1941, however, it could ill-afford such luxury. The new situation called for belt-tightening. Barely two weeks after La-Guardia's third election triumph, Christy Sullivan announced he was appointing a committee to find a new, more modest home for the organization. Christy wanted to save money.

The idea soon took root, though, that saving Christy was as damaging to Tammany as hanging on to its financial White Elephant at Union Square. Progressive circles wanted to put Christy into mothballs as well as the old headquarters.

Jeremiah Mahoney, Fifteenth Assembly District leader and LaGuardia's 1937 opponent, called for a meeting "to vote out the present leader of Tammany Hall." In a letter to Charles H. Hussey, chiarman of Tammany's Executive Committee, Mahoney also assaulted fellow district leaders. "When they attend the meetings of the Executive Committee of Tammany Hall," he said, "they seem to lose their initiative and their courage, and it has been the practice for them all, except myself, to follow the dictates of a stupid leader."

Mahoney also struck at the most festering sore in the organization's body—lack of jobs for its troops. He asserted that President Roosevelt had exhibited no enthusiasm for Tammany and that Governor Lehman "has indicated most plainly that Tammany under the present setup is not to be considered." Mahoney said his purpose in pointing this out was so "the leaders might see the light of day from the practical but more sordid standpoint of patronage."

Whatever the impact—or lack of impact—of Mahoney's seething letter, Christy's reign was drawing to an inauspicious end.

In February, 1942, as the Japanese swarmed over Singapore and the Philippines, and Nazi U-boats terrorized shipping along the East Coast, Christy bade farewell to big-time politics. At 5:25 p.m. on the seventh of February, Christy left his partitioned office at Tammany Hall for the last time as county leader. Slowly, he paced down the corridor to the Executive Chamber, his place of execution. Within an hour, several leaders dashed down the staircase, arms fluttering. "Out" they shouted to awaiting reporters, in umpire fashion, as they gestured appropriately.

The instrument of Sullivan's demise was a resolution, approved by a slim margin, by the district chiefs. In typical legalistic language, it read: "Resolved, that the Executive Committee of the County Committee of the Democratic Party of New York County hereby rescinds and revokes any privilege, power, prerogative or authority heretofore expressly or impliedly granted at any time to Christopher D. Sullivan to act as leader or spokesman or in any capacity whatsoever for and on behalf of the said Executive Committee and the regular Democratic Party in and for the County of New York."

It was quite a mouthful. Boiled down, it simply meant that Tammany Hall would have to go hunting for a new front-man.

The precedent for ousting the party's chief had been established in 1934. John F. Curry, on that earlier occasion, had fought bitterly to hold his office. Christy, by contrast, surrendered gracefully to the inevitable.

"It's all right," he announced, adding that he would remain in politics "in a small way." The snowy-haired, 72-year-old former county chief then departed for the South, where a vacation and the races awaited him. He left no real enemies behind.

According to the press, Christy Sullivan's successor was chosen at a meeting of the Executive Committee of Tammany Hall two months following his banishment. Supposedly, his heir, Representative Michael J. Kennedy, was chosen by a 14 and two-thirds to 9 and seven-twelfths vote over former Sheriff Dan Finn Jr. This was fiction rather than fact. The meeting that selected Kennedy was far smaller than the rambling 70 member conference at the Hall. And it drew considerably less publicity, too.

Clarence Neal was there. Kennedy was there. So were James H. Fay and a conspicuous non-politician, Frank Costello, whose broad interests encompassed a wide field of activities. Fay was Clarence's candidate for the vacant post. A one-time supporter of the New Deal, Fay had since run afoul of the administration.

Representative Kennedy, more rabid in his support of Washington, was reputed to be the choice of the President. A Congressman since 1938, he had followed Roosevelt's aid-to-Britain program down the line, despite misgivings within his Irish constituency. Such loyalty took political courage. This was recognized by the White House, and it did not go unrewarded.

Costello's undercover role in the contest was that of arbiter. He had paid for the privilege by acting as financial angel to the nearly insolvent Tiger organization. Tammany was not Costello's serf. The arrangement was closer to one of vassalage. It is certainly not to the credit of the Hall that in the dismal days of LaGuardia's third term, it turned to Costello for aid. Nonetheless, it did.

Roosevelt and Costello were unknown to each other. The President and the underworld leader had nothing in common. Yet, on this occasion, their minds were as one. Kennedy got the nod over Fay.

On April 14, 1942, the leaders of Manhattan assembly districts filed into Tammany Hall's Executive Committee conference room. Theoretically, they gathered to elect a new chief. In fact, he had already been chosen.

There was a last-minute scramble to induce Fay to rejoin the contest. He declined. Kennedy's opponents then clustered around Dan Finn, who had retained his position on the Executive Committee despite Carmine DeSapio's growing strength in their section of the First Assembly District. This "Stop Kennedy" movement failed, however, as the vote demonstrated.

Jeremiah Mahoney, who cast his ballot for Kennedy, urged sweeping changes in the Hall. He sought popular elections for district leadership and even the abandonment of the name "Tammany." He said that "only by so doing, can the people be made to realize that we are starting in the right direction and their confidence regained."

Willie Ahearn, our district's titular leader, did not vote. Willie frequently fell away. On this day, he collapsed outside the Hall, stricken by a cerebral hemorrhage. Dr. Paul F. Sarubbi, leader of the western half of the First Assembly District and a physician, immediately treated him on the sidewalk. The meeting was delayed while poor Willie was rushed to Bellevue Hospital.

Kennedy's victory was greeted by applause from Senator Robert F. Wagner Sr. Governor Lehman phoned his good wishes and congratulations from Albany. The county's Democrats, at last, seemed to have aligned themselves with the national administration.

In view of the events preceding his elevation, however, Kennedy's official acceptance statement may be dismissed as sheer window-dressing. "My election has been made possible," he said, "by the full exercise of democratic processes." He announced he was assuming office "committed to no man or group of men."

"Mike" Kennedy, like James Dooling, Eddy Ahearn and Bert Stand, inherited his taste for politics. Mike's father spent three decades in the "game" and Mike, the seventh of 14 children, was tapped as his successor. A round and jovial fellow, Mike was blessed with the gift of gab and a sparkle of wit. His formal schooling ended at the eighth grade. He regretted, occasionally, that he went no higher. "But I guess common sense and a sense of humor *is* equal to a college education," he mused. Mike fortunately found that the term "drop-out" had not yet become a stigma.

Mike began work at age 14 as a bellhop, advanced to elevator operator, then gave up the hotel business. By 14, he was ringing doorbells for his dad on the West Side. His first political job was in the State Superintendent of Election's office.

Next, he acquired a City Marshal's badge from Mayor John Hylan. Though he lacked the daring and dashing manner of Wyatt Earp, Mike created a booming business just the same. In his holster, he carried legal papers, not pistols. As an urban lawman, he worked closely with banks and insurance companies. After all, this was New York, not Dodge City. Mike hired several "deputies," other assistants and also a pretty, personable secretary. Later, she eloped and Mike tagged along as bridegroom.

In 1934, Kennedy became leader of his district, the middle portion of the Fifth, which took in Madison Square Garden and ran from 46th to 55th Streets. The location was strategic, for he could catch the Friday night fights and conduct business at the same time.

Kennedy was a close personal friend of James Dooling, who held leadership of the Fifth Assembly District's southern portion. When the ailing Tammany chief headed to Florida in a vain effort to regain his health in 1936, Kennedy went along. Following Dooling's death, however, Kennedy teamed up with the wrong faction and lost power and favor within the Hall.

Mike turned his attention from city to Washington affairs. He decided to go to Congress. This created a bit of a problem for him locally, though. He could not pass on his profitable Marshal's badge to his brother. Only Mayor LaGuardia, the Tiger killer, could do that. So Kennedy went to City Hall. The machine-hating Mayor listened to the Tammany district leader's personal request, then swore in his younger brother. The Little Flower, serving his second Fusion term, was still interested in picking up new friends.

As an addition to the House of Representatives, Mike was amiable and charming. His voting record was admirable. He went down the line in support of Roosevelt's foreign policy and preparedness program. Whether through conviction or expediency, he married the national administration. Motivation was unimportant. The result was more significant. The President, who had long since locked Tammany's decaying skeleton in the Democratic family closet, gave Kennedy his political blessings.

This halo from afar, combined with Costello's own vote of confidence, worked wonders for Mike. Twice blessed, he mounted the chair majestically occupied by Charles F. Murphy some years earlier. More recently, and less majestically, it had been Christy Sullivan's throne.

Like Christy, Kennedy was ruled rather than ruler. Bert Stand and Clarence Neal continued their joint regency. Unlike Christy, however, Mike gave the appearance of being his own boss. In his mid-forties, the portly, double-chinned West Sider seemed every meaty ounce a leader.

Another characteristic set him apart from his predecessor. Mike displayed a singular lack of concern for cultivation of fleet-footed thoroughbreds. That is, he usually stayed away from the local racetracks. Mike preferred dogs. At his Shrub Oak country home, he raised Irish setters and airdales.

A final dissimilarity between Sullivan and Kennedy involved their attitude toward public office. When Christy became leader of Tammany Hall, he did not bother to quit Congress, for he did not do much there anyway. He remained stationary in the House for another term. Kennedy, on the other hand, quickly announced he would not run for re-election in 1942.

Frankly, not many people really cared. In that wartime election year, attention centered on Albany. Herbert Lehman had finally left the state scene and Thomas E. Dewey was making another, more hopeful, bid for the office. As a prosecutor, Dewey had by now established an enviable national reputation. He had even unsuccessfully sought the Republican nomination for President two years earlier.

The crusading District Attorney's opponent, Democrat John J. Bennett Jr., was the personal choice of James Farley. As a result of a split with Roosevelt, Farley had become ex-Postmaster General and ex-Democratic National Chairman. Though he could still dictate Bennett's selection over the President's objection, getting him elected was not nearly as easy.

During the campaign, which many captains such as myself had to sit out because of the Hatch Act, I dropped over to Sam Koenig's clubhouse north of our district. "Hey, Dewey must *really* be in if Louis is coming around here!" joked one of Sam's workers. Sam still commanded respect throughout the area. His successors as county Republican leader, Chase Mellen Jr. and Kenneth Simpson Jr., had both disappeared from the grand political stage. But

Koenig remained. He held no formal robes and title and he needed none. To all, he continued to be "the Boss."

Relations between Democrats and Republicans at the district level continued to be amiable, except, of course, for one November day each year. In fact, arms-length inter-party relations were frequently better than intimate intra-party relations. Kennedy's election brought no era of good feelings to the Democratic organization. Before his first year in office was up, it was clear that some Tammany figures intended to make it his last.

Among this group was John F. Curry. Though he had been stripped of power a decade back, Curry was a very active political corpse. Some former allies remained loyal during the 1930s. Now, they prepared to do battle in his spirit, if not his name, against Kennedy. Philip J. Dunn, a lawyer, was undercover head of the movement, and several district leaders collaborated.

During the spring of 1943, they seized on the work of a "reorganization committee" and diverted it to their cause. The committee decided to "solemnly pledge and guarantee to destroy forever those causes which have brought the Democratic Party in New York County into public disfavor and under the shadow of public distrust." It also set out to break the century-old link between the Democratic Party and Tammany in language so pompous that it created a chuckle.

"Back in the early days of this nation," said the statement, "when Americans first fought for freedom, a group of Revolutionary soldiers formed the Society of Tammany as a patriotic and benevolent fraternity devoted to the cause of liberty. Let us once more robe it in benevolence and retire it to private life where it can serve as a constructive force in the preservation of the liberty it originally symbolized."

Kennedy survived the first effort to oust him. He even cheerfully welcomed this first thrust. "As long as I have to get in there and swing every so often," he said, "no one can say I'm the dictator of this outfit."

Kennedy was certainly no dictator. He more closely resembled a stenographer—taking notes from Bert Stand and Clarence Neal. They made a compatible trio.

Once, Bert showed Mike my precinct's voting record. I had molded my constituency into the "Banner Election District" of the "Banner Assembly District" of our party. The county leader assured me he was impressed. But he and I both knew that if I wanted to trade on my record, Bert and Clarence could grant a "favor" far easier than their nominal boss.

Although Kennedy continued to hold office throughout 1943, he literally could not remain in it. The walls, ceiling and floor passed to new ownership. The imposing Union Square structure was sold to the International Ladies Garment Workers Union, a more solvent organization.

Tammany Hall moved twenty blocks north to Madison Avenue and 37th Street. Its new home was comfortable, but not very splashy. Gone were the days of ostentatious glory. The new quarters consisted of an office for Kennedy, an office for Stand, a conference room, a library, two bathrooms and a women's lounge. As evidence of their respective influence, Mike's sanctuary measured 18 by 18 feet, while Bert's measured 24 by 24 feet. Naturally, as Secretary of the Hall, Bert had to share his space with filing cabinets and clerical help.

During the early forties, there were really two Bert Stands. One was our de facto district chief, a pleasant, open fellow whose friendship I treasured and whose confidence I enjoyed. The other Bert Stand was a behind-the-scenes leader of Tammany Hall, a man who played his cards close to his vest. He had weighty connections in circles that I never joined nor even wanted to become acquainted with.

Frequently, I visited Bert at Tammany headquarters, usually considered a private preserve for district leaders. There were no welcome mats out for precinct captains. Our conversations, however, avoided the sordid details of headline-making scandals. Bert was far from a Dr. Jekyll and Mr. Hyde type character. But he did have an uncanny and unembarrassing knack of carrying on the appropriate variation of shop talk with whoever sat across from his desk.

Another subject we rarely treaded on was the steady progression of Bert's brother, Murray, in public circles. Murray, who became a World's Fair official just after the 1937 Mayoralty election, and a civil defense official shortly before the 1941 Mayoralty election, was briefly unemployed in the spring of 1942. When LaGuardia chose to scrap his own title as civil defense chief at that time, Murray had to quit, too.

Murray did not remain out of "work" long. Again his City Hall guardian angel came to the rescue. During the fall, the position of First Deputy City Clerk fell vacant. Philip A. Hines, brother of the now jailed Jimmy Hines, resigned with three subordinates after an investigation showed he had accepted gratuities for tying marital knots in the Marriage License Bureau. The practice of accepting gifts had been an old one. Hines' predecessor, according to a Seabury investigation, had collected from $1,400 to $1,800 a month for the same chore. The Mayor was seriously thinking of reorganizing the department and abolishing the job. That is, until he remembered that a spot had to be found for Murray.

Though LaGuardia had no direct strings tied to the office, his opinion on who should fill it carried weight. Murray was sworn in at $7,800 a year. After administering the oath, the Mayor told reporters, "I think it was the best appointment I could expect, considering that I had no control over the naming of a Deputy City Clerk."

I do not know whether the Mayor kept his fingers crossed when he made that statement. But, offhand, I cannot think of anyone he would have preferred to install in that post. LaGuardia was already thinking ahead to the next Mayoralty campaign.

X

Fission in Fusion:
The Little Flower Withers Away

AS LAGUARDIA'S THIRD TERM IN CITY HALL PROGRESSED, IT BECAME apparent that the Little Flower was beginning to wither. One by one, the petals were coming off.

Although he sought, and found, friendships in strange quarters for a reform Mayor, all was not well within his own municipal family. Take the Police Department, for example. Years before, the Mayor had said, "I have had many a headache and have been discouraged many times since I took office . . . the fact that I have seen the courage and the high morale of the police improve has been one of the things that has sustained me in my efforts to continue."

Despite LaGuardia's boast about New York's Finest, few policemen I knew, and I knew many, cared affectionately for their boss. For one thing, he relieved them of their nightsticks. While no competent patrolman liked to go around bashing skulls, the nightstick was an essential tool. Look today at how many policemen have gotten into trouble for using their revolvers, their remaining defense, against hoodlums of tender age but matured muscles.

LaGuardia also hampered the police force in its control of mob violence. Concerned lest he alienate misguided blocs of voters, he once sank to the level of neutrality between law-enforcer and law-breaker. The situation under LaGuardia was a far cry from the days when George V. McLaughlin brooked no political interference and backed his men to the hilt.

Much of today's coddling of juvenile offenders stems from

154

LaGuardia's court reforms. "The first thing we did," he said in praise of himself, "was to remove all the dry rot from the proceedings in which children were involved, to transform the formidable black-robed judges into symbols of kindly but firm-minded fathers and mothers . . . In other words, it was our purpose to change the Domestic Relations Court from a hall of stone walls, wooden benches and wooden faces into a humane social agency for the benefit of unfortunate children."

During one of the Mayor's campaigns to humanize and de-fang the Police Department, I wandered into a local stationhouse for a chat with the captain, an old friend. As a loyal Tammany man, I jokingly hopped on top of a chair and set about removing a portrait of LaGuardia from the wall. "Don't do that, Louis," said the officer, "I'd like to smash it myself, but we're supposed to keep his face around somewhere."

I always found the police in our district cooperative. This cast no sinister reflection on their integrity. Whether a foot patrolman was asked to investigate strange noises in a cellar, or a truck had to be towed from in front of a synagogue on the Sabbath, service was prompt and efficient.

My year-round duties as an Ahearn club captain continued, despite the annual break imposed by the Hatch Act before election time. Occasionally, I worked with officeholders to fulfill contracts. Sometimes, I acted as an intermediary. In rare instances, I discovered a constituent was getting a raw deal from an elected official and saw fit to intervene.

Such a regrettable case involved our defective system of immigration regulations. One of the unfortunate legacies of the First World War had been a quota system designed to admit those foreigners who did not want to come, and geared to bar entry to those poor souls who did. Business at Ellis Island dropped sharply.

The sister of a constituent became ensnared in red tape over in Axis-dominated Europe shortly before our own entry into the Second World War. Without seeking my assistance, he went straight to one of the district's elected officials. Gladly, he paid $500 for expenses and influence in getting his sister across the Atlantic.

Three weeks followed with no results. Then came a request for $500 more to cover unforseen additional expenses.

The poor fellow, whose savings were barely able to cover the first outlay, finally came to me. "What can you do?" he begged. "Why didn't you see me in the first place?" I said with some annoyance. "Tomorrow, we'll go to ——— office and find out what is being done and what can be done."

The next day, he met me at the office of the official. The dignity of the surroundings bespoke the lofty position occupied by our host. A secretary punched away at a shiny new typewriter in a business-like manner as we entered. She announced our presence to her boss, but mentioned only myself by name.

"Stay put in one of these chairs," I cautioned my worried constituent. "I want to speak to him alone first. When you're called in, make believe you know what I'm talking about even if you don't. Whatever I say, just nod and don't look surprised."

I stepped into his inner office, shook hands, sat down, exchanged small talk, then got down to cases. "Do you remember Charlie ———, a constituent of mine?" I asked innocently. "I dropped by to put you wise to something that's going to involve your office. I've heard he's been told to write the authorities about an immigration problem concerning his sister. It seems someone around here—he didn't say who, mind you—has squeezed him for $500 already, and he's being pressed for another $500. You don't have anything to do with it, do you?"

"Well, to tell you the truth, Louis, I am a bit involved in the matter," he responded coyly. "Did he write the letter yet?"

"No," I said. "I pleaded with him to hold off for another 48 hours. As a matter of fact, he's sitting outside in the reception room."

"Gee, thanks, Louis," said the official as he sighed with relief and dropped all pretenses. "I'll cut the figure to $750 and you're good for $100 of it if you want a couple of suits for your trouble."

"What $750?" I said. "You'll get his sister here from Europe for the original $500. Otherwise, I'll not only have him send the letter—I'll deliver it myself. You shouldn't take a dime over what it really costs, and I don't want a penny of his money. After all, he's my constituent. He gives me his vote on Election Day. That's all I ever ask for. And, aside from expenses, that's all you have a right to ask for."

The preliminaries over, I called my constituent in. He nodded, according to previous instruction, at all the appropriate points as we resolved the immigration problem to his satisfaction. His sister was soon safe on these American shores.

This incident, thank heaven, was an exception rather than a rule. Rarely was I called on to checkmate the greed of an elected official. More often, I saw fit to keep hands off requests of constituents which, in themselves, skirted the limits of the law. There is a difference between a "contract" and a "conspiracy." Frequently, the gap is quite wide. One such occasion had an unusual twist and climax.

On a cold, winter day, a shabbily dressed woman, who was accompanied by a neatly dressed man, knocked at the door of my apartment. It was Friday, at suppertime, clearly no time to conduct clubhouse affairs. The man waited in the background of the hall while the woman unraveled her tale of woe through the half-open door. Her wayward son was in jail for burglary, she said, and she wanted to bail him out "for the weekend." To say the least, it was an unusual request.

"In the first place," I explained, "this is a fine time to see a judge. Do you think they hang around their courtrooms on Friday nights waiting for you? In the second place, you need a lawyer, not me."

"I have a lawyer," she signified. "He's already cost me $100 and I've promised to pay him another $100 before the trial. But he says I need a politician to get my son out of jail."

"How can you pay $200?" I asked. "You're a widow with four children. Every Easter I give you a basket of food, and, every Thanksgiving, my brother gives you a twenty-pound turkey."

At this point, the man in the hall interrupted.

"What widow?" he barked. "I'm her husband—and we have only one son, that no-good brat sitting in jail."

The woman turned on him in anger. In one sentence, he had destroyed an image she had spent years building up. Her cloak of poverty was now stripped, along with the disappearance of three phantom youngsters.

For five minutes, ignoring me, they argued violently in the hall. I gently closed the door and resumed my supper.

Several weeks later, she saw me at the clubhouse and apologized for her long-running ruse. She capped her appeal for forgiveness by making another request, however.

"I want you to put my son in jail," she said.

"Put your son in jail?" I replied in astonishment. "Why? The last time you came to me, you wanted me to get him out of jail. Now, you want me to get him back into a cell!"

"Oh, the situation is different," she explained. "When his case came up, the judge let him loose on probation. So what does he do? He comes home, steals my husband's pay envelope and takes off. He belongs in jail, all right."

There are some problems a Tammany captain cannot handle. There are others that are best left untouched. This was one of them.

On the larger Tammany scene, the year 1944 began with a bang, not a whimper. Michael Kennedy's reign ended quite suddenly, with a resounding crash. Upon this flabby West Sider's shoulders fell the misfortunes of the Hall. His guilt lay in being the man in the middle when intimate details of a local judicial nomination were revealingly dragged through the mud.

Gambler Frank Costello had provided a helping hand in securing the disputed nomination. And Republican leaders had provided a helping hand in assuring the candidate's election, in exchange for similar Tammany endorsement of a GOP candidate. This form of inter-party cooperation was not altogether unusual, especially in judicial contests. The principal figure indeed was well-qualified for his post. Down through the years, he has served with notable distinction. His integrity has never been challenged since he mounted the bench, nor has his impartiality been questioned within the courtroom.

In a moment of indiscretion, however, he phoned his thanks

to Costello. This five-cent call raised such a storm that Tammany Hall's entire structure was shaken, and its nominal leader ousted. Never did a nickel cause such political havoc.

True, Kennedy wielded about as much authority at the Hall as a grasshopper in the midst of a nest of army ants. That mattered not a whit. He was titular leader of the county's Democrats, and therefore the handsomest and most logical scapegoat. Less than two years after taking Christy Sullivan's place as leader, Kennedy was led to the sacrificial altar.

Like Christy's, Mike Kennedy's reign had been coated with failure. Unlike the aging Christy, he had assumed the Tiger's reign while in the prime of life. But Mike took merely the title of his office, never the command of it. He made no effort to clean the cat's wounds, nor could he, even had he wanted to. Until the judicial explosion, Mike was a personable figurehead. After the explosion, his sole use to his masters was at an end.

Bert Stand, too, paid penance for his acknowledged association with Costello. He surrendered his position with the New York State Athletic Commission. For Bert, this price was cheap and easily bearable. He retained the more important and more potent job of Tammany Hall Secretary.

A new face was brought forth to replace the discredited Kennedy. Unlike his predecessor, Edward V. Loughlin, the third Tammany leader in three years, had gone way, way past the eighth grade in public school. He held a degree from Fordham University, attended that school's Institute of Scientific Study and picked up a diploma from the Columbia Law School in 1921.

Loughlin served his country in World War I, and also served his city in the battlelines of the public school system. For a while, he taught health education. Loughlin later moved on to another arena of public activity. He stepped into the District Attorney's office in 1925, the State Assembly in 1933, then became secretary to State Supreme Court Justice Ferdinand Pecora. All the while, he kept his political footing in the Fourteenth Assembly District.

Loughlin ascended Tammany's vacated throne following an easy victory over Representative James Fay, the same fellow who had tried for the job two years earlier. He accepted the leadership with appropriate humility.

He also said, "Those who know me and my record know that no act of mine as leader or otherwise will cause anyone to regret the honor conferred on me." He noted that, as party leader, "I shall be called upon to make decisions, some of them of importance to all, regardless of party."

As a college man, however, Loughlin developed no illusions and labored under no naive notion that he would actually be in charge. "While these decisions shall be determined by the dictates of my conscience," he carefully pointed out, "I shall arrive at them only after I have consulted with my associates on the Executive Committee and other worthy Democrats outside of it."

The duet of Clarence Neal and Bert Stand clearly remained tall in the saddle. During the 1944 Democratic National Convention, anyone suffering from a severe case of myopia was offered easy evidence of this. No magnifying glasses were necessary.

When Tammany held its usual convention eve dinner, at Chicago's Drake Hotel, everyone who was Anybody in the county organization was there—at $10 per plate. Like banquets given in the world of diplomacy, rank and status determined the seating arrangements. And Neal, not Loughlin, occupied the place of honor.

Clarence was presented with a gold wristwatch. Loughlin merely joined in the tribute. Questions about the nature of the citation were brushed off, even laughed off. "Oh, it's for Mr. Neal's 56th birthday," someone explained.

As in the days of past glory, nominal leaders of the Hall were still made and unmade at meetings of the party's Executive Committee. Control of that unwieldy body was therefore essential. During Loughlin's tenure, Clarence moved to cement that control. The LaGuardia era was drawing to its close, and Clarence, with Bert at his elbow, intended to have a big say in the selection of his Democratic successor.

During this period, too, an arrow shot from far-away Albany lodged in the Tiger's hindside. The poison in its point took the form of reapportionment of the state's assembly districts. Since the changes were dictated by Thomas E. Dewey, a Republican Governor, and a Republican-dominated state legislature, it requires no imagination to figure out how Democratic strongholds were treated. New York County became a political disaster area. Manhattan's representation was sharply reduced.

Because Tammany's political districts coincided with assembly district dimensions, 36 leaders were crammed into the remaining 16 districts of the island. Under the new set-up, some leaders now held as little as one-sixth of a vote on the Executive Committee. The other five-sixths belonged to five other leaders squeezed into the same political boundaries. Our tight little island had become ever so tighter. The process of adjustment was painful but necessary. The only alternative would have been the voluntary resignation of some leaders and the surrender of their authority. But such noble acts of self-sacrifice belong to fairy tales. Like old soldiers, old politicians sometimes fade away—but rarely of their own accord.

Following reapportionment, the Fourth Assembly District did not fare too badly. It was divided into northern and southern portions. This act split the district, but it did not splinter it. The John F. Ahearn Association now bore the standard for the Democratic Party in the "Fourth Assembly District South."

Clarence Neal's old Twentieth Assembly District was totally demolished. Part of it emerged as the Sixteenth Assembly District, however, and Clarence could have kept it. Rather than cast merely one-half vote and accept a diminished role as lord over half an assembly district, Clarence chose to hand his Harlem bailiwick to a trusted lieutenant.

Clarence took on the newly created post as chairman of Tammany's Election Committee. In this job, he would again hold a full vote, just as if reapportionment never happened. Loughlin, as leader and Bert, as Secretary, also owned one full vote apiece. It became apparent that reapportionment fostered by Albany's Republicans might be put to good advantage by Stand and Neal in preserving the status quo at the Hall.

To further insure the continuation of Loughlin as titular head, another innovation was sprung. The county leader was permitted to name seven pliable Tiger stalwarts, each of whom would also be capable of casting a full vote at committee meetings. Naturally, their synthetic ballots would faithfully be thrown in whatever direction their sponsor proposed. This guaranteed a certain ten votes for whatever policies Bert and Clarence pursued through Loughlin.

The total voting power of the Executive Committee amounted to 26 ballots. With ten accounted for, only 16 were left for the 36 district chiefs. From the Neal-Stand-Loughlin trio's standpoint, the arithmetic was just four votes shy of perfect. That number, combined with their own ten, would automatically provide a majority of two.

If the average reader today finds even this brief analysis of Tammany's internal mechanics dull, so undoubtedly did the average city voter of two decades ago. The maneuverings within the Hall could not have interested people less during the fall of 1944. That Man In Gracie Mansion still dominated the city. Roosevelt was almost assured of a fourth term in the White House. Everywhere, news from Europe and Asia's battlefronts captivated the public's attention. Who could be concerned about local politics when the world's fate hung in the balance?

Day by day, the news was getting better. In Europe, Mussolini's Italy had already crumbled. The Normandy invasion proved successful and the Allies were now marching across the face of France. Berlin was being pounded into rubble. Halfway across the globe, our Marines doggedly slugged their way toward Tokyo. Even Justice Aaron J. Levy took time off from politics, when I visited him, to tune in a young CBS newsman, Eric Sevareid, whose war reports enthralled him. As nothing else, the fact that it could hold Aaron's interest pointed out the seriousness of the armed conflict.

At election time that year, I did not go canvassing. In fact,

Clarence called me shortly before the big day specifically to warn me to stay away from polling places. Behind his rough armor beat a heart filled with concern for those who loyally served him. Seldom did the press get close enough to apply a stethoscope, a misfortune that has forever blurred his public image.

Clarence was fearful lest I do a little vote-catching and get into difficulty with the government. "I know you are with Internal Revenue," he said, "and I don't want you to have any trouble. Don't worry about your precinct. Your people will get to the polls whether you lead them in by the hand or not."

I had no intention of tangling with the Hatch Act. Roosevelt, of course, won easily. Everyone connected with Tammany Hall knew he would, as did everyone else in politics, with the possible exception of Thomas E. Dewey. It was a shame for so much money to be wasted on campaign buttons and political literature. More productive uses could have been found for the funds, such as cutting a "Hang Down Your Head, Tom Dewey" record album.

A more exciting contest loomed ahead for 1945. Mayor La-Guardia was turning the final corner of his third term. He wanted to stay in City Hall, whatever his fiery protestations about the job. But, unlike Roosevelt, he could not expect a fourth term by virtual default. A political era was drawing to a close in this metropolis.

By the spring of 1945, the Little Flower's aroma had vanished. So had the hodgepodge of alliances, overt and covert, that had long guarded his fortunes. Deep and immense fissures opened in Fusion. Through these crevasses roared the winds of change.

The faucet of federal funds, which had gushed richly during Roosevelt's first two terms in Washington, finally dried up. Financing World War II was expensive, and New York City was far from the frontlines. Little cash was available for the Mayor's pet projects. Discouraged with this turn of events, LaGuardia, at one point, sought to exchange his Mayorship for military rank. But Roosevelt was unobliging.

Many of the Mayor's close colleagues were becoming disaffected with their boss. Getting along with him was no easy matter. Retaining his already acquired favor was even harder. LaGuardia's much-heralded loyalty to principles left little room for loyalty to people. Personality clashes inevitably developed, and bitterness was a natural end-product.

LaGuardia had long since deserted the Republican Party. For twelve years, he had slapped it in the face. For three terms, despite this, it had tolerated him. Now, finally, the GOP refused to turn the other cheek. In March, 1945, New York County Republican leader Thomas Curran, an alert and capable politician, prepared to edit the Little Flower's political obituary.

Curran pointed out that 80% of the party's district leaders in Manhattan opposed LaGuardia's renomination. Four years earlier, under Curran's astute leadership, the Manhattan GOP had provided a reservoir of strength, however lukewarm its temperature. But in the course of the Mayor's third term, even Tom feuded with His Honor. The county chief denounced LaGuardia as an ingrate to the party and the 'most artful political dodger" the city had ever known.

True, the Mayor still had the American Labor Party in his pocket. But this was small comfort. The ALP was no longer the potent political instrument of former days. The dismal spectre of Communist domination had rent it asunder. As the party's ship steered leftward, many moderates abandoned it. The Liberal Party, a safer and better balanced vessel, was launched by respected members of the city's labor movement.

Like the Republicans, this group looked for a potential candidate elsewhere than at Gracie Mansion. It sought a man who would bring about an "intellectually honest non-partisan administration." The Little Flower's regime had become nonsensical rather than non-partisan.

The Mayor could naturally count on the aid and comfort of his disciple, Vito Marcantonio. Over the years, this complex figure had spun a political cloth cut from both his own ALP and threads of the Democratic and Republican organizations. Marcantonio was one of the few men with whom LaGuardia had kept faith. It is therefore fitting that both their stars began to fade at the same time. Our nation's wartime alliance with Russia was weakening as victory approached, and the shingle on Marcantonio's door clearly read, "Paint Me Pink."

Of all the "minus" factors on LaGuardia's dismal political sick-chart, one stood out. His popularity among the city's electorate had nose-dived. The New York *Daily News* straw poll, usually an accurate gauge of voter sentiment, showed the Mayor as the choice of only 25% of those canvassed. William O'Dwyer, his 1941 opponent, drew 30%. Tops in popularity, with an almost startling 40% rating, was former Mayor James J. Walker! The wheel had certainly gone full-circle.

No longer the buoyant "Beau James," Walker chose not to run. It was probably the only time he had anything in common with Calvin Coolidge.

O'Dwyer, on the other hand, was no reluctant dragon. He did not wait for the office to seek the man. He went out huckstering for the Democratic nomination. And he courted it, as well, in some strange quarters outside of party channels. His search was not in vain. Despite moderate opposition within his own Brooklyn organization, he won his party's endorsement. In the coming campaign, Clarence Neal and Bert Stand would throw Tammany Hall whole-heartedly behind him. This was to prove the most disastrous mistake of their political careers.

The 1945 Mayoralty campaign turned out to be a dreary, lack-luster affair, well-deserving of the scant attention it receives here. Certainly, it was a poor echo of its resounding build-up. O'Dwyer won in a three-cornered race. LaGuardia's personal choice, Newbold Morris, came in second on a "No Deal" ticket. Judge Jonah J. Goldstein finished third, running as a Republican.

Goldstein had been an odd selection for the Republican Party candidacy, mainly because he had been a Democrat all his life. Goldstein had even been considered a likely Tammany nominee before the prize fell to O'Dwyer. There was cynical speculation that the GOP hoped his liberal record and philanthropic activities would draw him support from New York City's huge Jewish population. If so, it was a grave miscalculation. The O'Dwyer-Morris-

Goldstein contest, thank heaven, did not degenerate into a Catholic-Protestant-Jewish clash.

In our district, for example, only one type of "bloc" voting existed. It centered on a candidate's political faith, not his religion. My precinct scored heavily in O'Dwyer's favor.

Sometime after the contest, I ran into Judge Goldstein in front of the State Building in downtown Manhattan. Apparently, he had some recollection of the way my precinct had turned out in the recent election and in the 1939 General Sessions Court race, a few years earlier. In that contest, I had transformed a nearly solid vote against him in the Primary, when he ran as an insurgent, into a nearly solid vote for him, when he appeared on the regular Democratic line. Now, after six years, my precinct had again turned against him, even though the Hatch Act forestalled any direct campaigning on my part.

"You know, you let me down," he scolded.

"Let you down? What do you mean, Judge?" I asked.

"Well, look how poorly I did in your district," he complained.

"That's your fault, not mine," I pointed out. "You turned your back on your party by running on the Republican line. Naturally I opposed you."

"But even a son sometimes talks back to his father," said Goldstein, somewhat abashed.

"Maybe that's true," I replied. "It's a matter of upbringing, though. And in my house, we were brought up to respect our parents. We never forgot that lesson."

XI

O'Dwyer: A Knight in Rusty Armor

THE COMING OF WILLIAM O'DWYER WAS WELCOMED WITH EN-
thusiasm by Tammany Hall as well as by Democratic organizations
in other corners of the city. After twelve years of LaGuardia,
everyone in party politics looked forward to a square deal, a new
deal, a fair deal. O'Dwyer was destined to be the Sir Galahad
who would bring this shining new age to the city. Few Democrats
could dream, much less predict, that their knight was about to
shuffle a stacked deck and hand out a raw deal.

Edward V. Loughlin, whose head would soon become an
O'Dwyer trophy, innocently proclaimed: "It is needless to say
that I am happy and grateful about General O'Dwyer's overwhelming victory. It is a great tribute to him. The tremendous
plurality by which General O'Dwyer and the rest of the Democratic ticket won is a vote of confidence from the people of this
city in the progressive program of the Democratic Party."

Bert Stand and Clarence Neal sat at Loughlin's elbow as he
spoke. They had naively helped make O'Dwyer Mayor. In so
doing, they drove the nails into their own political coffins. Within
15 months after O'Dwyer's inauguration, all three would be
stripped of their Tammany posts and their party influence.

The "General" took office with millions of friends and barely
an enemy in sight. The storm that constantly swirled about
LaGuardia's head was missing from O'Dwyer's. His life story
patterned itself on an Horatio Alger novel. Only O'Dwyer and
his alter ego, James Moran, knew there was another cheap story
line between the covers, one far more sinister.

During the 1945 campaign, colorful comic books had been cir-

167

culated, which traced the candidate's equally colorful background. At 19, he migrated from County Mayo, Ireland, to New York with $23.35 in his pocket. He bounced from job to job, developing varied talents as a ship stoker, grocery clerk, deck hand, plasterer's apprentice, bartender and hod carrier. Taking into account, in addition, the two years he spent studying theology at Spain's University of Salamanca, he certainly brought with him to the New York City Police Department a wealth of diverse experiences.

While a policeman, O'Dwyer studied law at Fordham University. Then he traded his police badge for a clerkship in a Democratic Alderman's office. Acting Mayor Joseph McKee made him a Magistrate, Governor Lehman made him a Kings County Judge, Brooklyn's voters made him a District Attorney and his prosecution of Murder Inc. made him a national figure. Just how successful his sparring really was against the crime ring is still a debatable point. In any event, his crusading image won him Democratic endorsement in the 1941 Mayoralty contest and was the propeller of his campaign.

Defeated, he turned to President Roosevelt when the Japanese attacked Pearl Harbor. Roosevelt made him a major in the Inspector General's office, a colonel, a brigadier general and, ultimately, a Presidential envoy. O'Dwyer returned to this city at war's end with an impressive string of new laurels. It is evident that this political Horatio Alger carried imposing credentials when he took the oath of office as Mayor of the City of New York on the first of January, 1946.

After twelve long, lean years of starvation under the Fusion follies, deserving Democrats looked forward to the patronage that accompanied victory. It was neither an unethical nor unjustifiable expectation. No matter how much he screeched of nonpartisan government, Mayor LaGuardia had used his power of dispensing jobs as a quite potent political tool. So had Presidents Woodrow Wilson, Franklin Roosevelt—and Abraham Lincoln. Even Marc Antony had not been above lending an ear to the requests of a personal and political ally, Cleopatra.

During the first months of O'Dwyer's regime, I remained at my

Internal Revenue post. I had no inclination to fight rather than switch or fight in order to switch. I was content in the federal service. I had never acted without honor nor did I ever soil my conscience. No one in the service of his government ever should, and it surely is a badge of national shame that we read occasionally in the papers of men who do disgrace themselves and their offices of public trust.

Like any judge—and, in a sense, every revenue agent is a judge—I occasionally tempered justice with mercy. I rarely regretted it. But one case, in which I stretched the limits of discretion, left a bitter tang. The beneficiary was a young lawyer, a Republican, who later advanced to high political office.

At that time, just after the close of the war, he occupied an office on lower Broadway, several blocks north of the Customs House. Apparently, his office was not a very solvent one. I went there to collect withholding taxes that had not been handed over to the government. This, of course, was a punishable offense.

Several girls were conversing at one side of the office as I walked past the switchboard. "May I help you?" a chubby, youngish-looking man inquired. I told him the circumstances of my visit and asked to see the boss, Mr ———:

"Oh, he's in Washington and won't be back for two more weeks," he replied. "You'll have to return then." I made a note on my case history sheet and left.

When making my second call two weeks later, I was met by the same young man. I re-introduced myself and again asked to see Mr.———: "He's back from Washington now," the fellow said, "but he's tied up with a case in the State Supreme Court. Please come back in a few days." A bit annoyed, I made another note on my history sheet and left.

The third time around, I got the Washington story again. On this occasion, though, my patience was exhausted. "Look, every time I come to see your boss, you give me some excuse why he can't see me," I said. "What's going on?"

The young man promised that Mr.——— would be around on my next visit. "Okay," I agreed, "but this is the last time."

As I prepared to leave, the young man sheepishly inquired, "Do you have the authority to give him all these extensions?"

"That's my business," I answered. "I'll give him one more break. Make certain he's here next time. I'll phone ahead. We don't pull taxpayers by the scruff of the neck, but there's a limit to our endurance." Again I made a memo on the case history sheet.

On my fourth visit, I was jarred by the young man's greeting. "What can I do for you?" he asked.

With no effort to conceal my rising temper, I said, "You know who I am and you know why I'm here. Where's your boss?"

"I'm sorry, but Mr. ———, isn't here so . . ." he began to explain. He never finished.

"Forget the excuses," I interrupted. "This time I'm leaving a subpena for Mr. ———. Tell him to come down to the Internal Revenue office with his records, his bank books, everything!"

The young man glanced around the office, then startled me a second time that morning by practically whispering in my ear, "I'm Mr. ———." He asked me to follow him into one of the small partitioned offices.

Once inside, I demanded to know why he had lied and wasted my time on three previous trips to his office.

"I just didn't have the money the government wanted," he explained.

"What about the girls in the office?" I asked. "Do they work for nothing? How do you pay them?"

"I don't pay them regularly," he said. "There's no money. I haven't turned in the withholding taxes because I needed them temporarily to help get by. Give me just one more break on the warrant."

"All right, but this is absolutely the last time," I agreed. I made another addition to the already crowded history sheet on this case.

Evidently, he made the most of this last extension. Within a few weeks, his back taxes were paid in full.

This had been the type of favor for which a less ethical agent might have asked for, and expected, a "pay-off". I sought none.

At this point, I must run ahead several years in this narrative to explain why the incident left a bitter aftertaste. There are many ways in which a man in public life may honorably express his thanks or demonstrate his ingratitude.

During the 1950s, I attended a political dinner with a Republican friend. A district leader, he had helped the young man, by now a national figure, get his political start. When Mr. —— came to our table to greet my companion, the district leader introduced us.

"Your name sounds familiar," Mr. —— said, stretching his memory.

"I was with Internal Revenue years back when you had an office on lower Broadway," I pointed out as a refresher.

"Oh, yes. I remember now," he said. "It's been a long time since I saw you. We must get together sometime." He pulled out a pencil and small memo pad from his pocket. "Let me have your name again. I'd like to speak to you."

Because of his exalted position, I must admit I was pleased. Here was a man, I believed, who obviously did not intend to let a past kindness go unnoted.

When he left our table, however, the Republican leader advised me to ignore that just-concluded show of concern. "I know him much better than you do and much better than the columnists who keep harping on his liberal record. Three minutes from now, he'll forget all about you."

My Republican friend was right. I did not hear from Mr.—— again. When I took the initiative and asked for an appointment at his convenience, he replied through his secretary that he would get in touch with me. He never did.

As 1946 began, Bert Stand and Clarence Neal clearly enjoyed their views from the drivers' seats. Since the days of Christy Sullivan, they had called the turns at Tammany Hall. But, until now, they had merely captained a government-in-exile. While Fusionist LaGuardia had occupied City Hall, they basically depended on the meager job-offering of a Democratic Governor in far-off Albany and a Democratic President in farther-away Washington. Now, finally, one of their own sat behind the Mayor's desk, and Bert and Clarence logically assumed his gratitude for their help would be bountiful.

Bert even ignored a chance to go to Congress during this period, an opportunity most politicians would fight for these days. The occasion was the departure from the local scene of one of my good friends.

In 1946, Representative Sam Dickstein vacated his Washington post by moving up to the State Supreme Court. Sam had served our country and our district ably in the House for more than two decades. He never turned me down when I sought a favor for a constituent. Had he remained in Congress, I have no doubt he would have advanced to the chairmanship of a major House committee. But for Sam, as for most city lawyers, high judicial office was the ultimate reward of public life. He decided to exchange his legislative toga for a judge's black robes.

(This line of reasoning, incidentally, is one cause for so many Congressional committees being ruled by rural Southerners. Capable members from urban communities, such as Sam, look forward to acquiring their own courtroom. Cotton kingdom representatives lack similar aspirations back home. So they retain their Congressional seats year after year, decade after decade. They harvest the fruits of a political system in which seniority is the highest of public virtues.)

By the post-war period, our Congressional District took in a wider neighborhood than the Fourth Assembly District. Other clubhouses besides our own fell within its boundaries. Several contenders arose for Sam Dickstein's old job. Bert, no Solomon, could not satisfy all of them. Some thought it would be wise for Bert to take the elective office himself rather than risk the development of petty jealousies among the aspirants. That had been Eddy Ahearn's solution to a similar problem following State Senator Barney Downing's passing in 1931.

Bert, however, chose to stay close to city affairs. Washington was too far away a location from which to keep a careful check on the traffic between City Hall and Tammany Hall. Fortunately, apprehension within the district proved groundless. Without much bickering, the House position was given to Arthur G. Klein, who served capably for several years, then moved on, like Sam, to the State Supreme Court.

For myself, too, it was moving time. Though I enjoyed my work at Internal Revenue, the paycheck was thin. The rocketing price spiral of the post-war period appeared to thin it even further, and I engaged in no underhanded dealings to supplement it.

One day, Bert called and said Clarence Neal wanted to see me at Tammany Hall. I wondered what was up, so I immediately rushed over to find out.

"How much do you get from the federal government?" he asked. When I told him, Clarence asked how I managed to make ends meet on that kind of salary. Without waiting for an answer, he added, "To hell with it. Go down to City Hall and see O'Dwyer's aide, Louis Cohen. He'll have you sworn in for $150 a week as a city collector at the local racetracks."

I drove down from Tammany Hall to City Hall, briskly climbed up the steps leading to the city's capital and marched along the main corridor toward Cohen's office.

"I'm sorry, Mr. Cohen is too busy to see you now," said a rigid secretary, guarding the partition in front of his quarters.

"Are you certain?" I asked. "I have reason to believe he's expecting me."

She went into her boss' office, emerging moments later with the same icy response. I did not know why I was being brushed off as an unwelcome stranger. Maybe signals between the two Halls had been crossed. I intended to find out.

So I paced several feet down the corridor to Room Nine, the press room. One of the reporters there okayed my use of the outside wire. I called Clarence.

"Wait five minutes," he instructed. "Then walk back up the hall slowly. By the time you reach his office, he'll come running out to see you."

Ignoring three of the five minutes, I retraced my steps along the corridor back to his office. I guess those extra 180 seconds really counted. For when I halted for a second time before the partition, my reception was cold.

"I told you before that Mr. Cohen couldn't see you," the secretary said, obviously annoyed at my reappearance. I gave her my name again and asked her to check with her boss before sending me away once more. Persistence was apparently a virtue she did not appreciate, so she hesitated before performing her duty.

Moments later, Cohen came out of his office, as Clarence said he would. "Please tell Commissioner Neal that I was very busy. Now you go right across the street to the Municipal Building and see Mr. ———— at the Department of Finance. He'll be waiting for you and will see that you're sworn in. And please don't forget to tell Commissioner Neal that I took care of things."

The whole process at the Municipal Building took two minutes. When I walked out, I had exchanged a poor-paying federal post for a better-paying city job.

At that point, Clarence was still undisputed backseat boss of Tammany Hall, in company with Bert Stand, who acted as prime minister. Edward Loughlin, as chief of state, signed papers, issued statements and spoke for the record. He was the Tiger's "voice".

Traditionally, an implicit agreement had been subscribed to by Democratic occupants of City Hall and Tammany Hall. Only the personalities occasionally had changed at four year intervals. The division of authority was simplicity itself: elected leaders made public decisions; political leaders handled all patronage outside the Mayor's personal circle.

Late in 1946, Mayor O'Dwyer sought to upset this time-tested but unwritten rule. He launched an assault on Tammany's leadership, winning applause in the press for his well-publicized efforts. O'Dwyer pictured himself as a shining knight, charging the evil Tiger with a lance of civic virtue. He was out to reform the Democratic Party, he proclaimed in stentorian tones. And he was believed. Those who pointed out his armor was rusty were shouted down by his strident supporters. Who could then foresee that within four years he would himself be shrouded in scandal, resign the Mayorship under fire, engineer an ambassadorship and bid farewell to his beloved New York?

As Bert later pointed out, O'Dwyer sought to control Tammany Hall, not reform it. Bitter clashes developed between Clarence and the Mayor over appointments and judicial nominations. Election as Surrogate, for example, was a prize carrying not only good pay and long tenure, but also the authority to appoint receivers as guardians over estates. The value of this power is easily seen when it is recalled that the Ahearn club survived the vengeful Tammany reign of John F. Curry partly because of the trickle of patronage it received from Surrogate James Foley.

Clarence and Bert did not meekly surrender to O'Dwyer's whims. Neither was the type to open an umbrella of appeasement. But they lacked the Mayor's most formidable weapon, the ability to hand out jobs and take them away. District leaders dependent on the Mayor's favor were surely in no position to argue the niceties of the proper division of authority between public and party officials.

O'Dwyer's first move against Clarence Neal occurred in October, 1946. At a City Hall meeting with Loughlin, O'Dwyer insisted on eliminating the ten synthetic votes on the Executive Committee of the Hall. As a result, Clarence would be deprived of his membership in that group, since he had previously turned over his district leadership to a lieutenant. Loughlin walked out of the Mayor's office with his own crown and title still in place. Maybe he even felt a bit relieved.

But not for long. O'Dwyer whittled away at his position throughout the winter, ceased Tammany's full quota of patronage, denied it favors and hindered relations with the other Democratic organizations. By the first week of March, 1947, the game was up. A majority of the district leaders had been beaten into submission. Clarence and Bert were unable to rally enough support to hang on.

Though constant feuding and constant bickering had been the unmelodic theme within the Hall's ruling council over the past number of years, varied cliques briefly fused in the corner of an O'Dwyer favorite, West Side leader Frank Sampson. Their object

—to oust Loughlin from the nominal leadership, thus stripping Clarence and Bert of their "titled" junior partner. An Executive Committee meeting was arranged for this purpose. However, it never got the chance to commit the deed.

On March 3, 1947, Loughlin signed a curt note at his Madison Avenue law office and sent it one block north to Tammany headquarters. It read: "I have decided to devote all my time to the practice of law and hereby resign as Leader of the Democratic Party of the County of New York."

It was symbolic and fitting that Loughlin did not personally make the short journey to the Hall and preside over his own political funeral. Clarence and Bert handled the solemn details. The ornate desk of the resigned leader was bared of all trivia except a desk pad. A portrait of James Dooling still hung on the wall. So did a picture of a tiger wandering through the jungle. Bert tiptoed quietly across the red and blue carpet and red drapes were partly drawn over the window, perhaps in mourning.

Thus vanished Edward V. Loughlin from the political scene. Like Michael Kennedy, Christy Sullivan, John Curry and George Olvany, he did not leap—he was pushed. James Dooling, who departed the post in death, had labored under constant cross-fire. Nobody since Charles F. Murphy's day had really gripped the reigns of the Tiger tightly. Frank Sampson most certainly would not.

Two days following Loughlin's ouster, Sampson officially became leader of Tammany Hall. He quickly pledged himself to the cause of civic progress and his party's welfare. "Reorganization will be immediate," he proclaimed. He suggested that Bert and Clarence resign during a private conference.

Clarence, in turn, offered the new chief some unsolicited advice. "I also told him," Clarence explained to reporters afterward, "that he's going to be surrounded by the worst crowd there is in the world and for him not to go out for a walk near a cliff with any of that crowd near him, or they'll push him over. Any one of them. Unless he's got a couple of guys around him that he can trust, he'll have to spend his whole time as leader walking like this." Neal then pirouetted across the room, hands in pockets, to demonstrate his point.

As usual, Clarence was right. It would take Sampson less than a year and a half, the shortest Tammany reign in four decades, to find out just how right.

For the moment, though, it was Sampson who was swinging the axe and it was the collection of district leaders who had to keep their eyes open. The new leader moved swiftly ahead. At a luncheon of Tammany officialdom, Sampson served French vanilla ice cream, then offered a bitter chaser.

"It was delightful of you to come," he said. "I expect all of you to resign for the good of the party and in the interest of party harmony. Think it over for a couple of days and let me know your decision."

Clarence and Bert were thinking men, all right, but they did not think along the same lines as the new chief. So Sampson acted. He stripped them of their positions as party leaders. As far as he was concerned, Bert was no longer Secretary of the Hall and Clarence was no longer chairman of its Committee on Organization and Elections.

Neither Neal nor Stand eagerly stepped aside to make way for the New Order. They thumbed through the county organization's rule book for legal loopholes to marshal in their favor. Meanwhile, Sampson said Councilman Samuel DiFalco would "handle all duties formerly discharged by Bert Stand" and would occupy his desk. When someone asked Bert where he would now sit, he cracked, "My name is Stand."

For another month, the team of Bert and Clarence managed to keep a foothold, however slippery, at party headquarters. Then, Sampson's successful manipulations resulted in a change of the organization's rules. Both men found their jobs pulled out from under them. It was truly the end of an era.

For the moment, Sampson was boss. But only so long as he was able to hold together the various cliques that had united to oust Loughlin. And only so long as he could sup at O'Dwyer's table as court favorite.

Sampson, at 49, was a political Johnny-come-lately. Until a couple of years before, few had ever heard of him. An ex-waterfront checker, ex-ticket broker and ex-City Marshal, Sampson's chief claim to political weightiness came from his acuity in picking a brother named Eugene. Eugene Sampson, a powerful longshoremen's union leader, lorded over part of the waterfront, controlled a healthy number of votes and appeared his brother's most noteworthy political asset.

Much talk was made of how Tammany's new head would scrub the Tiger's black stripes from its back and de-odorize the jungle beast. Such boasts were mostly nonsense. Each leader since John F. Curry, with the exception of doddering old Christy Sullivan, had made the same empty claim. It was politically fashionable to do so, and cost nothing.

More accurately, Sampson set about turning the Tiger inside-out. To a large degree, under O'Dwyer's protective wing, he accomplished this. But the only thing "change" has in common with "reform" is that both words contain six letters.

Ever since 1934, the Hall had been led by men tracing their political lineage to Eddy Ahearn. James Dooling had been elevated by virtue of Eddy's cohesive block of votes. Christy Sullivan's own assembly district had been saved for him by Eddy's personal intervention. Michael Kennedy and Edward Loughlin were clearly the creatures of Bert Stand and Clarence Neal. And Bert and Clarence themselves had been Eddy's direct heirs.

Now the dynasty ended. Frank Sampson, of the West Side's Third Assembly District, owed no allegiance to the old Ahearn circle. I doubt that he had ever known Eddy. Certainly, had he lived these past 13 years, Eddy would not have approved of the underhanded practices that led to the downfall of his followers.

Sampson's oft-repeated and oft-praised plans to provide a new scent for the Tiger's lair, however, properly belonged with other animal stories in *Aesop's Fables*. If Sampson wished to form his own circle of intimates, that, of course, was his privilege. Even Bert and Clarence would not have denied him that liberty, much as they naturally yearned to remain in the inner circle. He began his reign neither better-off nor worse-off than many of his predecessors.

But Sampson soon committed the sin of excess. He designed a policy of total warfare against all of Bert and Clarence's supporters. Each and every jobholder bearing their stamp became fair game for his axe. Personal loyalty to himself rather than performance for the party became Sampson's theme song. Personal fealty became the basis for political punishment or reward. How many votes a captain piled up for the Democratic Party on Election Day no longer mattered. Certainly it did not in my case.

Sampson's campaign of ruthless firings was not fully unprecedented. But even if the new leader could point to the past and say he was following a path that had already been cut, this did not justify his actions one iota. Curry's political sins did not cleanse his successors of blame for similar misconduct. Samson's vindictiveness was eventually to spell his own ruin. He had an infinite capacity for creating political foes where none had existed before.

I became the first—or, at least, one of the first—of Sampson's victims. Shortly after Bert's removal from the Secretary's post, he called me and said Sampson wanted to see me at Tammany Hall. I asked what was up. "Believe me," Bert answered, "whatever it is, Sampson's up to no good."

We gathered up Willie Ahearn, who was still titular leader of the club, and hurried uptown. The three of us were ushered into Sampson's office and joined him at a table.

After the preliminaries, Sampson came straight to the point. "I want you to quit your job," he said.

I knew I had served well in the position that Clarence Neal had given me. During the past year, I had collected $16,000,000 for the city, far better than my successor would prove capable of doing. But the source of my job was purely political. I realized that Tammany's new ruler had the legal right, though not the moral right, to take it away.

"What other job do you have in mind for me?" I asked. Sampson assured me something would be forthcoming. However, I did not trust him, so I pressed further. "Look," I pointed out, "In my father's house, I was told never to spill out the dirty water before getting the clean. I won't resign until I know where I'm headed."

"I'm the boss here," Sampson snapped. "If you don't resign, I'll call City Hall and have you dropped from the payroll!"

Willie Ahearn jumped to his feet and smashed his cane hard against the desk. We all jumped back, for Willie's mental state was such that he could react violently to unexpectedly bad news. Fortunately, he calmed down and Bert pleaded my case more rationally.

But Sampson was adamant. "I'm running the show," he told Bert. "I do things differently as boss than you did. His job belongs to a district leader, not a captain. And district leaders have to be taken care of first. The job is going to McManus."

Bert scoffed at the idea. "Louis gets more votes for the Democratic Party in his precinct than McManus gets in his whole assembly district," Bert said.

Nonetheless, Sampson turned toward me and demanded once again: "Are you going to resign or aren't you?"

I glanced at Bert. He bowed his head and nodded. There was nothing else we could do. Later in the day, I composed the formal letter appropriate to such circumstances and dropped it in the mail.

A week afterward, Bert called Sampson to find out what alternate post he had in mind for me. "Nothing yet," Sampson replied, "but I'm still looking. Anyway, if McManus quits, Louis can have his old job back."

McManus *did* leave, but the post was not returned to me. Instead, it went to George Thompson, another district leader. George was a good friend of mine. So, within a week after he heard the job should rightfully have been mine, he went to Sampson and handed it back. "I won't take anything that belongs to Louis," he told me he informed Sampson. There indeed remained honor among some politicians of the old stamp.

Of course, the job was never re-directed back to me. Sampson never really had any intention of doing so. When Bert called the leader to remind him of his promise, Sampson merely replied, "I'll think about it."

"Stop that lying," said Bert. "I know you've already given it to a pal of yours."

"What makes you say a thing like that?" asked Tammany's startled leader.

"Listen," replied Bert, "You'll always find an enemy among friends. That's how I found out. I was tipped off. You're not going to be leader for very long."

Although Sampson retained the Mayor's support, he was far from a beloved figure among the district leaders and their captains. He maintained his position solely through the fortunes of the moment. More than most crowned heads, his had cause for uneasiness.

The fission and fusion of cliques within Tammany Hall's ruling councils was a continuing process. Realignments never ceased. Only their nature changed. Back in the early 1930s, when the Hall was dominated by Irish names, factions developed along geographical lines and clashes whirled around personalities. For years, the "Curry camp" and the "Ahearn camp" had been at odds.

Now, allegiances based on "national origins" dominated Tammany's internal affairs. Italian leaders banded together, first in self-defense, later to advance their interests. They were led through this period by a still youthful Carmine G. DeSapio. It had taken Carmine himself three disputed primary victories, years earlier, to break into Tammany's Irish-dominated ruling circle. When O'Dwyer entered City Hall, Carmine was not yet strong enough to bid for control of Tammany Hall. So the Italian bloc accepted— rather than supported—Sampson. Samuel DiFalco, who succeeded Bert as Secretary, was an honorable and talented lawyer, hardly the type to intentionally link up with the policies of Tammany's new leader. Later, Sam would move up to the State Supreme Court and eventually acquire Surrogate's robes.

Bert found a job for me as secretary to State Senator Elmer F. Quinn, from Sampson's own West Side. Elmer had replaced James Walker in the upper chamber when Walker became Mayor after the 1925 election. As Democratic Minority Leader in Albany, Quinn fought for the city's interests against the rural Re-

publican majority. He could justifiably point with pride to his
co-sponsorship of the "Ives-Quinn law" that wiped out discrim-
ination by employers based on race, creed, color, religion or national origin.

A politician of the old school, Elmer was interested in just two
qualifications when Bert introduced me. First, could I handle the
job? Second, did my record as a Democratic vote-getter warrant
my getting the job? Assured on both counts, he promptly hired me.

Elmer was a courageous independent. By virtue of his record,
he could afford this luxury. He had no use for O'Dwyer and even
refused to attend a meeting called by the Mayor to discuss city-
state affairs. He had just as little use for Sampson. Once, the
Tammany leader approached him and asked, "How many people
do you have on your payroll? Give me a list of who they are."

Elmer refused point-blank, then told Sampson where to get off.
"I'll pick my own people," said the Senator. "Don't try to tell me
who to hire and who to fire. I don't need your advice."

While Quinn lived, my job was safe. In fact, I lasted at Albany
far longer than Sampson lasted at Tammany Hall. The county
leader's high-handed methods had stirred a hornet's nest of resentment. Rebellion was in the air.

Vainly, he attempted to clamp down on the organization's district
leaders. At one point he issued a ukase which smacked of cen-
sorship. "Dear leader," began his directive. "You are respectfully
requested to refrain from issuing or making any statement in connection with any political matter or problem concerning the New
York Democratic organization without first consulting and dis-
cussing same with the County Leader."

Clearly, all was not well uptown. Bert Stand called me one
night, almost joyfully. "It looks like we're getting our wish," he
said. "Sampson's on his way out." And a short while later, he
was out.

Sampson retained O'Dwyer's backing to the end. Two weeks
before the deed, in July, 1948, the Mayor practically dared the
district leaders to act. He called the rebels "scavengers who belonged in the gutter." This, from a man who would himself desert

the sidewalks of New York in two years under a storm of criticism.

The leadership of Tammany Hall had become a brief, uncertain prize. The next man to discover this was Hugo E. Rogers, Borough President of Manhattan.

Hugo, 46 at the time of his coronation, held degrees from New York University's School of Engineering and the New York Law School. He had served on Tammany's law committee for 14 years and as a special deputy Attorney General in election cases for six years. He was no stranger to politics.

While bidding for the Borough President's job in 1945, Rogers made no speeches. An Army officer during the war, he had not yet been mustered out of the service. While in uniform, he was forbidden to participate in his own election campaign. So he merely attended rallies, was introduced, then had to sit back and let others do the talking. For a politician, this is difficult.

Hugo was also something of a scholar, hide the fact though he might. He authored several books with such saucy titles as *Minimizing Payroll Taxes* and *Legal Tax Savings*. An organization man to the core, his other book credits included *The Improved Order of Red Men*.

Rogers became leader of Tammany Hall almost haphazardly. He did not seek the job—really. A quartet of factional leaders handed it to him and were supposed to supply him with advice and buttress his hold on the job. Actually, they soon fell to bickering among themselves. The inevitable consequences were disastrous for Hugo. His brief term as leader, I am certain, was one of the less happy episodes of his life. Everyone wanted to use, or abuse, him. Nobody wanted to help him.

Sometime after his ouster, I met Hugo at a dinner and we reminisced about Tammany's hectic past. The Hall had certainly descended in stature among insiders as well as outsiders. Doubledealings were by now an established way of political life.

Hugo had been pressured by O'Dwyer into withdrawing as candidate for re-election to the Borough Presidency. He received, as compensation, the vision of judicial office. This turned out to be a mirage.

"Too bad you didn't get the judgeship," I said to him sympathetically.

"Well, that's the way things work out," he replied. "You also got promises and were left in the cold. You just don't know who to trust these days. It's not like it used to be."

The next head slated for the chopping block was that of Carmine G. DeSapio, who became the ninth Tammany leader since Charles F. Murphy and the sixth since 1942. Calmly, with a minimum of fanfare, Carmine mounted the scaffold.

The new county leader took office on a hot July day in 1949. There was no noisy opposition to his selection, but eight leaders of the "Irish" bloc abstained from voting. In the next decade, Carmine would prove himself the most able and distinguished Tammany chief since Murphy. No one who voted, however, had a crystal ball to foresee this. In fact, he even begged off for a day before outlining his plans as leader to the press. He said in apology that the honor had come so suddenly that he needed time to think.

Carmine's rise to political heights had begun, typically enough, with a captaincy in his local clubhouse. It took him three successive victories in district primary contests before Tammany's Executive Committee awarded him a coveted seat. Bert Stand's aid was instrumental, as I noted earlier, in gaining him entry into that exclusive club. Gifted with keen political intelligence, he quietly built a sturdy and cohesive train of followers. In 1947, Carmine helped Sampson become county leader. In 1948, he helped Rogers become county leader. Now, in 1949, he helped himself to the job. DeSapio was the first Italian boss of Tammany Hall, a summit that Albert Marinelli had aspired to reach, but never quite could.

Many cynics, grown accustomed to the game of political musical chairs, merely added him to the undistinguished recent list, under the names of former players, Sullivan, Kennedy, Loughlin, Sampson and Rogers. They considered the newcomer just one more unsteady Roman lawgiver, elevated by an unstable praetorian guard to a brief fling at emperorship. But Carmine fooled them.

During the next decade, while he firmly tugged at the Tiger's reins, DeSapio was analyzed and re-analyzed by the press. So much was written about him—complimentary and otherwise—that there is little purpose for repetition here. The publicity he freely welcomed set him apart from past leaders, who preferred to work quietly beyond the reach of microphones and floodlights. He was the very opposite of Charles Murphy, who said next to nothing for the public record and operated behind closed doors. He shook off the philosophy that the presence of Tammany leaders should be neither seen nor heard, only felt.

Perhaps Carmine's "modern" attitude led to his undoing. His dark glasses, which he wore as the result of an eye ailment, eventually became a sinister symbol of "bossism" under the glare of the communications media. Such spectacles may add glamor to a movie star's appearance. They added nothing but woe, however, to DeSapio's political image. Virtually every word this county leader uttered and every act he spawned found their way into a news item. Whereas public officials would have received accolades for taking, not avoiding, decisive action, Carmine was condemned for "imposing his will" when similarly decisive political measures were necessary. No Tammany leader, Carmine included, could forever shake off charges of "Boss Rule," which inevitably attach themselves to a man who openly makes large and controversial political judgements.

DeSapio's relations with O'Dwyer were somewhat better than Hugo's—but not much. Carmine, every bit as clever as the Mayor, kept his own counsel. And O'Dwyer could not abide by a Tammany leader who did not curtsy in his august presence.

O'Dwyer sought re-election in 1949. Tammany Hall, with no lavish enthusiasm, supported his candidacy. All the grievous errors made by the Mayor in his first term had been political, not public. To the average citizen his halo was still in place.

The Mayor's Republican-Liberal opponent, Newbold Morris, had been LaGuardia's fair-haired boy four years earlier, when he ran on the 1945 No Deal ticket. His chief claim to fame was his ancestry. Morris could trace his political heritage to pre-Revolutionary War days, a boast no Tammany candidate could equal. A graduate of Groton and Yale, he expressed a gentlemanly interest in "the science of government." Morris had many factors working against him, not the least of which was his name, "Newbold". It is an easily proven fact that no man christened with that name had ever become Mayor of the City of New York.

Morris also lived with the misfortune of having picked rich parents. This helps in state and national contests, but not local elections in polyglot municipalities. Furthermore, he held membership in Alpha Delta Phi, Phi Delta Phi, Scroll and Key and the National Golf Links of America, at Southampton. These befitted his station in life. But they also added to his unacceptability among those of humbler birth. Newbold Morris was licked before he could wave his first aristocratic finger at Tammany Hall's inequity.

Our Fourth Assembly District gave O'Dwyer approximately the same majority that it did back in 1945. This, despite his machinations against Bert and Sampson's shabby treatment of me. I worked for the whole Democratic line. But I was plugging for my party, not the man who, for the moment, dominated the city. Taken as a whole, about the best that could be said of this campaign was that luckily only one man would win.

O'Dwyer served only eight months of his second four-year term. Then Bronx leader Edward J. Flynn convinced Washington's Democratic administration that the Mayor could best serve his country by leaving it. New York City's loss was indeed Mexico City's gain when O'Dwyer took up residence there as our Ambassador. His popularity south of the border contrasted with the turbulence that marked the closing days of his reign here. Shortly after his re-election, flames of a growing Brooklyn scandal, involving bookmakers and police, had singed City Hall.

Fires of another kind swirled around O'Dwyer's closest associate, James J. Moran, whom he had once appointed as First Deputy Fire Commissioner. Before departing for his distant diplomatic post, the Mayor named Moran to a $15,000 lifetime job on the Board of Water Supply. Moran really did not need the money. He eventually wound up in prison, convicted of extorting currency while serving in the Fire Department—a matter of $300,000 or so.

According to a probation report read in court by the sentencing judge, "the strictly ethical aspects of his offenses do not seem to disturb him. His philosophy of life evidently has been that favors, preferences and special privilege are properly acquired by those who are smart enough and ruthless enough to advance themselves by such means."

This was the kind of man whom O'Dwyer kept at his side as a confidant and aide at the time he was casting stones at the Stands and Neals of Tammany Hall.

XII

War of the Halls:
City Hall Versus Tammany Hall

IN THE FALL OF 1949, VINCENT RICHARD IMPELLITTERI BECAME
Mayor of the City of New York by grace of O'Dwyer's self-
imposed exile and the 1945 city "Green Book." This pocket-size
volume, more accurately titled *Official Directory*, lists nearly
everybody who is anybody—and many who are nobody—on the
city payroll.

Edward Loughlin, Tammany's nominal leader at the close of
World War II, has since remarked that the name "Impellitteri"
caught his eye while he was feverishly thumbing through the "Green
Book" for a man of Italian ancestry to run for the Presidency
of the City Council. A crisis had arisen making this frantic search
necessary. Since the Democratic candidate for Mayor, O'Dwyer,
was an Irishman from Brooklyn, and the candidate for Comptroller, Lazarus Joseph, was a Bronx Jew, the logical choice for the
third city-wide office had to be an Italian from the island of
Manhattan. Thus, the ticket could be "balanced," a prime political
requirement. Queens and Richmond were of course unrepresented.
But they did not really count for much at Democratic parlays in
those days.

And so it came to pass that Impellitteri, an obscure law clerk
to a State Supreme Court Justice, was raised to exalted heights
as the President of the City Council. In this post, he was "Vice-
President" of New York City. When the freshly re-elected O'Dwyer
packed his bags and hastily retreated from the city, Impellitteri succeeded him.

Like Harry Truman, Impellitteri was virtually unknown when great public responsibilities were draped upon his shoulders. Like Truman, he had to wage, almost alone, an uphill campaign for the right to continue bearing these burdens. There the comparison ends. Impellitteri unjustly became the target for abuse and derision. These attacks came from enemies within the party, no great surprise. But they also came from learned political scientists, after his departure from City Hall. Theirs were cruel thrusts at his "indecisiveness," perhaps the unkindest cuts of all.

The professors claimed that he neither grasped the full potential of his office nor employed sound administrative measures. From high, ivy-covered towers, however, they completely ignored a basic fact that limits definition of the word "science" in "political science." The Mayor did not operate in a vacuum. He held office under a party system and alongside a powerful Board of Estimate. Political foes in his own party wanted his scalp, and the more ambitious of his colleagues on the Board wanted his job. Impellitteri was certainly not the most effective of Mayors. But he was undeserving of the damning criticism leveled against him. I am proud to count him as a friend.

No taint of scandal attached itself to his name. But throughout his administration, his position was undermined and his plans constantly sabotaged. Impellitteri's administration had as much opportunity for success as did the German Weimar Republic between the world wars. The odds against him were about as stiff.

The future Mayor was born on the island of Sicily in 1900 and brought here as an infant. Like his predecessor in City Hall, there was more than a touch of Horatio Alger in his rise from humble beginnings. He served aboard a destroyer in World War I, held various odd jobs, became a naturalized citizen and studied law at Fordham University.

Following five years of private practice, Impellitteri became an assistant District Attorney, then returned once more briefly to the defense table. In 1941, he became law clerk to a Democratic judge. It is from this position that he was plucked by Loughlin shortly before the 1945 election campaign got underway.

I sometimes wonder how a four-year chunk of New York City history might have been changed had the "Green Book's" printer inadvertently omitted the name "Impellitteri" in that year's edition.

Following O'Dwyer's resignation, Impellitteri automatically took over. But Tammany leader DeSapio had no intention of letting him remain in City Hall. A special election was slated to fill the Ambassador's unexpired term. The acting Mayor, like Joseph V. McKee under similar circumstances three decades back, wanted his party's nomination. Also like McKee, he did not get it.

The Democratic ticket carried as Mayoralty candidate the name of State Supreme Court Justice Ferdinand Pecora, a former counsel to the Senate Banking Committee and member of the Securities and Exchange Commission. A man of impeccable reputation and undeniable ability, he was certainly no doddering Joseph O'Brien. As well as our own party's endorsement, Pecora carried the label of the Liberal Party.

Bert Stand, far from a champion of Carmine DeSapio's, nonetheless stood behind the regular Democratic ticket. Earlier in that pivotal year of 1950, Bert had disavowed his long-standing political relationship with Clarence Neal. While reaffirming personal devotion to his old partner, Bert contended he would cooperate with Carmine. This, however, was to prove a very short and very unharmonious period of co-existence.

Impellitteri refused to bow out of the race. Though a mere two months separated his substitution for O'Dwyer and the oncoming Election Day, he set about building an organization and getting enough nominating petitions to insure his place on the ballot. Working under a tight deadline, this was no easy task.

Since he could not run under his own party's label, he cast about for another political tag, finally settling on the "Experience Party." But the acting Mayor remained a Democrat, no matter how unorthodox a Democrat.

A year earlier, he had trumpeted: "I have an ornery streak of independence which I am apt to assert from time to time. But, believe me, when I do it, it will not only be in the interests of the people but in the interests of the Democratic Party."

Impellitteri, in the heat of the campaign, said he was offered a tempting State Supreme Court judgeship as a consolation prize if he were to step out of the race. This judicial post would have brought him $392,000 over a 14-year period, based on the salary it carried back in 1950. Now, it is even higher.

Nevertheless, the acting Mayor kept his sense of direction. And he kept his furniture at Gracie Mansion, the Mayor's official residence.

Tough campaigns are not won by wishful thinking, though however positive a man's thoughts. There were few followers in his Experience Party camp. Help was needed. It came, and none too soon, in the form of dissident Tammany district leaders who broke away from the county leadership of DeSapio.

Harry Brickman, leader of part of Christy Sullivan's old bailiwick, the Second Assembly District, guided the inexperienced Experience Party through the muddy political waters of late fall. Robert B. Blaikie, maverick leader of the Seventh Assembly District, and former county boss Frank J. Sampson, of the Third Assembly District, also joined the Impellitteri entourage. This trio formed the core of his hopes.

I had grown to dislike and distrust Sampson, with ample cause, when he served as axeman under O'Dwyer. Brickman, though, was a firm and faithful friend. And while I have often disagreed with Blaikie, a perennial insurgent, it was impossible to dislike this scrappy, pixie-ish fellow no matter how cockeyed his views. All three would become prominent figures during Impellitteri's administration. Harry, remembering a favor I had done for him years before—one I had long since forgotten—would loyally prove an angel in distress when, in turn, I needed aid.

By throwing their support to Impellitteri, these three leaders took a calculated risk. Though his seemingly incredible victory assured them each a place in New York City's political sun, Pecora's triumph would have sealed their political coffins. At best, they faced certain excommunication by Tammany's present leadership.

Throughout the campaign, Impellitteri repeated the substance of one claim. "I have made one specific pledge," he said, "and that is that I'll be the people's Mayor, uncontrolled, unbossed, under no obligation to any man or group of men." Nonetheless, to his credit, the Mayor would demonstrate time and again his loyalty to those who stood loyally by him. This was a refreshing quality, lacked by many high officials both before and after him.

On Election Day, November 7, 1950, the Democratic Party was fractured. Impellitteri swept by the regular Democratic candidate, Pecora, by 1,161,175 to 935,353 votes. He even captured Tammany's Manhattan stronghold by a 246,608 to 214,610 margin. The Republican candidate, Edward Corsi, naturally finished a distant third.

The Fourth Assembly District as usual, supplied the regular Democratic ticket with its greatest plurality in New York County. The Mayor's Experience Party line took a sound trouncing in our part of the Lower East Side.

In the aftermath of the local political revolution, DeSapio's leadership of Tammany Hall, and perhaps the traditional Hall organization itself, appeared doomed. Losing to the well-regimented, well-financed Republican-Fusion-New Deal-backed steamroller of the LaGuardia forces in 1933 was one thing. Losing to the lonely figure of Impellitteri was quite another.

Years before, John F. Curry could not survive the drubbing handed to John P. O'Brien by a powerful combination of forces. There seemed little chance of Carmine's keeping his head above water following Pecora's submersion. Nonetheless, he began to drain the water from his sinking ship and prepared for a battle royal.

Impellitteri spent the day after his election triumph amidst the scent of floral wreaths that smothered his office and hundreds of congratulatory telegrams. Warily, he expressed hope for good relations among the Board of Estimate, the Democratic-controlled City Council and himself. He told supporters, "I was the spearhead of what you wanted— a poor man's candidate." But he also emphasized he was "still a good Democrat and always have been." Meanwhile, bandwagon-hoppers quickly put themselves at his disposal and set about the chore of disposing of Tammany chief DeSapio.

For his part, Carmine did not spend the post-election hours in quiet brooding. Though in no position to stage an immediate counter-attack, he could at least try to consolidate his shattered position. At a hastily-called meeting in the Hotel Statler, Tammany district leaders were presented with a carefully worded resolution. It said:

"Be it resolved that we, the undersigned, hereby pledge our loyalty to, and confidence in, the man who has been a tireless and unselfish worker for the Democratic Party in New York County, the Hon. Carmine G. DeSapio, chairman of the Executive Committee of the New York County Democratic Committee, and all of us hereby pledge to him our wholehearted support."

This was nothing less than an oath of allegiance to Tammany's ruler at his moment of disaster. Thirty-four of the 40 district leaders present signed the pledge. Carmine certainly had no intention of throwing in the towel.

In our district, Bert Stand waited eagerly to grasp whatever opportunities Tammany's turmoil tossed his way. Bert had been our de facto leader, of course, since Eddy Ahearn's death in 1934. But Eddy's brother, Willie, held the formal title and also the district's vote on the Executive Committee. This did not matter while Bert remained Secretary of the Hall and, with Clarence Neal, dominated its councils. But when Sampson gained control, Bert became an outsider for the first time. Ousted as Secretary, he could no longer attend Executive Committee meetings.

Willie normally cooperated in every possible way. But this did not alter the fact that Bert's vision was strained from his distant vantage point. Besides, Willie's precarious health often broke down. This made him unable to function, a handicap that could prove dangerous at crucial moments. For example, when Sampson took away my job, Willie was feeling ill at home. He was barely able to journey uptown for the decisive meeting with Tammany's chief.

It was therefore no surprise, and certainly no rebellion, when the symbol of leadership, as well as the substance, was passed into

Bert Stand's hands. The transfer took place shortly after the Election Day excitement had died down. Some opposition to the move existed among the district's county committeemen. Basically, this centered on the strong bond of sentiment that tied the Ahearn name to neighborhood politics. However, there was also growing distaste for the high-handed manner of Bert's brother, Murray, who was now City Clerk. Everyone knew that when Murray sneezed, Bert caught a cold. Many members were less than enthusiastic at the thought of any increase in Murray Stand's influence in district affairs.

On the balance scales, though, the plus factors overwhelmed the minus factors, so the move was made. By no stretch of the imagination was Willie's displacement personally motivated. Whenever poor Willie attended future clubhouse functions, he was ushered to a place of honor.

One of Impellitteri's first acts as Mayor, before leaving for a brief vacation, was to name Frank Sampson as his "political representative," that is, his job dispenser. Recalling my own experience with the man when he led Tammany Hall, I cannot say that his was a happy selection. The choice was logical, nevertheless, in view of Sampson's political stance. Carmine DeSapio, who had fought Impellitteri tooth and fang, certainly could not be assigned the task of churning out patronage. Thus, Sampson became the $15,000-a-year "Assistant to the Mayor" and a trustee of the Fire Department Pension Fund and the Police Department Pension Fund.

Harry Brickman was also rewarded. He became Deputy Treasurer in the Department of Finance. He had earned this compensation through his tireless efforts in the recent campaign.

Bob Blaikie, on the other hand, moved into no position of public responsibility. Hardly any had yet been invented that could hold him down long enough in one place. Bob has always been a charming screwball incapable of malice or set ways. Of his Stuyvesant High School football days, he once said, "I liked carrying the ball, but I got a bigger thrill out of tackling an opponent, hitting him hard."

Bob carried this philosophy into politics. After joining the Monongahela Democratic Club in upper Manhattan, he rebelled, formed his own club and eventually won his district's leadership. A rebel of many causes, he was soon denouncing the party's state chairman and national committeeman to their faces. Tackling political heavyweights became his chief hobby.

For some reason, Bob felt ill at ease on the favored side. I doubt he would have climbed into Impellitteri's boat if the acting Mayor had looked like a sure winner. Blaikie specialized in underdogs and embarked on periodic crusades against the city's political Establishment. He was a practicing reformer long before a professional reformer became the popular thing to be in New York City public life.

That Carmine DeSapio managed to survive his 1950 political Dunkirk was one of the marvels of local politics. In the years ahead, he would be saluted for judiciously selecting Robert F. Wagner as Democratic Mayoralty candidate in 1953 and Averell Harriman for the Democratic Gubernatorial nomination in 1954. But neither of these deeds surpassed his feat of merely staying politically alive after the crushing defeat handed him by Vincent Impellitteri. The Tiger had been skinned alive.

Bert Stand, whose political acuity matched anyone's in those days, expected Carmine's crown to shatter. Every so often, he threw a well-aimed rock to knock it from his head. Bert felt fully capable of picking up the pieces and molding them together again. He would never get the chance.

One major cornerstone used by Carmine to reinforce his position against Impellitteri's intrusions from 1950 to 1953 was the Mayor's political isolation. Strangely, this had been the very factor that had made Tammany's loss at the polls not merely a party defeat but also a party disgrace. Impellitteri had few allies. He was sole candidate on the Experience Party line during the campaign. Now, he was a solitary figure as Mayor.

True, the Mayor had ample sources of patronage in his hands and used them to win over other county structures. But Carmine could still draw from his own reservoir of patronage. This included jobs provided by county officials loyal to him, jobs available through judicial channels and jobs controlled by Tammany state legislators.

(Later, his ruthless use of this last-mentioned source would cut my own job at the State Senate from under me. I bore Carmine no grudge, for at the time he was engaged in a political life-and-death struggle against Bert. Besides, he would see to it that I was placed in a city job once his battle was won and he had realized the inequity of his act.)

In the spring of 1951, Senator Estes Kefauver's broad investigation of interstate crime concentrated on New York. The hearings drew a slash across city politics and politicians. Bert was asked to testify. So were Clarence Neal, Edward Loughlin, several district leaders and Ambassador William O'Dwyer. It was not precisely their Finest Hour.

Before the Kefauver committee and network television cameras, Bert and the former Mayor told conflicting stories of a 1942 meeting at gambler Frank Costello's home. Bert, O'Dwyer, Tammany leader Michael Kennedy and others had been present. O'Dwyer, an Army officer at the time, said he was there strictly on military business. Bert, on the other hand, said "It was nothing but a cocktail party—drinks and hors d'oeuvres" and that politics *were* a topic of conversation.

Still smarting under the abusive treatment O'Dwyer accorded him, Bert bitterly attacked the former Mayor's motives and methods. "Mr. Loughlin, Mr. Neal and I loyally supported O'Dwyer in his candidacy for Mayor," he said. "He asked for and received our support. Even in the face of the outspoken opposition to his nomination by Edward J. Flynn and the late Frank V. Kelly, leader of his own organization, we successfully advanced his candidacy and worked vigorously for his election."

Once in City Hall, Bert continued, "O'Dwyer's actions were always confusing, contradictory and irrational. He changed the leadership in Tammany Hall as often as he changed his mind. The public, however, was apparently misled by all his artful double talk into believing that O'Dwyer sought to reform the organization when, actually, his only objective was to control it."

Bert was only one of the many Tammany figures Costello acknowledged as acquaintances. The names of Harry Brickman and Hugo E. Rogers also came up during the hearings. Harry, as Deputy Treasurer, and Hugo, as special counsel to the Traffic Department, both held their purely political posts through Impellitteri. They had served their Mayor staunchly and faithfully.

All sorts of public and political pressures were exerted on the Mayor after aspersions were cast on their backgrounds. He gallantly resisted this coercion and refused to fire them. Such loyalty was not geared to win him favorable press notices. Lesser men would have taken an easier course. But Impellitteri stuck by his guns, even though it damaged his own public image.

"There is not one iota of proof or even a suggestion," he said, "to indicate that these men have ever been remiss or have been influenced in the performance of their duties as public officers." Impellitteri also pointed to his "personal reluctance" at "penalizing those who were loyal to me" when other public officials had not been asked to discharge men who were similarly mentioned in the course of the Kefauver hearings.

Whatever may have been said of their past associations, neither Hugo nor Harry compromised his integrity as a public official. Nor did either ever engage in a political double cross. These are sure tests of any man's personal worth.

Politically, of course, both men opposed Carmine DeSapio. And Carmine, in turn, rightly did all he could to eliminate their political roots, even though they retained their public positions. Harry Brickman was vulnerable. His home ground, the central portion of the Second Assembly District, was sandwiched between the western portion, ruled by Louis DeSalvio, and the eastern portion, ruled by Prosper Viggiano.

Both leaders, like Harry, honorably and skillfully served their constituents and their neighborhoods. But good men often take opposing sides in any conflict. Unlike Harry, Louis and Prosper stood behind Carmine in his struggle against Impellitteri.

During the primary contests for district leaderships in the late summer of 1951, Harry merely squeaked by in the 11 election precincts of his sector. This gave Carmine his chance. Using parliamentary methods as county leader, he realigned political district geography, merged the eastern and western portions of the Second Assembly District and squeezed Harry Brickman's central sector out of existence.

Other opponents of DeSapio similarly vanished. The number of district leaders was reduced from 41 to 35, and the voting power of dissidents on the Executive Committee dropped to three votes of the 16 total. Carmine could now do battle against the Mayor without worrying too much about his rear.

As Impellitteri's administration progressed, the gulf between the Mayor and the Tammany leader widened. Neither side considered reconciliation possible. The only way out seemed unconditional suurrender by one party to the other. But who wanted to buy peace at *that* price? Both men still continued to jockey for position, with unfortunate consequences for precinct workers such as myself— the narrowest, most vulnerable stripes on the Tiger's skin.

Temporarily, my own job at State Senator Quinn's office was safe. Elmer, made of stern stuff, would ignore all attempts at coercion or intimidation—from whatever their source. Some other office holders, on both sides of the dispute, were less secure. In the late fall of 1952, 16 persons, whose salaries ranged from $4,000 to $9,000 were lopped off the city payroll. Frank Sampson handled the details. Similar undertakings for O'Dwyer had trained him well for this task.

Although Manhattan Democrats were not totally shut off from jobs, these were channeled through Sampson rather than the county leadership. Democrats in other counties by contrast, were cared for by their borough chiefs. These had smoked peace pipes with Impellitteri. No such truce was attempted with DeSapio, partly because of Sampson's opposition. His entire influence within the administration would have disappeared had Carmine sought and gotten the Mayor's ear. In any event, Carmine was none too eager to sign a peace pact that would surely have left him something less than the Tiger's sole rider.

As a result, Impellitteri continued to denounce the Tammany leader as a sinister figure, which he was not, and DeSapio continued to assail the Mayor as incompetent, which he was not.

At one point, Impellitteri refused an invitation to the annual $50-a-plate fund-raising dinner of the New York County Democratic Committee. "I will not attend DeSapio's Tammany dinner," he said, "because my presence there might be interpreted as an indorsement of his leadership. That I will continue to oppose. In my judgment, his continued domination of the Democratic Party in New York County is harmful to the welfare of the party."

No example of Sampson's influence over patronage rivals the selection of a 33-year-old political novice as a city Magistrate in late 1952. It was excusable only by reference to the old adage that blood is thicker than water. Chief Magistrate John M. Murtagh protested to the Mayor. "When a Frank Sampson can make a wedding present to an old friend by appointing her husband a judge," he said, "our system of selecting Magistrates is seriously defective."

Sampson meekly shrugged his shoulders and pleaded innocent. "I did not recommend it and had no connection with it," he maintained.

During this period of stress and strain for Manhattan Democrats, Bert Stand gravitated to the Impellitteri camp, taking our club with him. His distaste for Sampson possibly exceeded his distaste for DeSapio. But Bert's main interest was his personal stake, and that of the Fourth Assembly District, in the Hall's power structure. These considerations overwhelmed any minor qualms over personalities.

Therefore, for the first time in memory, the John F. Ahearn Association was openly enrolled in the list defying the will of Tammany's majority. Years earlier, Eddy Ahearn had borne no love for John F. Curry, who ruled the Hall. But Eddy fought him from within the Tiger's cage, never from outside of it. Eddy's father, John, once quarreled with Charles F. Murphy. But this, too, was kept strictly a family affair.

In a sense, Bert tried to reap the harvest in both worlds. First, he aligned himself with the Mayor outside the pale of the Hall. Second, he used his membership on Tammany's Executive Committee to challenge Carmine's leadership. This second move had been made possible by Bert's elevation to the titular leadership of the Fourth Assembly District, which I noted earlier. While Willie Ahearn had occupied that chair, Bert was not even on the committee.

Bert Stand crossed his political Rubicon at the meeting of August 27, 1952. Until that date, he had straddled the fence. He had not previously joined forces with Harry Brickman, who disliked him, or, of course, Sampson, in support of the Mayor. Now, however, Bert chose to nosedive from the rail and stridently denounce DeSapio's leadership to the press as "helpless, hopeless and useless." He issued a statement acidly reviewing Carmine's record and demanded his resignation.

"This is no fight against the organization," alleged Bert. "It is a fight to preserve it." He charged that "DeSapio has his own F.E.P.C.—he forgets every political commitment."

Carmine immediately responded that "Mr. Stand would have no objection to my leadership if I had adhered to his choice of a candidate for the Supreme Court."

DeSapio was referring to the party's nomination for the State Supreme Court. Both Municipal Court Judge Saul Price and Joseph A. Cox, counsel to the Public Administrator of New York County, wanted the job. Cox got it. While no doubt well-qualified —he later even advanced to Surrogate—Cox was not from our Fourth Assembly District. Saul, on the other hand, had grown up on the Lower East Side, was a member of the Ahearn Club, a good friend and already an able, experienced jurist. Bert had led him to believe the nomination would be his, and now Bert had failed to secure it. Saul deserved a better break, and the blow was bitter.

Stand took a second long step in his campaign against DeSapio within a few days. He began circulation of a petition calling for the Tammany leader's ouster. Members of the Executive Committee were invited to pick themselves a new county chief.

Bert's claim that he did not want the job for himself was not indicative of any lack of ambition. Even in the days when Christy Sullivan staggered and Michael Kennedy stumbled, Bert had never sought the title. He always had preferred a behind-the-scenes role. Bert's talents lay in fields other than speechmaking.

Among other nasty things he said about DeSapio, Stand charged the Tammany leader with unsuccessfully trying to block Elmer Quinn's renomination for the State Senate. He also charged him with aiding O'Dwyer in his "phony" reform drives. As for Carmine's durability in the county leadership, Bert said "it is not what you would call a steady job." Christy Sullivan, Mike Kennedy, Edward Loughlin, Frank Sampson and Hugo Rogers could all attest to that.

Such talk was not geared to make Bert Stand welcome within Carmine DeSapio's circle of friends. So I do not think Bert felt too slighted when he was omitted from the guest list of an Executive Committee luncheon at the Commodore Hotel.

I had far greater cause to feel slighted by Carmine early in 1953. He took away my job as secretary to a Manhattan State Senator. Carmine had nothing against me personally. He called me aside sometime later to explain this. And, in the years since, I have gotten to know him better and today consider him a good friend. But, amidst the turbulence of that period, he found it necessary to strike at me to hurt my district chief. There was no malice involved.

Unlike Sampson, who in 1947 enjoyed the full measure of Mayor O'Dwyer's devotion, DeSapio was in a desperate position. Every job he could give one of his own people could prove a valuable pawn in his struggle against Impellitteri at City Hall and against Stand at Tammany Hall. In order to hang on to his own position he had to lick both.

State Senator Elmer Quinn's death immediately made possible Carmine's control over my job. The Senator's successor, new to

Albany, lacked Elmer's tough streak of independence. When Carmine snapped his fingers, the new man jumped. Thus, in March, 1953, I found myself out of work.

Bert Stand, of course, quickly capitalized on my being fired. He used it as a weighty hammer to crack over Carmine's skull. Soon a full-page letter appeared over my signature, complete with statistics, which outlined my service to the party and reported my dismal fate. Bert distributed it to about 1,000 Tammany figures in clubhouses throughout the borough. It was a strongly worded missive, containing such language as "My reward from DeSapio is the bread and butter taken from my mouth" and "I won my district and lost my livelihood."

I had been Banner Captain for nearly three decades. On Election Day, 1952, several short months before, the victorious Republican Presidential candidate, Eisenhower, had polled just 69 votes in my precinct to Democrat Adlai Stevenson's 696. I had done even better for Tammany's State Assembly candidate, Leonard Farbstein. I swung him 694 ballots to the 51 garnered by his Republican opponent.

Bert used these statistics to demonstrate the inequity of my fate. To make certain the point was not lost on other captains throughout the city, he included in bold capital letters, "TODAY IT IS ME, TOMORROW IT WILL BE THEM."

The letter created a storm in some Democratic clubs, according to the press. It did not serve Stand's purpose of helping to topple DeSapio from the Tiger's back. Indirectly, though, its coverage in a local newspaper helped me get a city job.

Shortly after a news item about it appeared in an evening paper, I ran into Harry Brickman at the Municipal Building lobby. Harry, as I have pointed out, was Deputy Treasurer and a close ally of Mayor Impellitteri. He was on the outs, however, not only with DeSapio, but also with Stand.

"Is it true you're fighting Carmine DeSapio?" he asked.

"What, me buck Carmine?" I answered. "How could I do a thing like that? I'm just a captain and he's the county leader."

Harry then showed me a copy of the newspaper carrying the item about my firing and the subsequent letter.

"I'm sorry to hear about the job," he said. "You sure didn't deserve that kind of deal. What are your plans?"

I told him the whole thing had come about so suddenly that I had no plans.

"Come on upstairs," he suggested. "I think I can find you a spot in my department."

I followed him into the elevator and we went up to his office. He glanced through some filing cabinets, looked up smilingly and announced, "Louis, you're going to be a comptometer operator."

"A what?" I asked.

Harry repeated the name again. "It's some kind of office machine," he explained. "But don't worry about it. You'll go out on field investigations, the same as you did for Internal Revenue."

I felt relieved, but asked why we simply did not call a machine operator a machine operator and an investigator an investigator.

"Oh, you'll have to keep the other title for a little while," he said, "because that's the only vacancy on the list now."

I thanked Brickman, and he knew I would do my job efficiently. Harry did not have to give me the position, of course. As a captain in the Ahearn Club, I was Bert Stand's responsibility, not his. But there are some politicians of the old school who do not forget past favors. Harry was one.

Years before, I had given him a helping hand when he needed it. Now, with no solicitation on my part, he returned it with interest. In a way, this is the best gauge of a man, whatever his station in life. Making fancy speeches may impress the public, but it takes no pain to put one meaningless word after another, sentence after sentence. Deeds are less fickle a measure of judgement.

As a courtesy to Bert, I told him of Harry's act.

"You're not even in his district. Why did he do a thing like that?" Bert questioned me.

"Go ask him," I responded.

Bert and Harry were barely on speaking terms as the result of an old quarrel. Neither would voluntarily approach the other, as I well knew. Bert quickly lost interest in the subject.

As the Mayoralty campaign of 1953 neared, DeSapio and the Mayor prepared for their imminent collision. Impellitteri was determined to seek re-election on the Democratic ticket. Carmine was equally determined to deny him the nomination. In April of that year, at another $50-a-plate New York County Democratic Committee dinner, the Tammany leader warned his foe, "The people want a candidate who will see to it that Thomas Dewey is not re-elected Mayor of the City of New York this November." Clearly, Vincent Richard Impellitteri would have a primary fight on his hands before he could seek a second term—two Days of Judgement, not one.

Carmine DeSapio viewed the Mayor from the standpoint of a devout political enemy. Naturally, he could be expected to unleash a barrage of abuse against the Mayor at the least opportunity. That is politics. But others, notably colleagues of Impellitteri on the Board of Estimate, authored unkinder cuts. These members of his own municipal "family" charged he was a "do-nothing" leader. Assailed from both Tammany Hall and by associates at City Hall, the Mayor tried to ward off the blows of each.

"How can I do a good job when most of the Board members are running for my office," he said ruefully. "They don't want me to have a successful administration so they block me and take it out on the people."

The accuracy of this statement was brought home when two of them eagerly threw their hats in the ring and others wistfully wished they could, too.

As the inevitable handwriting became faintly inscribed on the wall, peace "feelers" were stretched toward Tammany Hall. DeSapio rejected these indefinite bids. He distributed 41,000 postal cards to enrolled Democrats in a one-question poll—did they want Impellitteri as Democratic nominee in 1953? The resulting tally ran four to one against the Mayor, as Carmine expected it would. The search for a fresh, sparkling candidate got underway.

The hunt ended when Carmine joined Bronx chief Edward J.

Flynn in settling on Manhattan Borough President Robert F. Wagner, Jr. Young Wagner had an illustrious name, a result of his judicious selection of Senator Robert F. Wagner, Sr. as a parent. He also had a competent, if not spectacular, public record of his own. He was no "puppet," even though he was the hand-picked candidate of what reformers would later come to denounce as the "bosses."

Leaders of the other three county Democratic organizations decided to stick with Impellitteri. Evidence mounted that the upcoming primary would decide something more than the next-four-year occupant of Gracie Mansion. It shaped up as a battle that would resolve, as well, the future of Tammany Hall and the relative power to be exercised by each of the city's five Democratic county leaders.

When The Bronx leader, Edward Flynn, died a month before the day of reckoning, Carmine suddenly became the single weighty prop under young Wagner. A Wagner victory would therefore cast him in the role of the city's Number One Democratic Leader. A Wagner defeat, though, would surely break him. No one expected that he could pull a second miracle to equal his feat in retaining power after 1950's setback at the polls.

Bert, having cleanly broken with Carmine in 1952, backed Impellitteri in 1953. The Mayor gratefully accepted Bert's support, but probably had little concern for Bert's motives. The Bert Stand of the 1950s, sorry to say, was not the Bert Stand of the 1920s, and 1930s, nor even of the 1940s. Then we were close associates and even closer friends. The Bert Stand of the 1950s, under the Rasputin-like influence of his brother, Murray, followed the course carved by personal advantage. When he cast his lot with the Mayor, it was not that he loved Impellitteri more, but that his future in a DeSapio-led Tammany Hall would be nil.

Several Ahearn Club captains, sensing the winds of change, deserted the Mayor's cause. They openly supported Wagner.

I worked for Impellitteri's candidacy, but broke with Bert before the election on more personal an issue—a political maneuver in which I was victimized. This devious undertaking will be outlined later for, as night follows day, its mushrooming consequences led to Bert Stand's decline and fall as leader of the Fourth Assembly District.

In the September primary contest, Impellitteri was soundly beaten. His personal political world turned upside-down. So did that of his supporters.

The Mayor felt that he had embarked on a worthwhile program for the city and deserved the opportunity to finish his task. "When I came into office, I inherited some corruption, some messes. But I've cleaned them up," he had declared some time earlier. "I have raised the level of public confidence in city government. It was pretty low when I came into office. If people will take time to look at my record instead of listening to its being recited by a political opponent, I'll continue in office."

Now it was over. The disappointed Mayor gave some thought to unfurling his Experience Party banner again. When the shock of his stunning defeat sank in, however, he bowed to reality and left the field to his conqueror. Impellitteri had lost his three-year battle against the Tiger. Tammany Hall had finally whipped City Hall.

In a period of comparable length, William O'Dwyer had tamed the striped cat and made himself ringmaster. Had Impellitteri acted as mercilessly and as ruthlessly as his predecessor, DeSapio's job of unleashing it would have been all the more difficult, if not a sheer impossibility. But Impellitteri was a "nice guy." He used a carrot rather than a stick, soft bait rather than a harpoon. No lover of baseball, he was probably unfamiliar with Leo Durocher's dictum that "nice guys finish last."

Some of the Mayor's closest political allies fell by the wayside after the debacle. Between the primary and the general election, eight district leaders who supported him were cut from Tammany's Executive Committee. Frank Sampson felt the sharp blade, rather than his accustomed handle, of the axe when he was ousted from Third Assembly District rule. Bob Blaikie, too, was dropped. Harry Brickman had of course lost his Tammany post two years back. Of Impellitteri's principal backers, Bert Stand still hung on. His turn would soon come, though for reasons less noble than picking the wrong candidate.

Wagner, naturally, had no difficulty winning on Election Day. The LaGuardia nostrums by now were distant history. Republicans had gone back to sleep. Their nominee, Harold Riegelman, general counsel to the Citizens' Budget Committee, was honorable, respectable, decent and dull. He sacrificed himself willingly at his party's altar.

The young, monotonous-voiced Rudolph Halley, who had become President of the City Council in the wake of the Kefauver hearings, also ran. But that is all he was, an "also ran." The former chief counsel to the Senate committee had ambitiously traded on his television fame. But he found that the viewing public liked him better as a performer than as a potential Mayor. In our district, he polled 6,644 votes to Wagner's 16,473.

Wagner's victory raised Carmine DeSapio to dizzy heights. With Flynn dead, he was not merely head of Tammany Hall. He was overlord of the entire city Democratic machine. Surely a remarkable turnabout, indeed, for a man whom many critics were prepared to write off just months earlier as a political has-been.

All the young Mayor-elect had, he owed to his father's reputation and the Tammany chief's political cunning. Within another year would come another important contest, for the Governorship, that would raise DeSapio to still dizzier heights—this time, as a prominent state and national figure. By almost single-handedly forging the nomination, and fostering the election of Averell Harriman, Carmine would become potential Presidential king-maker at the 1956 Democratic National Convention.

Who would have guessed that a post-LaGuardia-era leader of Tammany Hall could mount such a majestic perch? And who would have guessed that, having reached that summit, he was destined to be hauled down by the very Mayor whose career he had helped launch?

XIII

"Bashful Berty's" Last Stand

SOON AFTER YOUNG WAGNER'S ELECTION DAY TRIUMPH, I MET
Carmine DeSapio at a charity affair. My job at Harry Brickman's
office would end, of course, as soon as Impellitteri's administration
packed up at City Hall on December 31, 1953. Harry himself
would be out of work. That is the way the spoils system works.
Carmine knew this. He realized, though, that his blow in taking
away my Albany job earlier in 1953 had been a bit below the belt.

"I'm sorry about what happened, Louis," he said. "I had nothing
personal against you."

"That's the way politics goes," I acknowledged. "Others would
have done the same in your place."

DeSapio also realized that the bitter letter which followed had
been the product of Bert Stand's pen, not mine. He told me to
see him after the new Mayor took office. "I'll make it up to you.
I'll get you something else," he said.

As usual, DeSapio kept his word. In January, after arranging
an appointment, I went to Tammany Hall. I was certainly no stranger there. But I had rarely visited the Democratic county headquarters since Frank Sampson took command. Carmine came forward with a cheery greeting and ushered me into his office.

"I've got something for you," he said. "Next Tuesday, at 9:30
a.m. or so, go down to the City Treasurer's office. You've worked
there before. See George Bragalini. I'll speak to him over the
weekend. He'll have you sworn in as an investigator."

The following week, I went down to the Municipal Building and
began my new job, which, in a sense, was my old job. My new
boss, City Treasurer George M. Bragalini, was a mustached former

bank official. During the waning days of the Truman Administration, he had served as acting Postmaster for Manhattan. He seemed vaguely to recall my name.

"Say, aren't you the fellow who swiped those 47 post office jobs I gave Bert Stand?" he asked.

"Yes," I admitted. "I gave them to my constituents. They needed the work."

"No wonder you're Banner Captain," he laughed.

Bragalini proved himself an executive of high caliber. He was to be sorely missed at the city's Department of Finance when Governor Averell Harriman "swiped" him the next year. Harriman put him to work as President of the State Tax Commission, a post in which he served with notable distinction.

Meanwhile, in the Fourth Assembly District, a decisive change was in the making. For two decades, Bert Stand had led our Lower East Side Democratic Banner District. For half that period, he had shared with Clarence Neal control of the entire Tammany machine. Now, he prepared for his Political Judgement Day.

The situation Bert found himself in, as January, 1954, dawned, was neither better nor worse than Eddy Ahearn's plight in 1929, a quarter of a century earlier. Mayor James J. Walker and Tammany chief John F. Curry had been just as hostile to Eddy's interests as Wagner and DeSapio were to Bert's. Yet Eddy survived sturdily, while Bert would fall by the wayside.

The difference in their fates stemmed from the difference in the men. For all his cleverness, and not even Carmine would have denied his craft, Bert lacked Eddy's key quality—loyalty to his captains. Through thick and thin, we had returned this loyalty. Eddy used to remark time and again, "The captain is the backbone of the Ahearn Club. Remove me and you can find another leader. But remove the captains, and the club will disappear."

Bert Stand forgot this elemental dictum. It was a strangely pathetic error, for Bert had himself been an excellent captain. I knew. For years we had shared the same election district. We had made the rounds together.

There were several reasons for his inability to hold the captains in his corner. Bert would prefer to think he was undone by Carmine DeSapio. It sounds less ego-damaging than the truth. There is no shame in losing to the acknowledged champion, the man who controlled the Democratic Party's county machinery. In reality, however, Bert Stand was undone by Bert Stand, with the able assistance of his brother, Murray.

By the early 1950s, Murray Stand had become one of the most disliked men in the club. The honor did not come easily. He really worked hard at it, perhaps even harder than he did to get admirable press clippings. Murray's name often appeared in the papers. He was the cheerful fellow at the Municipal Building who churned out marriage licenses. As City Clerk, he sometimes even conducted the ceremonies himself. To the public, he was a name. To reporters, he was good copy on a dull day when a wisecrack or marital anecdote was welcome. But to his colleagues, Murray was a symbol of what was wrong with the club.

Many years before, when he was an Alderman, Eddy Ahearn had chided him for acting too big for his britches. Murray candidly admitted his shortcomings later when he declined to run for membership on the City Council. His election-time relations with La-Guardia, and his subsequent "rewards", were whispered about at the clubhouse. His lack of enthusiasm for the Democratic ticket on those occasions was known and felt. Murray never seemed to have time—or make it—for a colleague.

Bert was influenced by his older brother. Over the years, he grafted strains of Murray's character. I would like to think that the Bert Stand of the 1950s was some other fellow, certainly not the cheerful, roly-poly friend I had known since boyhood.

The beginning of the Decline and Fall of Bert Stand can be traced to several abrasive incidents. Perhaps the most significant of these centered on myself. As I noted toward the end of the previous chapter, I had broken with Bert during the 1953 primary election campaign. Though I continued to work for Impellitteri at the time, my friendship for Bert shattered.

Late in August of that year, a deputy commissionership had fallen vacant. It had been held by an Ahearn club member for several years. Since Bert, at the time, was one of Impellitteri's key backers, the job would unquestionably stay in our club. The retiring deputy commissioner made known his intention of leaving some time in advance. There had been no doubt about whom was in line to succeed him. As Banner Captain of our district, I had not merely been offered the post. Bert had repeatedly "promised" it to me.

There had always been something sacred about a political promise in our club. John F. Ahearn never broke one and ruled unchallenged for 30 years. His son, Eddy, also kept faith with his captains and maintained their devotion till death, and even beyond —that is why poor Willie was permitted to hold the honorary title of leader. Now, the lessons of the past ignored, Bert not only let me down, he did it in a manner of which I had felt him incapable. In the process, he drew first blood from himself, as well.

My ordeal began on a hot, late summer morning. Vincent Impellitteri was still Mayor, and the Stand brothers were riding high. It started with the ringing of my phone in the Treasurer's office.

"Louis, you better watch out," said the caller. "You've just been sold out by Bert and Murray on the deputy commissionership."

The caller did not sound as if he were kidding, so I immediately tried to reach Bert. Unable to do so, I contacted Murray instead. Dealing with one, at this stage, was the same as dealing with the other.

"Oh, we couldn't get you the job," said Murray Stand almost matter-of-factly. "The 'Imp' wanted a lawyer. Besides, you've already got a job in the Treasurer's office."

"What do you mean I've already got a job?" I replied. "Did you get it for me? Harry Brickman saw me through after Bert's fight with Carmine. What have you ever done to deserve your $15,000 plum besides double-crossing your party? You may think you're high and mighty now, but you'll come down from your perch fast enough. Just wait and see. You and your brother are through."

At night, when I entered the clubhouse, everyone said Bert

wanted to see me. That was fine, because I was looking for him, too. The shock had worn off. The anger remained.

"I'm sorry about the job, really sorry," Bert said. "I did my best. But what's this I heard about your insulting my brother?"

"Insulting him?" I countered. "What did he have to do with my job in the Finance Department?

"My brother and I didn't have anything to do with it," Bert admitted. "We know Harry Brickman was responsible."

"Let's get down to the point, Bert," I said. "What was the deal for the deputy commissionership? You know you promised it to me."

"Well," Bert insisted, "like my brother said, the 'Imp' wanted a lawyer."

"Don't pull that nonsense with me," I snapped. "He'd have sworn in anyone that you sent up. The man who held the job all these years was certainly no lawyer. When he said he was retiring, you gave me your word on it."

"Well, I plugged for you but the 'Imp' wanted a lawyer," Bert repeated lamely.

"If that's all you have to say, then we're through, Bert, and you won't be leader very long," I said.

"Now, Louis, take it easy," Bert urged. "We've been friends for 40 years. Your father, my father—they were kids together."

"Let them both rest in peace," I replied. "This matter is between you and me. What you just did to me I never would have done to you."

The next day, Bert went to see my aged mother at our Attorney Street flat, where my parents and their family had lived for more than half a century. She refused to intervene.

Half in English, half in Yiddish, she said, "I can't tell my son to forgive you. Not after what you owe him. In the middle of dinner, he'd get up if you called and get dressed and leave. When you wanted someone to go someplace with you, it was always Louis. You wouldn't trust anyone but him. And now, this!"

The wheels that eventually rolled over Bert Stand were oiled and slowly began to turn. I made a long-distance call to Judge

Henry Schimmel, the most respected living member of the John F. Ahearn Association, the man who had introduced me to politics back in 1917. He was vacationing in Pennsylvania at the time. After listening to my story, the judge returned to New York City. Within hours, a majority of captains had rallied around him. From that time on, Bert was finished, even if he could not bring himself to realize it.

Officially, Bert Stand's ouster as leader would not take place until the 1955 September primaries, a long, long way off. To the newspapers, he was still "Leader of the Fourth Assembly District (South)". But not to those of us close to neighborhood affairs. Bert was determined to fill out his legal term, then seek re-election. Before long, however, he was a lonely, almost solitary figure at the 290 East Broadway headquarters of the John F. Ahearn Association. The clubhouse had become a skeleton without meat.

By mid-1954, almost all the district's captains were established in our own club, barely a block away. Some dissidents, who had broken with Bert earlier, joined us. We called our rented brownstone quarters the "Lower East Side Democratic Association," for we could not yet use the Ahearn name. This was the only remnant of the past that Bert had retained.

Temporarily, we were leaderless. I preferred a background role for myself and considered Judge Schimmel the best qualified candidate for the leadership. Since he was to retire soon from the bench, no problem of eligibility would have arisen. There were two other aspirants, City Marshal Michael "Mitch" Bloom and a sly lawyer, whose name shall not be graced by mention here.

Before reaching a decision, we agreed to meet uptown with Carmine DeSapio. As county leader, he naturally took more than a slight interest in district affairs. A crucial conference was arranged with Carmine at Tammany Hall. Many captains were present. I was not.

Judge Schimmel called me immediately after the meeting and asked why I had missed it.

"When was it scheduled for?" I replied. "No one notified me about the time."

The Judge was taken aback. He had tried to reach me earlier in the day, he explained. Unable to do so, he had asked the sly lawyer to tell me the precise hour to be at the Hall. The Judge, an aging and honorable man, neglected to consider that this ambitious fellow wanted the leadership for himself. And my presence at the conference, as a strong supporter of Judge Schimmel, would possibly have smothered the cunning attorney's chances. So he ignored the Judge's simple request and never called me.

As it turned out, his selfish tactic hurt Judge Schimmel but did not aid his own cause. Carmine wanted no lawyer as leader. Instead, he looked favorably on "Mitch" Bloom, a fresh figure, untested but apparently personable. Though DeSapio's word was by no means law, his approval or disapproval of a candidate carried weight.

The crafty lawyer, turned down despite my absence, belligerently returned to the clubhouse. He decided to fight Bloom for our new club's leadership, with or without the blessings of the county leader.

I was in the middle, uncommitted to either man. I did not know Bloom well. He was far younger than myself, and had joined the Ahearn Club long after Eddy's passing. He came from another assembly district, one that had been merged with ours as the result of a Republican redistricting scheme in the early 1940s. On the other hand, I knew the lawyer who opposed him all too well. By no stretch of the imagination did he deserve my support.

I called Judge Schimmel and agreed to back Bloom. Unknown to me, Mitch had snuggled up to the telephone booth, eager to hear what I was about to say. He was, of course, elated.

'I'll never forget you for this," he said afterwards. "The first good spot that comes our way after I become district leader is yours. I won't forget!"

As with Bert earlier, I took Mitch at his word.

The election in our temporary clubhouse quarters at 278 East Broadway was close. Gifted with a coating of surface sincerity, the lawyer had cultivated many friends. Besides, others who knew Bloom better than I did were opposed to the young man's selection. A large bloc of captains, lifelong friends, followed my lead, however. Because of this cohesive support, Mitch squeaked in as winner.

The Primary Day contest was still many months off. But Bloom was now in fact, if not title, leader of the Fourth Assembly District South.

The seeds of Bert Stand's personal political disaster were sown long before September, 1954, when the press reported the circulation of a petition demanding his resignation. As I have stressed at some length, Bert had planted them himself. None of us would have rebelled had he kept faith with us. But Bert had been goaded into betraying his political trust, a responsibility no less sacred in our neighborhood's past than any position of public trust. "Your brother Murray is ruining you," I told him long before this uprising. "If you keep listening to him you won't last. He's the most hated man in the club."

Bert, underestimating the gravity of his recent conduct, grimly clung on to his vaporized title. "They can have the captains," he told a reporter, "I think I'm going to have the people."

Stand had apparently forgotten another canon of Lower East Side politics—that the district's Democrats voted for their captains. True, this rule had faded somewhat over the past few years and would fade further in the next few. But it still had substance. People offered allegiance to their captains, not a distant, lordly shadow called "The Leader".

"My opponent is not really Michael Bloom," Bert contended. "It's Carmine DeSapio." Here, too, he had misjudged the nature of the contest. Bloom was a political nobody. Carmine lent him his support and Mayor Wagner lent him his hand, for the benefit of press photographers. But almost anybody could have licked Stand in 1955.

Shortly before the primary contest ended, Bert stopped me in the street and asked for forgiveness and another chance. "Anyone can make a mistake," he said. Even then, he still had hopes of holding on to the leadership.

"Everyone is entitled to one mistake," I pointed out. "But

you've made more mistakes than you have hairs on your head. I
was brought up by my parents to play squarely. I don't say one
thing, then turn around and do another."

As a final, desperate measure, he circulated *The Bert Stand News
Letter*. This four-page pamphlet denounced Carmine DeSapio as
the instigator of his misfortunes. The allegation was pure hogwash.
More significantly, Bert accused a certain deputy commissioner of
treachery in backing Bloom. This was the man who got the post
I had been promised. It seemed off-key and odd, indeed, that the
fellow felt no loyalty toward his benefactor. This fact confirmed,
in my mind, suspicions about the circumstances of his elevation.

On Primary Day, September 13, 1955, enrolled Democrats of
the Fourth Assembly District South trooped to the polls. When the
ballots had been counted, the score was 4,697 for Bloom to 806
for Stand. By nightfall, Bert was a forlorn, bowed figure on the
stoop steps of the old Ahearn Club.

An era of Lower East Side politics and a slice of Tammany Hall
history vanished with him that evening. Strangely, I felt a bit
sorry, for at such moments a person's perspective becomes wrapped
in sentiment. The many long years of our friendship seemed fresh
and clear, and the recent act of betrayal was temporarily dimmed.

If this were a novel, there could be no more appropriate place
to end my story than here. Unfortunately, the Fourth Assembly
District did not become a Political Fairyland in which Justice
reigned and Fairness ruled. Only an Eddy Ahearn, returned from
the grave, could have brought about that happy an ending.

To Carmine DeSapio, concerned with the larger political picture,
Bert's dethronement was just one of many local victories, though
perhaps the most significant. Carmine tightened his control over
the Tammany organization throughout Manhattan. His triumph
had come in the wake of the party's first try at "direct" election of
district leaders. DeSapio proudly viewed his achievement. Of the
nine district primary contests in 1955, Tammany's chief participated in eight and lost only one of them. He termed the results
"a clear mandate for the programs and policies" of his organization.
With some justification, he boasted: "The enrolled members of our

party have expressed their support for those principles which advanced the candidacies of Mayor Wagner and Governor Harriman, and which brought the Democratic Party to an unprecedented position of public trust and confidence."

Only one non-Tammany insurgent won election, but he ran unopposed. So DeSapio had little reason to express regret. An obscure "reformist" Democrat, Edward N. Costikyan, now led the Eighth Assembly District South. Within several years, he would replace Carmine as county leader, an absurdity that entered no one's mind at that moment of exhilaration.

As 1955 closed, the political star of Carmine DeSapio sparkled brightly. He was hailed as Tammany Hall's greatest sovereign since Charles F. Murphy. This was not too praiseworthy an accolade, considering the mediocre caliber of men who had ridden the Tiger's back since Murphy's death in 1924. But it was something of an accomplishment, anyway. As James J. Walker might have put it, Carmine had removed the brains of Tammany Hall from Calvary Cemetery, where they were interred, and brought them back to Manhattan Island.

There were vast differences, however, between the two political commanders. Whereas Murphy was tight-lipped and ran a taut organization, Carmine removed the bars from the Tiger's cage and let the public have a good look. He transformed Tammany virtually into an "open society". The muddy cries of "Boss Rule" that splashed across DeSapio's closing days as county leader unfortunately obscured his earlier sound achievements. These were real enough, indeed, to anyone who had grown up with Tammany during the first half of the century.

DeSapio introduced several "reforms", if use of *that* word may be excused, over the objections of some lieutenants. This was a risky business. In fact, the very method by which Carmine was to be eventually ousted from rule in his Greenwich Village home district stemmed from one of his innovations—the direct primary. Until 1955, leaders had been selected by county committeemen in each district, acting as a form of "electoral college". DeSapio brought democracy with a small "d" to the local Democratic party structure. Now. all enrolled Democrats could have a hand in selecting their district chief.

Carmine also introduced New York City's newest ethnic groups to the political spectrum. Considering his own difficulty, as an Italian, in gaining acceptance on Tammany's Executive Committee, it is not insignificant that he helped bring in the first Puerto Rican district leader. He also pressed for the appointment of Harold A. Stevens as the first Negro to mount the General Sessions bench. Stevens, an able jurist, advanced later to the Appellate Division on his own.

Carmine raised Harlem leader Hulan Jack to the Borough Presidency. At the time, this Manhattan position was the highest elective office held by a Negro. Later, poor Hulan was to be publicly crucified for a blunder, rather than a crime, that would have rolled off the back of a less conspicuous political figure. Such is the penalty occasionally imposed on a city official when unwarranted conclusions are drawn about an acknowledged error.

By late 1955, Carmine was probably the most influential big-city political leader in the country. Even Adlai E. Stevenson, playing hide-and-seek with the White House, remarked: "If it were my ambition to seek the Democratic Presidential nomination next year, I would welcome the support of Tammany Hall and Carmine DeSapio."

Stevenson got the nomination, of course, but not with Tammany's help. Carmine threw the weight of his organization behind Averell Harriman, New York State's liberal, capable Governor. So did former President Harry Truman. When Harriman dropped out of the White House picture, Carmine's national prestige naturally took a dip. Despite this setback at the 1956 Democratic National Convention, he remained king locally.

In the role of district leader, Mitch Bloom proved to be no miracle worker. Forty-six and a snappy dresser, Mitch looked clean-cut and spoke good, progressive thoughts. As a political personality, he had little else to recommend him. Once victory had been achieved, I had asked Mitch to restore the "John F. Ahearn Association" name to the club. But he wanted the break with the past to be complete. Thus disappeared the Ahearn name from district politics.

In retrospect, it was perhaps for the best. The name had not deserved the abasement of the past few years. Nor would it deserve the tarnish of the next few. Our new leader would certainly add no luster to the district's rich tapestry of political history. Better that the Ahearn name become a source of sentiment rather than a subject of scorn.

One early omen of Mitch Bloom's mettle had been his oratory during the recently concluded primary campaign. When asked why he had supported Impellitteri in the 1953 Mayoralty contest against Wagner, he replied, "We followed our leader, who was Bert Stand. He told us Impellitteri was the party organization's choice for Mayor." He then added proudly, "Impellitteri lost my district (precinct) three and one-half to one."

Once in power, the new leader fashioned for himself a trademark of self-assurance. He knew that, after going through the ordeal of putting him into the leadership, we were not likely to turn right around and wrest his symbol of authority. As for the annual inter-party November sparring match, Mitch could look forward to losing no sleep on Election Day. The word "Republican" was still an epithet in the Fourth Assembly District. Any man who sought office here under the banner of the GOP did so to symbolically keep alive the tradition of our two-party system. Mitch had ample cause, therefore, for complacency during the early part of his reign.

Take, for example, the biennial contest for the office of Congressman. In 1956, incumbent Arthur Klein prepared, as had Sam Dickstein before him, to move up to the State Supreme Court. According to the district's political promotional policy, Assemblyman Leonard Farbstein was to fall heir to the Washington post. Lenny had toiled in the Albany legislature since the early 1930s. He was no stranger to the district, though he might have been to much of the electorate. Like other elected officials, he depended on the precinct captains. And we saw to it that he was returned to the state legislature like clockwork every two years.

In 1956, when Lenny was awarded the party's nomination, he faced no problems. Our Congressional geography, it may be noted, had become a bit more expansive. The Fourth Assembly District was now one corner—though the most overwhelmingly critical corner—of the Nineteenth Congressional District. That year, its boundary ran from East 20th Street down through our neighborhood, then dipped farther south to the Battery. At the tip of the island, it turned north again and crawled up the less populated West Side to 21st Street. (The gap between its East and West Side pincers consisted of the lower portion of the GOP "Silk Stocking" oasis.)

Some 336,000 persons lived in our Congressional District in 1956, yet the man picked by the Republicans to oppose Farbstein was a 26-year-old lawyer, Maurice G. Henry, Jr. The poor fellow tried hard. He even issued a pamphlet called *Facts About Henry.* It was a waste of paper. Lenny was on record in favor of labor legislation, social security, full employment and aid to Israel. We captains plugged for the complete Democratic line, and Lenny won almost inadvertently—by a two to one margin.

The same story was repeated in 1958, when Farbstein won by three to one, and again in 1960. During that latter year, the District's boundaries were still unchanged. His opponent on the Republican line was a bit older than Henry—two years older, according to the press. Thomas O'Callaghan was also a bit more confident. His optimism was based on the recent construction of middle and upper income housing for some 25,000 persons in the district. This turned out to be wishful thinking by the young man. Once more, Lenny did not have to stay awake for pulsating long hours on Election Night. He was again the winner by a landslide.

In 1962 and 1964, the biennial November tale would be the same—but with cliff-hanging prologues in the Democratic primaries. These suspense-filled contests would be attributable to the geography of Congressional redistricting, a haunting spectre that makes many a "safe" candidate shudder. They will be described at a later point in this narrative.

Large Election Day pluralities had little to do with the personal popularity of particular candidates. If they ran on the Democratic ticket, they won. If they ran on any other ticket, they lost. For that matter, Mitch Bloom's own personal popularity was virtually non-existent. His "success" as leader was based on his captains' canvassing and the electorates' force of habit. As we reach the end of Tammany Hall's road, though, even the importance of the captain has rapidly diminished. Only the strength of force of habit remains. If this, too, fades, New Yorkers may one day wake up to find that they live in a two-party town.

By the mid-1950s, the cold water flats of the past were giving way to the skyscrapper cooperatives of the future. This development had mistakenly inspired young O'Callaghan's optimism. For a different reason, it similarly hypnotized our district leader.

"You know, Louis, once those new buildings go up, we won't have to worry about a thing," Bloom said. "No more staircases, no more hard work. They'll all vote for us."

"What makes you think so?" I asked.

"Oh, they'll need favors," he said.

"Look," I pointed out, "the people moving into those buildings won't depend on you for anything. They may vote for us, but it won't be because they owe you anything."

"Give me one reason why not," he proposed.

"First of all, they won't need home relief," I said. "Second, co-op apartment buildings don't have landlords that have to be bargained with. Third, the only help they'll ask for is getting a jury notice squashed or a summons torn up. And you can't do either of those, anymore. So why do they need you?"

Mitch thought for a few moments, then looked puzzled. "Gee, that's funny," he said. "I never figured on that."

The state of our local Democratic "family" is best manifested by the fact that in 1957, two years following his formal ouster from the leadership, Bert Stand smelled the aroma of political demoralization and sought to capitalize on it. He set up a rival clubhouse over a restaurant on Delancey Street. He even approached me and promised his support if I would oppose Mitch

Bloom in the next Democratic primary. My distaste for Mitch had grown, but not to the extent that I would depend on another of Bert's "promises". After paying a few months' rental, he quietly folded his "club".

XIV

The Captains and the Kings Depart

SOME TIME BEFORE HIS DEATH, EDDY AHEARN HAD REMARKED that politics had "lost its kick"—it was not "fun" anymore. Whatever truth that statement had in the grim days of the early 1940s was magnified tenfold by events of recent vintage. The Bert Stand Era had accelerated the process of local political decay. Under the current regime, no hope of a glittering renaissance beckoned.

My personal reappraisal of Mitch Bloom followed his appointment as executive manager in the Manhattan Borough President's office. By prearrangement, I had been first in line for the job. Though no Bible was in sight, Mitch had sworn I would get the first good job that came our district's way, provided no attorney's sheepskin was required. Instead, he took it for himself. The circumstances closely resembled those of Bert Stand's dark deed in 1953.

This shock, too, began when my office phone rang at the Municipal Building. The caller was anonymous. "Louis, you better get upstairs to Arty Greeninger's office in a hurry," he said, "you're about to be double-crossed."

Greeninger, a key aide to the Borough President, was quartered several floors higher in the building. When I got to the reception room, there was Mitch, sitting impatiently. He looked as if he were eager to get something over with, and over with quickly.

"What are you doing up here?" he asked as I entered.

I answered that I would like to ask him the same question. I was in no mood for fencing. I related the anonymous caller's tip that he was waiting to be sworn in as executive manager in the Borough President's office. Bloom blandly confirmed the news.

"Are you a lawyer, Mitch?" I asked.

"No," he replied.

"Then what was our agreement?" I continued.

He said he remembered his promise but that he had to make a living too.

"What about your City Marshal's job?" I asked.

"Well," he replied, "I'm going to give that to my brother."

"Your brother!" I snapped. "What right do you have to give that to your brother? It's a political job and he's never done a thing for the party. He's not even a captain."

Mitch had no alibi. He lamely promised me the next thing that came to the club. As an afterthought, he added, "Anyway, Carmine insisted that I take this job."

"Look, Mitch," I said. "Don't go passing the buck to Carmine. I was in politics before you knew what the inside of a clubhouse looked like. When a county leader makes a job available to a district leader, he doesn't say 'give it to this man or give it to that man.' If Carmine wanted a specific individual, he'd hand out the job personally without covering up. But it seems you want everything for yourself."

The "next thing" for others as well as myself rarely came along. Of Mitch, much was expected. He produced next to nothing. Excuses however, were plentiful and freely given. "Carmine crossed me," he would apologize, or, more mildly, "Carmine didn't come across" and "Carmine let me down." Mitch never took the blame himself. Carmine DeSapio was always the arch-villain. From this theme there was no deviation. If Carmine were as Captain Blighish as Mitch made out, it is a wonder Tammany's Executive Committee did not mutiny and throw him off the Tiger long before the "reformers" got the chance.

There were times, though, when Mitch Bloom did have his hands full—with no scapegoat in sight. An impartial observer could almost, but not quite, sympathize with him in his plight. By way of contrast, Bert Stand had never picked up an evening newspaper and discovered a page one headline and news story (with a photograph, no less) depicting his role in a $99,000 blunder. Mitch

Bloom did. It came following his "promotion" to the job of Assistant Commissioner of Borough Works.

Not only did Mitch preside over this costly goof; he did it within three blocks of his new Lower East Side Democratic Association clubhouse on Grand and Clinton Streets. In defense of Mitch, it might be said that he probably did not really pay enough attention to borough works to be aware of what was going on in his department.

In any event, four blocks of sidewalk, running along both sides of East Broadway from Grand to Rutgers Streets, were torn apart before hardly anyone knew what was going on. The gutter was also uprooted in preparation for widening the roadway. One day after work began, someone in public employ remembered to remind property owners what was happening. Notices were sent out telling them they had better remove underground oil lines, tanks and other obstructions within 20 days. According to the blueprints, sidewalks were to be narrowed to 13 feet. Since most of the old buildings had stoops, this meant there would be only six feet, or so, of clearance for pedestrians.

Cries of anguish from the local citizenry were heard all the way down to the Municipal Building. As the saying goes, the people spoke and they were heard. Before very long, destruction and construction work ended, and reconstruction work began. The mission —to restore East Broadway to its former width.

Over at the Municipal Building, excuses and flimsy rationalizations flew thick and fast. At least the street was repaved, someone pointed out. And if the city should ever decide to tear up the sidewalk there again, the experience gained in the dry run might prove useful.

Mitch, for once, offered no alibi. "A mistake was made," he admitted. "They should have started after they gave sufficient notice to the people in the neighborhood. What are these? Second-class citizens? They wouldn't do it this way on Park Avenue or East End Avenue."

Mitch could almost be applauded for his candor except for one little point. Why did he use the pronoun "they" instead of "we"?

After all, he was Assistant Commissioner of Borough Works. More important, as district leader he was supposed to know what was going to happen in his own neighborhood. Such a snafu never would have developed in the days when Eddy Ahearn kept his eye on every niche and corner of the Fourth Assembly District.

A startling change had overtaken Tammany Hall's Executive Committee by the late 1950s. When Carmine DeSapio was re-elected county leader in 1957, only 14 of the 41 district leaders who had put him in power back in 1949 were still around. Now, over half the members were college men. Many of these were lawyers by profession. No saloon keepers were on Tammany's ruling body, though one district leader maintained a package liquor store. Only one undertaker remained on the committee.

Another, more significant, transformation had come about within the Hall. Unfortunately, it was marked by the advent of a new stripe of man in place of the old-time district chiefs. This change had little to do with age or educational levels—it was a matter of personal values, the two-way bond of faith between the leader and his captains. In the 1950s, the process began. In the 1960s, it gained momentum. There were few leaders left by the mid 1960s, at the time af reapportionment, whose reputations for square-dealing with their subordinates matched those of bygone days.

On the Lower East Side, Prosper "Duke" Viggiano, of the Second Assembly District, was one. His colleague in the other half of that district, Louis DeSalvio, was another. In the northern half of the Fourth Assembly District, Hyman Solniker, who was since traded in his leadership for a judgeship, had always played fair with his captains and their constituents. The same may be said of Frank Rossetti in upper Manhattan's Sixteenth Assembly District, and Angelo Simonetti in the Thirteenth Assembly District. There were no doubt others, but these come immediately to mind.

Closer to home, on the Republican side of the ledger, Henry Steinberg, of the Fourth Assembly District, and Vincent Albano, the Sixth Assembly District leader who had moved into his party's county chairmanship, also typified the old-style, straight-shooting neighborhood politician.

Why had these men survived the assaults of reformers and the thrusts of insurgents? Louis DeSalvio's case is exemplary. Any district leader with a letterhead could dash off a note of protest to a government bureau. With appropriate fanfare, many do whenever the city embarks on a project that would trample their area's interests. Stationery is cheap. But how many would buttonhole a Mayor and haul him through their neighborhood to show him at first hand the havoc it would wreak on hundreds of families? Louis DeSalvio did. State Senator Joseph Marro, now a Civil Court Judge, also acted as guide. The tour brought results. Appeals made in this manner cannot be crumpled and discarded in a wastepaper basket. This is why their people respect them. Louis and Joseph did not have to collect a scrapbook of press clippings attesting to their popularity. All they had to do was walk through their neighborhood.

Louis DeSalvio's colleague at the other end of the Second Assembly District, Prosper Viggiano, was better known as "Duke". He held a law degree from Fordham University, and was on the Dean's List, no less. Nonetheless, he was still one of us. He grew up on the Lower East Side and never forgot his heritage. He stayed close to his people. That is why no "reformist" invader managed to dethrone him. One vigorously tried—an Ivy Leaguer who labored as an advertising executive and relaxed by yachting. The Duke beat him easily.

Though our ranks were thinning, many precinct captains carried on in the old tradition. The constituents who counted on us were never let down, and they, in turn, never let us down at the polls. Despite my obvious disenchantment with my own district's leadership, I continued to do my neighborhood job. My precinct, which included none of the new skyscraper apartment buildings, had absorbed a mixture of newcomers. It was no longer 100% Jewish, and my friends had given me the title of "Captain of All Nationalities". I was Johnny-on-the-spot at nearly all hours for all reasonable requests, be they personal favors or those of broader community concern. If an increase in street lighting were needed, I got it. For such odds-and-ends as having one-hour parking privileges substituted for half-hour parking privileges, the Clinton Street Merchants Association offered me a dinner. The thought was nice. But I declined the fete. I was merely doing my job as a Tammany captain, a tag that still carried no discredit for me. If the above passage seems slightly immodest, I offer no apologies.

On the larger scene, Tammany chief DeSapio was caught in the whirlwind of change that swept through the county organization. He failed to take into account its ultimate target, which inevitably led to his ruin. Instead, he tried to fit himself into the mold that the new reformist clique sculptured. This was an impossible chore, for the more he contorted, the more they squeezed. When he was forced—as all leaders are—to make a big decision, one with which they disagreed, they used the consequences of his act to discredit and politically destroy him.

As already noted, DeSapio was the most public relations-conscious leader in Tammany Hall's history. Charles F. Murphy had been taciturn. Most successors had been similarly reserved, some with good cause. Christy Sullivan was tightlipped, perhaps because he had nothing to say. But from Carmine, words flowed in a steady stream. He spoke at dinners, he spoke at charity affairs, he spoke at conferences. One district leader complained that it was harder to reach Carmine for a personal chat than it was to see him on television.

He also delivered lectures on the political processes at New York University. In every possible way, he tried to improve Tammany's "public" image. Even a learned article in the *Harvard Law Record* appeared bearing his name.

For a while, DeSapio managed to draw guarded praise from newspaper columnists and magazine writers. Sometimes grudgingly, they acknowledged his efforts to give the Tiger's reputation a scrubbing. But, politically, it was a vain performance. The reformers, his eventual conquerors, would not be satisfied with any achievements he could bring about. They wanted total revolution —with themselves in the cockpit after the smoke had cleared.

The spark that ignited the rebellion was DeSapio's choice of Manhattan's capable District Attorney, Frank S. Hogan, as Democratic candidate for Senator in 1958. Carmine flexed his political muscles, no innovation, but he did it openly at an all but closed State Democratic Convention. The result was shocking to reformist sensibilities. Cries of "Boss Rule!" and "Dictatorship!" reverberated throughout the state. Newspaper article was piled upon newspaper article in a damning pyramid of condemnation. Carmine's dark glasses became the symbol of political evil. His past good deeds were all but forgotten. It would have been laughable had it not been so serious. Overnight, he was transformed into the modern Madison Avenue equivalent of "Boss" Tweed and "Boss" Croker rolled into one.

Back in 1953, DeSapio had plucked a rather obscure young man, Robert F. Wagner, Jr. from a political hat and forged his nomination for the city's highest elective office. For this he was honored, since Wagner successfully entered City Hall. In 1954, Carmine performed the same feat, using his political muscle to put Averell Harriman across as Democratic nominee for Governor. Formidable pre-convention opposition from Franklin D. Roosevelt, Jr., who also wanted the job, was drowned. Harriman successfully entered the state's Executive Mansion, another feather in Carmine's cap. Roosevelt, on the other hand, showed himself incapable of even winning the post of New York State Attorney-General, running on the same ticket.

No one denounced DeSapio as a high-handed dictator then. He was a wise, benevolent ruler. Some even credited him with strokes of political genius. It is difficult to quarrel with success.

The story in the fall of 1958 was different, however. Carmine now made the monumental error, that most cardinal of political sins, of picking a losing candidate. He did it in the same autocratic manner that had led to earlier triumphs. Frank Hogan might have gone on to become a truly splendid United States Senator. But, in defeat, he also pulled down Harriman, seeking re-election. It made no difference that the Governor's conqueror, Nelson A. Rockefeller, was an extraordinary campaigner who would later dream wistfully of sleeping in the White House. DeSapio's ticket had lost the state. Therefore, Carmine was no longer the state's wise Democratic pilot. To many party opponents, he was no longer even a reputable Democratic leader. They viewed him as just an archaic Tammany boss.

It was at this time that the reformist movement shot into high gear. The word "insurgent" was mislayed. The designation "reformer" seemed a more meritorious emblem. A sharp line—more artificial than real—was drawn between the "good guys", the reformers, and the "bad guys", the party regulars. (Who knows? If the reformers had fought the Republicans in the 1958 election as hard as they had assailed the image of their own party's chief, maybe the Democratic ticket would have come out ahead. Albany returned to the Republican fold in the wake of Tammany's being dragged through the mud.)

In the coming years, Herbert H. Lehman and Eleanor Roosevelt served as rallying points for the "reform movement". Both were distinguished Democrats and distinguished New Yorkers. Neither was personally ambitious, for each had long since secured an honorable place in history. Both truly acted in the conviction they were fighting the good fight. But they were only the summit of this new insurgency.

Beneath them was an assorted, less noble, mixture of local citizenry. Almost all of them spoke in the name of the same high ideals. What these men of varied backgrounds, Ivy Leaguer and grade schooler, lawyer and beatnik, would actually do with any new-found power was a blunt question mark. Militant nobility is an easy virtue when an individual is seeking, not exercising, authority.

In any event, Mayor Wagner saw fit to enlist himself in their ranks. To His Honor, DeSapio was no longer "a stalwart friend of decency, honesty and integrity in government." This is the description he had once accorded his benefactor in happier days.

For Carmine, the future held no bright promise. In 1959, his leadership of the First Assembly District South, in Greenwich Village, was challenged. He accepted this bid to oust him by declaring that a man is "unworthy of holding any position of trust in politics if he fears a fight, cringes at the prospect of defending his record or complains he is being persecuted when his political philosophy is questioned."

Carmine won this first local fight. But the race showed that Greenwich Village was hardly what British members of Parliament would describe as a "safe constituency".

In the Fourth Assembly District, Mitch Bloom faced no immediate challenge. Something called the "Roosevelt-Lehman Independent Democrats" was formed in February, 1959, issued a few brochures, then silently vanished. Similar clubs have sprouted and withered with noticeable frequency as the late 1950s merged into the early 1960s.

Bloom's "staying power" was by no means an accurate index of his popularity. Voting the straight, regular Democratic ticket was a well-established automatic reflex in the Fourth Assembly District South. For decades, we captains had cultivated this reflex. Now, we could virtually sit back and relax during what used to be a hectic pre-election period. Mitch reaped the harvest. As leader, he could proudly boast of the area's returns the morning after each election. Certain of victory, he felt less obliged to look after his captains. In a very real sense, we had "automated" ourselves out of our previous indispensability.

A new breed of captain thus found it easy to develop in the channel we had laboriously carved in years past. These men, of a later generation than my own, were usually lawyers. Eddy Ahearn had always hated to depend on attorneys as captains. He believed many were too impressed by their own sheepskins to deal with constituents as equals. But Eddy's antiquated objections no longer counted. He was dead and so were his political notions. Events were to show that old ideas are not discredited by age alone.

The "modern" captain of the soaring 'sixties no longer remained close to his constituents. It was, and is, a far cry from the days when I climbed six flights of stairs to see voters in squalid tenements. My old colleagues and I used to work our way up one building, across the roof and down the next. Now, staircases have become obsolete in the soaring structures whose elevators haul tenants up and down. Yet many of my young colleagues hesitated even before pressing a button that would comfortably lift them to the apartment of a constituent. Would they ever consider huffing and puffing their way up six flights of steep staircases, as was necessary in bygone days?

To many of these young men, a captaincy is the launching pad for a public career or handsome court patronage. They ask not what they can do *for* their constituents, but what benefits they can derive *from* the clubhouse. Few captains remain who graduated from the old school of politics. They are indeed a vanishing breed.

There came a point, in 1961, when I could no longer accept the conduct of my leader. I therefore saw no course open other than leaving the Lower East Side Democratic Association. For 40 years I had served my party, my neighborhood and especially my precinct's constituents faithfully, while serving my conscience as well. My whole adult life had revolved around my corner of Tammany Hall, the Fourth Assembly District. Recent events, though, had left a bitter taste.

When Eddy Ahearn was lowered into his grave, the neighborhood lost a vital, even irreplaceable, organ of its political body. Now, after three decades, the rest of its anatomy was fast withering away. It was therefore with mixed emotions that I quite cleanly broke with the club, successor to the old John F. Ahearn Association.

My letter to the organization's secretary was brief: "Please accept my resignation from the club as a member, captain, and from the County Committee as of this date, July 12, 1961." I added a postscript to the official notification—"Mitch Bloom knows about it".

Before resigning, I had made certain that Mitch knew precisely why I was dropping out of the club. I had stayed away from meetings for several weeks before acting. Then I called on Mitch at his office in the Municipal Building.

"Come on in and sit down, Louis," he greeted me. "What's on your mind?"

I thought he had a pretty good idea, so I came straight to the point: "Mitch, you once admitted that if I decided to go against my leader I would let him know why to his face. Well, I'm here to tell you that we're finished. My influence among the fellows six years ago gave you the leadership. That lawyer didn't grab it only because I pulled enough votes your way. Other captains who knew you better said I'd regret it. They were right. In appreciation, you crossed me—more than once . . ."

"I tried," Mitch interrupted, "but Carmine didn't stand up for you."

"You didn't try very hard," I replied. "It's your job as district leader to stand up for me, not his. Carmine carries the whole county on his mind. What's keeping your head occupied besides your own district? You never worked for anyone but yourself. The milk has been spilt. If there's anything I can do for you apart from politics, you know where to reach me. And you know I'll play straight with you."

On that note, I ended my attachment with the Lower East Side Democratic Association. During the hectic period of late summer, 1961, I supported Mayor Wagner in his bid for a third term. His continued establishment in Gracie Mansion was by no means assured. A primary contest for the office loomed.

Carmine DeSapio, Bronx leader Charles A. Buckley, successor to Edward Flynn, and Brooklyn leader Joseph T. Sharkey had split from the Mayor on ample personal grounds. Wagner had noticeably warmed to "reformist" elements within the Democratic organizations, certainly no friends of the borough chiefs. He had snubbed Carmine and snuggled up to the Liberal Party, heir to the old American Labor Party of LaGuardia's day.

Nonetheless, Wagner had not deserved being barred from renomination on the basis of his record over his first eight years in office. (Similarly, Impellitteri had deserved a better fate back in 1953.) I therefore plugged for the Mayor before the Democratic primary and, then, before the November general election. No one's crystal ball could foresee what paths he would turn down during his next four years in office.

The same September Primary Day that virtually assured Wagner's continuation as Mayor was responsible for snapping DeSapio's

political roots. His Greenwich Village corner of the First Assembly
District was torn from under him. The reformist drive that mis-
carried in 1959 gave birth to success in 1961.

DeSapio's defeat at home, as everyone including Carmine realized, would inevitably lead to his ouster from the Democratic
County Executive Committee, and, thereby, from its leadership.
(At this point, use of the term "Tammany's Executive Committee"
would be a misnomer.) Eventually, his post as Democratic National Committeeman from New York State would also fall by the
wayside. For one title—in practice, though not theory—rested on
his ability to retain the title beneath it. Once Carmine had been
pried loose from his little corner of Greenwich Village, his entire
pyramid of authority would topple.

Many newspaper columnists and magazine writers sought to
explain the reasons for DeSapio's fall. This is no place to go into
detail about the goings-on of a West Side assembly district. But
one point might be stressed here. Many of the area's inhabitants
were no longer the same people who had established Carmine as
district leader back in the early 1940s, when he successfully challenged and re-challenged Dan Finn, Jr.

Greenwich Village, always a quaint, unworldly point of gravita-
tion, had become the mecca for a group of newcomers whose revolt against society centered on politics as well as the arts. Like
"Banning the Bomb" and "Marching for Peace," the "Beating of
Boss DeSapio" had become a noble "cause". As such, it was ripe
fruit for the collection of beatniks, enthusiastic youngsters and pur-
poseful lawyers of the community.

Our Fourth Assembly District leader was not drowned in any
such chorus of discontent. His very insignificance made it impossible to classify his ouster as a "cause" of heroic proportions. So
no crusade was launched. Mitch Bloom blissfully remained safe—
at least for the immediate future..

Our Congressman, however, was less fortunate. The western
borders of the Nineteenth Congressional District, which sneaked
north as far as Twenty-first Street in 1960, had shot up all the
way to Eighty-sixth Street by 1962. This had the effect of the

Roman Empire's opening of its gates to Alaric's Goths. Virtually this entire northwest territory was infested with reformers.

Poor Lenny Farbstein certainly had his work cut out for him. Either that, or his job would be cut from under him by some ambitious young malcontent. Dauntless, he took up the cudgel of battle. This was not easy for Lenny. At middle age he had become so used to winning by default that over-strenuous campaigning might prove too exerting. Fortunately for him, our Lower East Side assembly district, the Banner District, was the most formidable prop for any "regular" Democratic candidates. Lenny Farbstein lived here and, after three decades as an elected official, most voters at least knew his name.

His 1962 opponent in the Democratic primary contest was Bentley Kassal, a denizen of the congressional district's turbulent northwest frontier. Kassal, a six-year veteran of the State Assembly, carried impressive reformist credentials and an even more impressive list of endorsements. Herbert H. Lehman addressed a campaign letter to "Dear Fellow Democrats" praising Kassal as "an outstanding liberal." The former Governor predicted that "Kassal will not only vote right in Congress—he will fight right. He will fight hard, with imagination and purpose." Kassal also drew unmeasured praise from Eleanor Roosevelt, the *New York Post,* "Americans for Democratic Action" and the Liberal Party.

Nonetheless, he labored under distinct handicaps. For one thing, hardly anyone in our part of the Nineteenth Congressional District had ever heard of him. For a second, his parents had boldly selected "Bentley" as his given name. Now, "Ben" would have proved no handicap, and "Benny" might have been a decided advantage. But "Bentley"? Never! Furthermore, Kassal ran as an "insurgent" and "reformer," while Farbstein wore the tag of "regular" Democrat.

On Primary Day, 1962, Lenny Farbstein probably sweated a good deal more than at any November Election Day. But he won his reprieve. When the final tally was made, he was assured of another two years in the House of Representatives. His seat was secure.

In the spring of 1964, Lenny, by now well-rested, calmly prepared for a new Democratic primary contest. His opponent this time, if anything, was even stiffer competition.

William Haddad, like Kassal, hailed from the northwestern frontier of the Nineteenth Congressional District. His reformist credentials were even more impressive than those of his predecessor. Haddad had not only been a champion of the reform movement—he helped found it. His glossy campaign pamphlets were superb, the products of superior craftsmanship. In one, he visioned himself as "A VOICE FOR THE FORGOTTEN DISTRICT." In another, a photograph showed him squatting before a television set at Hyannisport beside a more renowned public figure. "This is the exact moment that John F. Kennedy knew he would be President," said the accompanying caption.

Haddad did not depend, however, on greatness by association alone. To his credit were listed a long string of worthy achievements, all gathered by the candidate before he reached the age of 35—"a founder of the Peace Corps and its Associate Director . . . a personal troubleshooter for President Kennedy . . . a crusading *New York Post* reporter . . . a Senate expert on juvenile delinquency."

Aside from tooting his own horn, Haddad attributed to Farbstein's trumpet an uncertain sound. He charged Lenny with absenteeism. He charged that Lenny passed no bills except private immigration measures. He charged Lenny with moonlighting. He charged Lenny with "brazenly disregarding his public responsibility."

Poor Farbstein really had a whirlwind blowing him around in 1964. But he held some trump cards of his own. First, he was again a neighborhood product, while Haddad was an outsider. Second, Lenny's hand had been graced by the clasp of President Lyndon B. Johnson's hand. There was proof of this on photographic record, and the pictures were not hidden from the voting public. Third, the President had written Lenny an appreciative letter. This, too, was put in circulation. So were brochures lauding him as a "courageous fighter" for the "Better Deal," whatever that meant. Similar pamphlets affirmed his support for a domestic peace corps, disarmament, housing, cultural exchanges, medicare, new immigration legislation and everything else a New York City Congressman is supposed to favor.

More than ever before in this neighborhood, both sides heavily relied on the printed word and the devices of the public relations man. The captain was no longer king. He was no longer even a knight on the political chessboard. He no longer maintained the bond of mutual trust with his constituents that I had enjoyed in years past. He was now just a petition gatherer and an errand boy for pamphlet deliveries.

Regretfully, in the Fourth Assembly District, the outcome of the Farbstein-Haddad contest was not decided on public issues alone. Few issues divided them, in the final analysis, because both men said they favored the same things. Only the question of who could best carry out the policies they both said they cherished with heart and soul could be placed before the electorate. It was not enough.

Another, more sinister, "issue" became a topic of local conversation—religion. Young Haddad's father had committed the unpardonable sin of being born in Syria—or Egypt, depending on which story you believed. The fact that the upper West Sider said he was of Jewish extraction made no difference. Everyone knew that Arabs outnumbered Jews by about forty to one in that part of the world. Logically, therefore—denials to the contrary—the odds were 40 out of 41 that Haddad was the enemy in disguise.

The candidate could be forgiven for not being Jewish enough. But he could not surmount the broadly hinted charge of "Arabism". On the Lower East Side, that term is far more abominable than all the epithets thrown by reformers, such as "Tammany thieves" and "Boss Rule", put together. Haddad was even referred to in some quarters as "El Haddad." The effect was devastating throughout the Fourth Assembly District.

When the polls closed on Primary Day, June 2, 1964, the complete tallies for the six assembly districts forming the Nineteenth Congressional District showed Lenny the winner by a sparse 3,151 votes. He pulled 19,851 ballots to Haddad's 16,700. But in the

Fourth Assembly District, Haddad did not merely take a beating. He was swamped—2,997 votes to Farbstein's 7,403. Once again, Lenny could drift back to the House of Representatives. Since his opponent in November was to be a Republican, the general election may be dismissed as an epilogue. He beat his GOP challenger by a comfortable, even relaxing, margin of 84,481 to 24,901 votes.

Young Haddad had waged a vigorous primary campaign and deserved a more satisfying fate than relegation to political obscurity. No doubt he will be heard from again. But just as the saying goes about the way to a man's heart being through his stomach, the way to Primary Day triumph on the Lower East Side is through the district leadership. Capture the vital machinery he controls and half the battle is won. This is the route that reformers, insurgents or any other rebels with a cause will have to follow if they expect success when reaching for the more glamorous public offices on the annual day of political judgement.

As for Lenny, he drifted amiably and uneventfully through the next two years. When Primary Day, 1966, approached, he stirred hesitantly from his traditional Washington lethargy. Once again the turbulent West Side spewed forth an articulate, vigorous gladiator—this time reformist City Councilman Theodore Weiss. Once again Lenny stretched his creaking political muscles and tried to avert dislodgement. Past experience had shown that the Lower East Side could pull him through. Ignoring his Congressional District's openly hostile northwest frontier, he counted on a heavy turnout in his old stamping grounds to tip the ballot scales in his favor. Once again, he hoped history would be repeated. But East Side, West Side, all around the town, a lively contest for Manhattan Surrogate dominated the political scene. Councilman Weiss latched his reformist star to the reformist candidate for that judicial post, who, in turn, was firmly harnessed to Senator Robert F. Kennedy's entourage, very fast company indeed. Kennedy's magnetism signaled triumph for his judicial entry. Weiss, appearing on the same ballot line, almost squeaked to victory as a by-product. In fact, unofficial tabulations gave the contest to the reformer on Election night. Three days later, however, a recount showed Farbstein the winner in a near photo-finish. Less than a 200 vote margin out of the nearly 35,000 ballots cast had saved Lenny from being turned out to political pasture. While his opponent cried "foul," Lenny returned to Washington to do his bit in preserving the Republic.

But the end was not yet in sight. Weiss belligerently refused to quit. He took the matter to court, charging that voting irregularities influenced the election results. A State Supreme Court Justice listened to the reformer's gripe, noted that the number of invalidated ballots constituted "almost eight times the margin of victory," and ordered a new primary. By now, Lenny had become used to biennial challenges in the Democratic Primary. But never before had he been placed in double jeopardy. He again straightened his weary bones, transfused his tired blood and set off on the second campaign within six weeks. He quickly announced his intention of introducing a bill in Congress to impose a 90-day freeze on food prices. (All consumers may not vote but all voters are consumers.) Meanwhile, back in New York City, Councilman Weiss denounced a move by the City Council to hike expense allowances of its own members by $2,000 per head out of city revenues. (All taxpayers may not vote but all—well, most—voters are taxpayers.) As August and early September wore on, so did the candidates.

Somehow, the campaign got entangled with the war in Vietnam. Weiss, a militant "dove", criticized the administration's Asian policy. Farbstein, whose foreign policy interests normally centered on Gamal Abdel Nasser's sword-rattling and the scarcity of Passover matzoth in the Soviet Union, suddenly found himself the champion of Lyndon Johnson and the State Department. Weiss annoyed many folks with his sharp darts directed at fellow Democrats in High Places. Farbstein, albeit accidentally, emerged as a voice of moderation, with undertones of statesmanship. Even if the President's popularity had slipped somewhat in the neighborhood, Lenny could safely identify himself with the "policies" of Ambassador Arthur Goldberg, whose stature remained undiminished. Throughout the campaign Weiss harangued and harped on the Vietnam issue. So did the press. Frankly, I doubt Nineteenth

Congressional District voters were stirred much—at least on the
Lower East Side. Muggings on Delancey Street, not ambushes in
Saigon, were of immediate concern. Enrolled Democrats in our
corner of the borough regarded Weiss as the enemy, not the Viet
Cong. In their eyes, Weiss' sin was not in running on the Vietna-
mese war. It was in running, period. He was an invader from the
district's northwest limb. And he personified reformism in its most
virulent stage. By contrast, Kassal and Haddad had been portraits
in moderation.

Weiss was a toxin. Farbstein was the antidote. Whatever else
could be said of Lenny's Congressional record, none could deny
he was a neighborhood product. Those snooty uptowners who argue this is small reason to vote for a man might well remember President Franklin Roosevelt's reported defense of Rafael Trujillo—
"He may be an s.o.b., but he's *our* s.o.b." Lenny and Trujillo, of
course, had little in common. Trujillo spoke tolerable Spanish and
lived on a large private estate called the Dominican Republic.
Lenny lived in an apartment building. Both men, however, could
be relied upon to do what was expected of them and not rock any
boats. This is important. Unlike upper West Siders who wanted
to overturn the world and set it in motion in some other direction,
Lower East Siders preferred the familiar to frenzy. In large droves
they turned out at the polls between the hours of three and ten
p.m. on September 28, 1966. The afternoon set for the run-off
election was damp, chilly and gloomy. Nightfall brought no
meteorological relief. Lenny, though, could not have cared less.
By 11:30 p.m., it was clear he had managed another narrow escape.
The vote was close—17,269 to 16,177. But, close or not, it was
final. Lenny's continued employment in the nation's capital was
assured.

XV

A Wagnerian Opera Without Music

ALTHOUGH THERE WERE MANY NASTY CHARGES HURLED BY Bentley Kassal and William Haddad against Lenny Farbstein in their bids for his Congressional seat, neither could rightfully call him a "boss-dominated" candidate. By 1962, and even more so by 1964, there was no mighty "boss" left on the island of Manhattan. At least not in the traditional sense of Tammany Hall politics.

Following Carmine DeSapio's defeat in the 1961 primary, his authority vanished. His once-magnetic influence on city and state officials dissolved. Though an eclipsed Tammany chief may retain his circle of friends, the same cannot be said about his circle of political vassals.

Carmine's successor as Democratic leader of New York County was Edward N. Costikyan. I did not know the man. Since 1961, I had taken on the role principally of an interested political bystander. The new leader was 37 years of age, which meant that he had not yet opened his eyes when Charles F. Murphy passed from the political stage. A trial lawyer, Costikyan's ability to articulate his views on television was impressive. His ability to command the respect earned by his predecessor was another matter.

Back in 1949, Carmine had been acclaimed as the "first" Italian leader in Tammany history. His ascension was the product of a virtual revolution on the Hall's Executive Committee. During the 1940s, it had been an open secret that the Tiger had been split into "Irish" and "Italian" blocs, with "Jewish" district chiefs gravitating from one clique to the other.

Using the same criteria, Costikyan's elevation may also be considered a "revolution" of sorts. I have read he was of Armenian

241

extraction, certainly another "first." Since there is no Armenian bloc in the party, his selection may have symbolically represented progress in one of two directions. On the one hand, perhaps a man's national origin, and that of his ancestors, no longer worked for or against him in the party's hierarchy. Or, on the other hand, maybe the position of county chief in the Democratic Party had become so meaningless, and the title of "Tammany leader" so hollow, that it was no longer worth more than a brief sparring match between competing blocs. This was a far cry from the days when the titanic struggle between Eddy Ahearn and John F. Curry rocked New York's political community and aroused banner headlines.

At 31, Costikyan had captured the leadership of the Eighth Assembly District South, where he headed the "New Democratic Club." During his first days on the Executive Committee, the young reformer must have felt lonely, for at the time, DeSapio was at the height of his power.

By 1960, though, Costikyan was aggressively calling for Carmine's ouster on grounds of "Bossism." When success loomed two years later, the newcomer proposed a "program of reform and democratization of the party." Though he considered himself a reformer, he must have gained some perspective in the six years he spent on Tammany's ruling council before his selection as county leader.

In any event, by the time he mounted Tammany's decaying throne, Costikyan was an "older" reformer, and many of the "newer" reformers complained he was too mellow. They opposed him during the decisive balloting of March 3, 1962. You might say they considered Costikyan a "conservative reformer." Or, looking at the dispute from the other side of the coin, a "reformed reformer." Costikyan, in turn, warned the new breed that "unless they were ready to understand that diversity doesn't mean disunity, we're going to have trouble."

Already there were problems in the new, more democratic Democratic county organization. Carmine must have laughed from the sidelines.

In the months ahead, Costikyan need not have greatly concerned himself with the problems of power. He held none. Despite the Mayor's reputation as a reluctant dragon, Wagner intended to make the important political decisions himself. One of these was to grant the tacit support that made possible the installation of Costikyan as titular leader in the first place.

Mayor Walker had acted similarly in John Curry's behalf back in 1929. But, having done so, Walker then sat back and let Curry resolve questions of patronage. Wagner had no intention of letting Costikyan enjoy this latitude.

In 1962, Robert M. Morgenthau, a competent and capable, but also modest and reserved, United States Attorney was selected as Democratic candidate for the Governorship. He did not really go out and earn the nomination. Nor was it handed to him by the Democratic county chief in consort with other borough leaders. City Hall, not Tammany Hall, was the architect of young Morgenthau's candidacy. The November result was a disaster paralleling that which had helped undo DeSapio four years earlier.

No one even bothered to demand the resignation of Costikyan. Nor could anyone, tongue in cheek, attribute the blunder to his indiscreet policy of picking candidates. Not since his own elevation to the county leadership had anyone thought of denouncing him as a "Carmine DeSapio without dark glasses." Clearly, the man in the driver's seat was not Edward N. Costikyan.

For better or worse, the Mayor had seized the crown formerly worn by Tammany chiefs. He was now the city's political chief as well as the city's Chief Executive. It could be a term of endearment when he acted wisely, or a term of reproach when he acted otherwise. The soundness of any decision would naturally depend on whose ox was being gored. As for Tammany Hall, its fortunes were at the lowest ebb since O'Dwyer's days. If anything, its condition was now even worse. Apathy prevailed as it lapped at its restraining collar and leash. The Tiger had gone out of the cat.

Costikyan, far too young to be an authority on the Hall's background, saw fit to remark: "Even in 1955, a lot of people thought that Tammany was a good, affirmative thing. Now, no one feels any attachment. Tammany Hall is completely gone."

If Costikyan could not name people to the jobs normally channeled through his organization, he could at least try to rename the organization itself. The unofficial label of the New York County Democratic Organization became "Chatham Hall." But the name did not stick. Tammany Hall remained Tammany Hall, a designation that brought dishonor only to those who brought dishonor to it.

By the spring of 1964, with the Tiger gravely ailing, or, according to some, already dead, reformist rebels were looking for a new "cause." At the City Council chamber, they found one. When Mayor Wagner used pressure to secure his choice for Majority Leader, they verbally stoned him for ramming his man through. Wagner's participation was a perfectly natural act for any Chief Executive who wants to dominate his legislative partner. Years earlier, Vincent Impellitteri had failed to master his co-ordinate branch at City Hall. As a result, governmental processes were stalemated and he became the scapegoat. The present Mayor wished to avoid a similar fate.

And so it came to pass that Mayor Wagner had to take his place on the receiving end of the charges he had orated against other men in other days. "We repudiated bossism in the past," screeched one reformer, "and I refuse to submit to bossism now."

Costikyan, too, was unhappy, but for a far different reason. He thought the Mayor was dealing too freely with the new breed of reformers, who sought to displace the old breed of reformers, who had made an unsteady peace with the still older breed of party regulars. It was the old story of the reformist stick beating the dog that bit the Tammany cat that ate the lamb that the voters had elected.

Not so oddly, discontent and soreness centered on the ancient practice of patronage. Costikyan threatened to resign when job vacancies were filled with neither his advice nor consent. Then he withdrew from taking this drastic step, following President Kennedy's assassination. It was a postponement, though, not a cancellation. Costikyan, according to some sources, was fed up with the job. If a county chief cannot distribute patronage, of what use is he?

The new breed of reformers, many of them attorneys, usually feigned scant concern for the vistas that politics held open to holders of law degrees. But they were interested, all right. The beautiful vision of a patronageless world of reformed politics proved a mirage. Their "Situation Wanted" requests were answered on the doorstep of City Hall, though, not party headquarters, or "Chatham Hall."

What these reformers did to deserve political reward somehow escapes me. Their effectiveness in getting city dwellers registered is perhaps best demonstrated by the fact that on October 6, 1964, the New York County Democratic Committee found it desirable to place a full-page ad in the city's most widely distributed newspaper. The purpose of its message was to urge readers to sign up in time to vote. If modern precinct captains were half as intimate with their constituents as we Tammany captains had been, no need would have arisen for such gimmicks. Imagine Charles F. Murphy, or even James Dooling, for that matter, buying advertising space to announce there was an election coming up!

Two days after President Johnson's landslide November triumph, Costikyan finally and formally quit as leader of Manhattan's Democrats. Reportedly, he resigned in order to spend more time at his law practice.

As his successor, Mayor Wagner installed J. Raymond Jones, leader of the eastern half of Harlem's Thirteenth Assembly District. In a sense, Jones was another "first"—the first Negro leader of Tammany Hall. At 65, however, the gray-haired Jones was no stranger to party intricacies. He had been active in Democratic politics before his predecessor was born. And he was good at it. Not for nothing did he earn the nickname, "The Fox."

Jones' principal error, committed before the turn of the century, had been in being born into the wrong race. "The first time I put my foot in a Democratic clubhouse—Martin Healy's Cayuga Club in Harlem—in 1921, I couldn't have conceived what happened today," he said at the time of his election. "In those days, there were two clubs, the whites upstairs and the Negroes in the basement."

Born on St. Thomas in the Virgin Islands, he stowed away at age 16 aboard a schooner bound for Puerto Rico, than came to New York. Jones slowly worked his way up through the party ranks, the path being all the more tortuous because of the informal color bar that limited the value of the "D" in Democratic Party. To paraphrase the words of Winston Churchill, when the British leader addressed the United States Congress, "if Jones had been born white and his intra-party opponents black, instead of the other way around, he might have made it on his own."

Jones announced to reporters, "I hope to make Tammany a working organization within the framework of my experience and knowledge." (It was refreshing to find a Tammany leader who did not shy away from being known as a Tammany leader.)

Whatever Jones' more pertinent qualifications for the county leadership, however, the major requirement for the job was obvious. Any prospective candidate would have had to meet it, and the Harlem Councilman was no exception. This requirement was an oath of fealty to the lord and master of Gracie Mansion. Jones would have to follow orders. No touch of a silver-edged sword upon his shoulders signified this status of vassalage. None was necessary. While Jones might rightfully expect to have the Mayor's ear, he was in no position to tug at it.

As 1965 dawned—the final year of his third term in office— Robert F. Wagner hoarded power like a political Silas Marner. He kept the intoxicating fluid tightly corked. Others might be allowed a quick peak, but never a sip. He was—if the expression may be excused—Boss of New York City. Moreover, he had indicated quite clearly his intention to remain so for another four-year stretch.

Until the 1964 Democratic National Convention, the Mayor had been a long-shot possibility as Vice-Presidential timber. Within hours after President Johnson tapped Senator Hubert Humphrey as his running mate, however, Wagner announced he would seek a fourth term at City Hall. "I have always said I probably will run," he said. "That is my intention. There is a lot of work to be done in New York City."

The Mayor then set out both to run and work. Everyone knew that Lyndon Johnson had sparked many a blowout in Washington by dimming the White House. Wagner, ever mindful of the President's popularity, ambitiously adapted part of the Johnson public utility policy to the local level. Among the New Year's resolutions required of city workers, one shined brightly—thou shalt not burn lightbulbs excessively. From the inner recesses of the Municipal Building to the most unpolitical elementary school plant in distant Staten Island the word went out. An executive order directed city department chiefs to appoint "light wardens" in each public edifice. These guardians of the city purse were to conduct daily room-by-room patrols. Their mission: turn off all lights, fans, air conditioners and other power-gobbling monsters after business hours.

According to the Mayor's instructions, summonses were to be issued in two colors. The first, to indicate a preliminary warning, the second, to present a final warning. Third offenders were slated to face the wrath of their department heads.

I, for one, loyally sought to obey this municipal ukase. My nephew, a high school teacher, was, alas, less diligent. At 2:45 in the afternoon of a date that will forever remain nameless, he dismissed his class, strode absentmindedly toward the elevator and pressed the "down" button. Just as the door opened he heard a cry: "Wait! you forgot the lights!" Fortunately, he received no demerit for his wasteful conduct. The panicky screech was uttered by one of his faithful students, not a lurking floor warden.

No one knew how much money this economy edict was supposed to save the city. Operating on the theory that a penny saved is a penny to be spent, the Mayor set out to redirect anticipated earnings along politically useful channels. A $7,500 raise was directed to the Budget Director, whose principal job is to keep the budget in check. Some 116 judges received across-the-board $2,500 increases. This brought the salary of one Appellate Division Justice to a level $1,500 higher than that earned by the Chief

Justice of the United States Supreme Court. Bountiful financial
blessings also rained down upon the wallets of numerous bureaucrats. These ranged from $400 to $10,000 per year. (One of
Wagner's chief beneficiaries, housing and redevelopment head
Milton Mollen, was to make news later in the year by turning upon
his benefactor and running for elective office on a fusion ticket.)

Meanwhile, back at the office, I dutifully clicked each light switch
to an "OFF" position at closing time. I am certain that thousands
like myself were filled with satisfaction by the thought that each
penny we saved was a step toward fiscal sanity and a more prosperous New York City.

In far-off Albany, an indirect challenge to the Mayor's over-
riding authority was brewing. Upstate Democratic leaders joined
forces with Bronx chief Charles Buckley and Brooklyn's Stanley
Steingut, holdouts from Wagner's New Order, to push aside his
choices for key posts in the New York State Legislature. At a party
caucus, the Mayor's men were rejected. Had this alliance of upstaters and dissident downstaters worked, the opening salvo at the
state capital would surely have been followed by assaults within
the city limits.

Wagner could not risk a major setback. No "boss" can. Therefore, while he pompously pressed for the "binding up of party
wounds and a restoration of party harmony within a framework
of continuing progress in party democratization," he tyranically
set out to undo the work of the Democratic caucus.

Having cast his die and crossed his Rubicon—in this case, the
Hudson River—the Mayor stormed the capital's ramparts. Defeat
was unthinkable. He could not afford to lose. And he did not.
However, the propriety of his methods raised many an eyebrow.
Wagner did not play the political game according to Hoyle. In the
absence of crystal balls, though, no one could foresee the fateful and
fretful consequences for the Democratic Party in New York State
and for the man who steered its personnel. Wagner's men won the
Assembly Speakership and Senate Majority Leadership which he
had staked out for them. Like their opponents, both victors were

highly competent professionals. But from this bitter contest poured a torrent of grim allegations and poisoned feelings.

It took the Mayor nearly five weeks to accomplish his goal. During this period of family squabbling, the state legislature did no legislating. And when triumph finally came, it was conveyed solely through the votes of Governor Rockefeller's brigade of Republican lawmakers.

Cries of "sellout" quickly rang out. After all, why would the GOP step in and rescue a Democratic Mayor from a whirlpool of embarrassment? Especially in an election year! According to a press aide, Wagner's reaction to the upstate coup was: "What's happening in Albany is news to me."

State Chairman William H. McKeon, an intra-party foe of the Mayor, charged an inter-party deal had been arranged between Republican Rockefeller and Democrat Wagner. In return for putting the Mayor's leadership candidates across, the Governor was assured his controversial budget and tax programs would later be passed by the legislature's Democratic majority.

More cynical observers even envisioned the Rockefeller-Wagner axis extending beyond the legislative session. According to one tale, the Governor was to guarantee clear sailing for Wagner in the 1965 Mayoralty race by backing a pathetically decent and respectably dull sacrificial lamb as his GOP adversary. Later, when the 1966 Gubernatorial race loomed, the Mayor was to return favor for favor by backing a similarly anemic Democratic opponent for Rockefeller. If the story could be taken with more than the proverbial grain of salt, few knew and fewer would tell. In any event, Congressman John V. Lindsay was charting a political course of his own, one destined to make the rumors circulating through clubhouses a waste of wordage.

For the moment, however, Wagner's Albany machinations kept him firmly perched atop New York City's political nest. At least it seemed so at the time.If the unpleasant affair had left his public image somewhat stained, were not the results worth a little mud? Having brought Tammany and the Queens and Richmond organizations to heel, he now appeared on the verge of eliminating the last vestige of Democratic opposition within the city boundaries—the shattered Steingut and Buckley camps in Brooklyn and the Bronx.

I do not know whether the groundhog saw his shadow in February, 1965. But for Robert F. Wagner, shadow or no, political winters seemed far behind. His route to his present eminence was indeed a winding one. In 1953, he had been hoisted into City Hall upon the "bosses' " shoulders. In 1957, their doorbell pushers kept him there. In 1961, however, he had cast his allies aside like shoes that fit well once but no more. Instead, he courted and wed a curious mixture of partisan reformers, non-partisan civic leaders and anti-partisan crusaders. Miraculously, he turned the trick of winning re-election by vigorously running against much of his record instead of "on" it. Of course he willingly accepted plaudits for whatever blessings fell upon the city during his first eight years in office. All municipal evil, on the other hand, was passed off as the residual waste-product of "bossism."

These past campaigns were ancient history. In 1965, it seemed Wagner would neither need to seek out new friends nor rely on old ones. As the month of February wore on, no grand challenge or challengers appeared on the Mayoralty horizon. "Bossism" was dead, or at least almost dead—if you consider only the nasty kind bearing an anti-Wagner label. The GOP could be expected to field a safely orthodox and honorable chap who would no doubt impress sweet old dowagers and the Citizens Union, but few others. Of course, a few zealous reformists within his party might harbor faint suspicions that the Mayor was not really one of them. But what of it? Costly campaigns are not waged by a handful of professional malcontents with small appeal, smaller purses and no organization.

In a local fireside chat and interview, telecast directly from Gracie Mansion, Wagner reiterated he would "most likely" seek an unprecedented fourth term. To reinforce his words, he pressed back into service Debs Myers, an ace public relations man, as his secretary. Myers, a former aide, ostensibly was rehired to "initiate a reorganization of many city public information functions with the view of achieving substantial economies." That is what the Mayor said—really and truly, he did. But the description masked Myers' real task, namely to bloat the Wagner image into Samson-like (though not Goliath-like) proportions. At this stage of the Wagnerian drama, the day-by-day labor of precinct captains counted for nothing, while a good press agent was worth his weight in gold. Or, if not gold, at least a substantial pile of legal tender from the municipality's shrinking treasury.

At the surface level, the Mayor had every reason for supreme confidence. On March 1, 1965, John V. Lindsay, the Silk Stocking District's tall, articulate and politically attractive Congressman, made crystal-clear his preference for Washington's rarified atmosphere over New York's polluted air. Along with Jacob K. Javits, Lindsay had been considered the only Republican capable of giving the Mayor a run for his backers' money. Inasmuch as Javits was already a United States Senator, a more prestigious job to which Wagner himself once aspired, it was highly unlikely he would step down to do battle with Wagner in the city gutters. Thus apparently vanished any potential GOP competition even before the winter frost had thawed.

No intra-party primary threat beckoned either. J. Raymond Jones, who had been lifted into the county leadership by Wagner, was not Carmine DeSapio. He had no able alternate hidden in the wings. Nor could the Steingut and Buckley organizations field a "bossed" candidate capable of whipping the city's Boss of Bosses. Both county leaders had been rocked by the Rockefeller-Wagner coup in Albany and grimly held off rebels within their own dis-integrating camps. They had all to do building dikes along the Harlem and East Rivers to ward off the Mayor's final assault.

Further proof of their plight came later that Spring during the annual political dinner season. On May 6, hardly anyone of consequence showed up at the yearly dinner of the Bronx Democratic organization. As the story went, to honor Buckley was to antagonize Wagner. Two weeks later, 13 of Brooklyn's 22 Democratic assembly district leaders stayed away from a party tendered county leader Steingut. Many friends of mine within the Brooklyn organization no doubt realized the seating plan lists would be carefully scanned by Wagner's patronage aides. Jobs earned through years of faithful party service could well be lost by an evening's indiscretion. Few could enjoy a hearty appetite under such circumstances.

At the other end of the Democratic spectrum, the only fellow brazen enough to seriously consider challenging the Mayor in the September primary was Congressman William Fitts Ryan. He hailed from upper Manhattan, just north of the perennial reformist pocket that had spawned Leonard Farbstein's opposition in 1962 and 1964. Ryan was less a party reformer than a party revolutionary. If he were to make Gracie Mansion his home address, New York City's county Democratic organizations would not merely have undergone corrective surgery and a drastic change in personnel. The party system faced decapitation and the accession to power of political delinquents. Such a man, no matter how pure his motives and noble his soul, was dangerous. In such a setting, Wagner could rightfully expect even his most critical foes to rally to his side in defense of peace and municipal tranquility.

This, then, was the situation in early May, 1965. Wagner, though not necessarily a beloved figure among his fellow Democrats, appeared at least an unbeatable one. No constitutional amendment barred a fourth term for His Honor. He would evidently breeze to victory in the September party primary, walk over his Republican opponent in November and settle comfortably down for another four-year stretch in office.

The GOP plight was so pathetic at this point that its state chairman told newsmen the five Republican county chairmen "had not closed the door" on a possible fusion ticket headed by an independent Democrat!

At this stage of the text, a half page of blank space might be a prudent device to emphasize the contrast in outlook for Robert F. Wagner's Mayoral career between May 12 and May 13, 1965. On that latter day, Congressman Lindsay announced a change of mind. "After long and deep consideration," he said, "I have decided to run for Mayor of our City of New York."

The news was a local political bombshell. It chased the international crisis from the lead position in many a newspaper. Unfamiliar as I am with internal Republican intrigues, I do not know why John Lindsay turned around and accepted his party's nomination. As a lifelong Democrat, I frankly am somewhat baffled by why any capable young man would make the Republican Party his home, much less welcome its endorsement. My friend Vincent Albano may have a partial answer. As New York County Republican Chairman, he no doubt did a little arm-twisting in getting Lindsay into the race. But Vince will have to tell his own story.

Before the week was out, city papers had churned out well-illustrated features on the photogenic candidate. Similarly, Luce publications were busily preparing a matinee-style cover story about the attractive chap who, in the city, the Republican sword was wielding. One morning daily prophesied in a headline: "Wagner vs. Lindsay: the Best Bout Since '33."

Whether or not it would be the best, it certainly shaped up as the most exciting in a long time. In one corner, the Republican challenger—43 years old . . . six foot three-inches . . . Yale man . . . Representative from the Seventeenth Congressional District since 1959 . . . no political scars detracting from an infectious smile . . . recorded victories included those over the Japanese in the Pacific (as a gunnery officer aboard a Navy destroyer) and Eleanor Clark French (in the 1964 Congressional election).

In the other corner, the Democratic champion—55 years old . . . height irrelevant . . . a Yale man, too . . . Mayor since 1954 . . . one major political scar (a loss in the 1956 Senatorial race) . . . recorded victories included those over the German Wehrmacht in France (as a member of the Eisenhower team, military, not political) and Harold Riegelman, Robert Christenberry and Louis Lefkowitz (at four-year November intervals).

Two weeks after the bout was arranged, however, a snag developed. One of the contestants announced he might be missing. "I know what the Mayor's life is," the Mayor said. "I've been through it for 12 years and it's a very grueling one, and I'm not decided that I'd want to face it for another four years of hard work." He outlined personal reasons for his attitude and added, "For a number of months now I've been weighing the question." He promised a decision in two weeks.

Many observers, political and journalistic, believed that Wagner was playing it coy. William O'Dwyer had followed an apparently similar "No—No—No—Maybe—Yes" technique before "accepting" Democratic renomination in 1949. Despite unofficial polls that showed Lindsay running ahead of him, the Mayor surely would have gone into the November contest an odds-on favorite to retain his job. Wagner indicated this himself. While admitting that his challenger might make a fascinating foe, he scoffed at the prospect of defeat. He asked City Hall correspondents if they could imagine "ANY Republican winning in New York City."

During the two week period of tense expectation, Wagner certainly behaved like a prospective candidate. "We are only at the starting line of a race that must be run against forces which, if they overtake us, will overwhelm us," he told a union convention tightly packed with potential supporters. This was hardly the type of statement a public official would make if he were backing off from a fight.

And yet it came to pass that on Friday, June 11, 1965, His Honor stunned the political community by pulling out of the Mayoral race. The decision, announced at a jammed, floodlit press conference, was "final and irrevocable." He said it was based on personal rather than political considerations, thereby earning him the good wishes of political foes as well as political allies.

The impact of Wagner's withdrawal eclipsed Lindsay's own change of mind one month earlier. After 12 years in office, like him or not, the Mayor had become something of a municipal fixture. He had held the City Hall hotspot four years before his young GOP challenger had sought public office for the first time. The terms "Mayor" and "Wagner" had almost become glued together.

Under the circumstances, any book dealing with Tammany Hall and Democratic politics could not avoid delving into the subsurface factors that led to this dramatic abdication. As for his personal considerations, Wagner must—and should—be taken at his word. But there were other pressure points of a political nature, as well.

In an earlier chapter, I have shown that minor elected officials often forgot how they got into office, who put them there and what obligations to their supporters and constituents they could rightfully be expected to meet. What a distinct pity that this failing was not the exclusive property of minor public officials! An inconsequential assemblyman or state senator or city councilman could be quickly set straight, a chore I tackled on many an occasion. But who is to serve the Mayor of the City of New York this bitter pill. Certainly not a precinct captain or district leader. Back even in the 1920's, when Tammany mounted a still virile Tiger, Eddy Ahearn's fingers were singed when he frankly set forth the facts of political life before a startled Jimmy Walker. How Eddy and our district suffered during the rest of that decade for his necessary indiscretion!

There were no Eddy Ahearns around in the 1960s, men capable of courageously and bluntly explaining his duties to His Honor. There was no Tammany organization around, either. Wagner had suffocated it midway along his 12-year route to this final reckoning. During the last four years, he had kicked the corpse and tugged at its limp tail. With the prospect of future political triumphs bright, Wagner fell into the fatal trap that awaits any man in high elective office. He assumed an unwarranted stance of independence.

"No man is an island," suggests a venerable poet. And to no man is this description more apt than to a political man. Just as an ill person needs constant treatment and attention, a nominee needs the care and support of precinct and district workers. But a successful candidate, like a discharged hospital patient, often forgets the "doctors" who pulled him through. While a cured patient may never re-enter the hospital for the same illness, an elected official again and again must turn to his political medicine-men at two or four year intervals. If he ignores them, if he discards them, if he repudiates them, how can he expect the same loyal service that was once tendered him on faith? Robert F. Wagner, feeling fit and unconquerable, accustomed to easy triumphs, had torn up his political Rx.

The Mayor's recent political conduct had left many long-time party professionals dismayed and bitter. Scars of the much publicized Albany clash, for one thing, remained unhealed. On that occasion, the Mayor had not only left himself open to charges of making a deal for Republican support, which would have been bad enough. He also had broken a major rule of political behavior —thou shalt not break a party confidence.

Everyone in politics knows that a certain amount of horsetrading is necessary in picking up votes and support in a legislative body. It happens in state legislatures, the House of Representatives and even in the august chambers of the United States Senate. But few talk about these bargains outside the circle of their political peers. Although an essential part of the give-and-take of political life, they appear vile and dirty and evil when presented starkly on the printed page.

Wagner scooped up the alleged facts of one such arrangement made by his intra-party opponents and spread them—like dirty linen—before a shocked public. In other days and in other places the Mayor himself had engaged in similar barters. (Not for nothing does the Liberal Party lend its good name on the voting machine.) But, now, he chose to cloak himself under a banner emblazoned "I am holier than thou" and hurl charges of "bribery" at his adversaries. These opponents were not Republicans, mind you, but fellow Democrats dwelling in the same political house.

The Mayor was certainly not naive and obviously not a political innocent. Could such a man be trusted ever again with a political confidence? This was not a question which greatly worried the general public. But you may be certain it concerned—and concerned mightily—the Mayor's uneasy collaborators. (The angry reaction of some national office holders to historian Arthur Schlesinger, Jr.'s recital of uncomplimentary things he heard the late President Kennedy say about his Secretary of State might give some indication of the resentment Wagner's conduct aroused at the local level.)

The Mayor's mastery of the legislature had given him the power over nearly a million dollars in patronage plums. But it did nothing to earn him the respect of foes or the admiration of followers.

Much as the Albany goings-on shattered the possibility of healthy co-existence at the upper echelons of the Democratic Party, the ethical factors did not directly stir the souls of the average party worker. A precinct captain has little fear of seeing his confidences broken by a Mayor, since he rarely has access to a Mayor's ear to offer them. (On occasion, when requesting an appointment with Wagner, I was told by one of his aides he would contact me shortly. More often than not, no response was forthcoming.)

To the lower Democratic echelons, His Honor's political heresies were on a different plane. For decades, clubhouse captains had been the backbone of the city's Democratic Party skeleton. Eddy Ahearn repeatedly acknowledged this fact in Tammany's glory days. And until the Wagner administration, the fact remained an unchallenged principle. Wagner did not shout, "Beat the Precinct Captains!" with the gusto that had marked his crusade against "Bossism." Vocal outbursts were unnecessary. His eccentric patronage policy simply ignored these loyal workers, thereby forcing the clubhouse system to fall apart. This, in my judgment, was his most flagrant abuse of political power and his most callous breach of the political code.

These nameless men had painstakingly cared for their constituents' interests through hot summers and dreary winters. As an inevitable by-product, they had maintained the supremacy of their party on Election Day year after year, decade after decade and generation after generation, with time out only for periodic bursts of reformism. These men had not simply pressed doorbells a few days before election "to get out the votes." They had earned those votes by constant and concrete service. Their labor had won young Wagner his seat in the New York State Assembly, lifted him to the prestigious Manhattan Borough Presidency and plopped him in the imposing chair at City Hall. Their labor had failed to win him a seat in the United States Senate in 1956 solely because upstaters voted as well as city folk, and the clubhouse system ended where urban New York faded into the countryside.

By his fanciful, capricious use of patronage machinery, Wagner pushed many reliable old-timers into retirement. And their natural political heirs, who would have carried on, shied away from the dismal fate they saw before them. This left the field to others, often lawyers with less interest in their precincts than in their pocketbooks. These "captains" all too often slept 11 months of the year and merely distributed brochures during the twelfth.

While man does not live by bread alone, he must have bread to live. In years past, hard-working captains such as myself did not consider the political positions we held as "gifts." We had earned them by fruitful work for our party and our constituents.

Three decades before, when Fiorello LaGuardia hurled verbal brickbats at "clubhouse loafers," we naturally felt resentful, for LaGuardia knew better. Nonetheless, the Republican-American Labor Party-Fusionist Mayor was a political foe and such charges were to be expected. On the other hand, Robert F. Wagner, a Democrat Mayor, was one of us. His calculated neglect cut far deeper. Wagner's most tragic error was not that he pilloried his major foes within the party. It was that he cast aside loyal precinct captains, the very backbone of the political system that installed him in office.

Like a football coach bent on filling his bench with new blood, the Mayor increasingly turned away from party regulars. Instead, he placed his fortunes in a breed of "politicians" who, for want of a more picturesque phrase which would include them all, must be referred to here as "Wagner men."

It is often said that a man may be judged by the company he keeps. It is equally true that an elected official's political strength may be judged by his political allies. Who were the Mayor's closest confederates during his last four years in office? To whom could he have turned for aid and comfort now that his opponent was to be no sacrificial lamb?

First of all, Wagner had caressed the Liberal Party. In the 1961 general election, more than 200,000 votes had been cast for him on the Liberal line. This was a formidable figure. But lest anyone be deceived by raw statistics and draw incorrect inferences about the nature of Liberal support, some cold water must be liberally splashed on that number, hefty though it is. Like the American Labor Party from which it sprang, the Liberal Party is a political operation rather than a political organization. At its head are several leaders of potent labor unions within the city. They dictate the policies pursued by their party which, in essence, consists of union members, not party workers and their constituents. The Liberal Party also embraces an assortment of college professors. They make handsome figureheads and are impressive theoreticians. But they count for little in the candidate-selecting process. This all-important chore remains the preserve of a small cabal of more practical men. The mass of union members they control are expected to pull the Liberal lever on Election Day through labor loyalty, not party loyalty, with the same automatic motion with which they punch their time-clocks. As for precinct captains? A fantasy! The Liberal Party is all head and no body.

For a Democratic Mayor, the importance of the Liberal Party is basically negative. In its absence, most union members would surely vote Democratic rather than Republican. But the fact that it does exist allows its leaders—I almost feel tempted to use the term "bosses"—to approach the Mayor with an ultimatum that no county chief of his own party would dare make. The language, of course, would be more civil, but the message boils down to this: "If we don't get a healthy share of patronage, we'll take our party over to the opposition camp in the next election." A variation of this threat might be: "If we don't get a healthy share of patronage, we'll run our own candidate, split the Democratic vote, and let the opposition sneak across in a three-cornered race."

Men who hold political jobs under the aegis of the Liberal Party rarely feel any loyalty to the man whose successful candidacy made those jobs possible. They have attained their positions through a levy extracted from the Mayor, a sort of political tax. In any event, they are not precinct captains or year-round workers in their neighborhoods. They cannot go out and hustle votes. They probably would not know how. Their "constituencies," for the most part, are limited to their own families—or those members, at least, over the age of 21.

A second major prop under the Mayor during his last four years in office, if indeed it were a prop, was the reform movement within the Democratic Party. The reformers split into two camps—the savage, impulsive species and the moderate, tamed variety. The first class included the Edward Kochs, men who stood at the forefront of the "Beat Bossism" crusade and any other crusade in vogue at the moment. To the second class belonged the Edward Costikyans, men who had mellowed with age and proved more or less amenable to Wagner's New Order.

Merged almost imperceptibly into this group of reformed reformers were several representatives of the New Breed of organization men—the Mitch Blooms. These district chiefs held court in clubhouses whose heritage could be traced to Tammany Hall's dynamic past. But they lightly regarded their heritage, if, indeed, they had even a vague understanding of what they were heirs to. Titans of Tammany's heyday would surely revolve in their graves were they to realize that the merits and demerits attributed to the Hall by young reporters, fresh out of Journalism School, are based on the record of the current crop of tribal chiefs.

Whether screeching reformers, calm reformers or coated nonreformers, the three groups shared one characteristic in common. None could deliver a weighty bloc of votes for the Democratic ticket unless the head of the ticket could draw them on his own.

One last bloc in Wagner's political entourage deserves mention. It consisted of a small cluster of organization men who were old enough to remember their political legacy and respectful enough not to dishonor it. These district leaders—the Prosper Viggianos— stuck with Wagner not through admiration, or even respect, but because they were Democrats. For the most part, their own positions were beyond the Mayor's reach. But they knew the jobs of their captains rested on the Mayor's whims. So, with a singular lack of enthusiasm, they strung along with the man in City Hall, thereby keeping their clubhouses intact.

Wagner's key to maintaining his New Order—patronage—was the same key used by every political executive since men came out of caves and instituted systems of organized rule. But there is no magic formula capable of automatically converting patronage into votes. The man who is given a "political job" must know how to "get out the vote." And, as I have taken pains to point out, there is far more to this task than handing out leaflets listing the academic achievements and philanthropic activities of office-seekers. Patronage directed to a man who could distribute literature and do little else would no doubt guarantee the patron one vote if the beneficiary were single, two if he were married and an additional vote for each child born of the union at least 21 years earlier. Such a man's greatest political asset would be an immense family.

This is not to say he is a worthless individual. He might prove an admirable addition to some engineering department of a city agency, if he knows a little about math. But does he qualify for a patronage post? Never!

Nonetheless, as the Wagner regime wore on, such men frequently fell into positions that in other days were preserved for deserving precinct captains. Many district leaders, ground in the ABCs of partisan politics, bit their lips as they read of vacancies being filled by people who had never seen the inside of a clubhouse. All too often, posts that had been rotated for years by members of the same club were handed out—almost haphazardly—to outsiders. Neither the advice nor consent of district leaders was sought.

This erratic policy of job distribution resulted in a virtual community of political strangers. The situation became so chaotic at times that insiders no longer asked what clubhouse a new appointee came from. They asked what city he came from!

The Mayor's political caprice could be forgiven, perhaps even praised as virtuous rather than vicious, if the result had been a corruption-free, efficiently run and safe New York. But how many citizens could honestly acclaim the city as a better place to grow up and live in today than in bygone days when government offices were traditionally filled on a political merit system?

The ability of precinct captains to carry out commitments to their constituents tragically suffered as a result of unpolitical appointees holding political jobs. This especially applied to the captain's ability to cut through masses of red tape in clear cases of bureaucratic injustice.

Take, for example, the ordeal of a man who loses a licensed position because his license has been cancelled on a technicality. One such crisis began with a painfully prodigious search by an examining board. It revealed that a young fellow who had been serving competently in a job for a full year had lacked two appropriate college credits (apart from the more than 160 which were acceptable) at the time he received his license. Although he had met all eligibility requirements, including completion of these two credits, at the time of his actual appointment, he was nevertheless stripped of his license and, hence, his livelihood. The unfolding drama might have been farcical but for the grim consequences. Even a letter from his supervisor stressing the competency—even the superiority—of his work availed him nothing. The municipal bureaucrat to whom it was addressed merely produced a paper clip, attached it to the fellow's folder, put it away and slammed both the filing cabinet and his career shut. Not a trace of human compassion or understanding faintly glowed in the office where the economic execution took place.

Years ago, captains could insure that their constituents' lives would not be ruined by such ludicrous technicalities. They could go above the heads of robot-like bureaucrats, if these failed to see reason, and reach the ear of someone with heart and mind and soul. The captains did not have to know this power-that-be personally. For they could always make contact with someone who did.

Walking automatons inhabit many city offices today. If anyone is willing to applaud the domineering impersonality of government they symbolize, let him for one moment step into the position of the poor fellow whose career, like Cinderella's coach, turned into a pumpkin at the very hour he received his license. Years ago, the touch of a captain's magic wand would have saved him.

We cling tightly to the belief that a "government of laws" is vastly superior to a "government of men" because laws are just while men are corruptible. The Constitution of the United States is indeed an admirable document, short, comprehensive and vague enough to allow for changing interpretations in changing situations. Municipal codes, rules, statutes, ordinances, regulations and by-laws, however, have little in common with the mother document of our nation. A Philadelphia lawyer might plow through them with a measure of understanding—but only if they happened to be the codes, rules, statutes, ordinances, regulations and by-laws of his native city. For every loophole through which a cagey lawyer might slip a wealthy client, there are ten knots to tighten against the average citizen.

All too often, the choice at the municipal level is not between a "government of laws" and a "government of men," but between a "government of red tape" and a "government of equity." The choice is not so cut-and-dry, especially if the right men could be fitted to the right jobs.

I realize the preceding paragraphs have strayed from the topic of ethics and morality in politics over to the area of humanity and compassion in government. But I make no apology for this meandering course. If, as the saying points out, politics is the father of government, then the practitioners of both crafts should share a common trait—a sense that they exist to serve their fellow man, not create artificial obstacles to justice.

During the last four years of the Wagner administration, individuals had been shoveled into political jobs who, in Tammany's heyday, would have filled the corners of private law offices and corporate suites instead of being inflicted upon the general public. At 5:00 p.m. each evening (4:00 p.m. during the summer months) these appointees snapped shut their briefcases and disappeared into the growing darkness. No political nightwork marred their evening hours. Yet, on the narrow shoulders of these political ciphers, Robert F. Wagner unwittingly staked his own future at City Hall.

Had the Grand Old Party nominated a grand, old, stodgy nonentity as seemed likely earlier in 1965, the Mayor could have floated back to office in November on a cloud. No help would have been sought or needed. When John Lindsay, a not-so-grand-nor-so-old, unstodgy entity accepted his party's designation, an Elephant of a far different color took the field against His Honor.

During the four weeks that spanned the dates between Lindsay's decision to run and the Mayor's decision to bow out, Wagner probably took a long, hard look at what his political gymnastics had wrought in the way of political support during the preceding few years. The panorama was dismal.

Liberal Party officialdom, of course, would have had little reason to stray from his corner. But the party's leaders could probably have delivered only the votes of those union members who would have voted for Wagner anyway, Liberal line or not. (Ten votes for the same candidate are ten votes whether they are cast on one line or two lines or eight lines.) Those union members who preferred Lindsay, on the other hand, would have switched their votes without a care about party loyalty. There were no Liberal precinct captains to be loyal to.

However potent this third party might have proven, one basic fact stood out in this election, as it does in all city elections. Ultimately, a Democratic Mayor must turn back to his own party for succor in times of stress. Indeed, this is as it should be. But New York City's Democratic Party was, by 1965, a party of loose ends. No strong tie of loyalty to the man who had arrogated all party power unto himself knotted the various factions together. In the face of such disunity, the solid backing of the Liberals would have been small consolation.

Back in 1961, Wagner had defeated Republican Louis J. Lefkowitz by 1,237,421 to 835,691 votes—a spread of 401,730. But these raw statistics were misleading in terms of Wagner's appeal within his own party. Only 970,383 of his total had been cast on the Democratic line, a bare 134,692 more than his major opponent's figure. This, despite the fact that 2,202,162 New Yorkers were enrolled in the Democratic Party that year while GOP enrollment was a paltry 767,526.

Now, four years later, Wagner would have had to rally around him a party that was far less cohesive and far less inspired than when he pulled his little miracle of 1961.

Many in the reformist camp—especially the rash and reckless breed that spearheaded his crusade against DeSapio—had deserted the Mayor and had set sail on other courses. Some raised the Jolly Roger flag of Congressman Ryan and joined his swashbuckling pirate fleet. Youngsters old enough to campaign, but not old enough to vote, were even more audacious. They dropped efforts to reform the Democratic Party and set out to reform the city instead. They hopped aboard the Good Ship Lindsay.

The more conservative reformers, the reformed reformers and the New Breed of organization men did not leap from the Wagner ship. They were his closest political kith and kin. They were among the chief beneficiaries of his regime. They and their ilk had filtered into practically every agency, bureau, department and municipal office. Their desertion would have been something more than treason. It would have been foolhardy. As I indicated earlier, however, the effectiveness of their vote-getting support was a moot point.

The only group of Democrats who really knew the ABCs of drawing ballots for the party, whether its candidates were vibrant, plodding or downright dull, was the "out-group" of old-timers. They occupied the fringes of the Mayor's New Order and never really melted into it. When Wagner first sought public office, these district leaders and their captains had been the workhorses that assured his victory.

Now, vilified by reformist holy men within the party and snubbed by their Democratic commander-in-chief, their efficiency plunged. They could no longer provide a measure of tangible service to their constituencies. Weekly meetings at local clubhouses, by contrast with former days, were dismal and poorly attended affairs. A generation ago, captains could have pulled a Nero or Caligula to victory in their own precincts. But no more. Wagner had never met many of these silent figures, anonymous to all but their tiny constituencies. Yet, by bringing them to a state of prostration, he inexorably crippled his chance to serve an unprecedented fourth term in City Hall.

This, then was the political scene surveyed by Wagner as, Hamlet-like, he pondered the question: "To run or not to run?" Victory was by no means out of reach. The very tag "Democrat" assured him of a better than even chance of hurling back his Republican challenger. But the Democratic Party of 1965, like another local institution, the New York Yankees, was not the unbeatable team of bygone days.

During the four week period he spent weighing his political future, the Mayor may have hoped that all party factions would somehow fuse or glue themselves to his person and cause. If so, the dream lacked realism. No "draft" movement materialized. Not even a slight breeze stirred the air around Gracie Mansion.

The sorrowful scene on June 11, 1965, which signified the Mayor's abdication, stirred many witnesses. Robert F. Wagner, Jr., was no monstrous despot, no political cutthroat. Had he been, his passing from the political stage would have been a moment for jubilation by a grateful city. Yet many New Yorkers reacted with mixed feelings. Personally, he was a likeable individual. In his public conduct, he was well-meaning. From a political standpoint, however, he had inevitably come to this moment not because he burned his party's bridges behind him, but because he had left them to rust and rot away.

The Political Tragedy of Robert Wagner traced on the preceding pages may not seem to warrant the expenditure of several thousands of words. The cast is not of permanent importance. But the purpose of spelling out the political errors which led, in part, to his sad decision is educational, not merely historical.

Perhaps the simple truths conveyed by this lesson have not been stressed in political science texts because they are so basic. Defying them would seem a breach of common sense. In any event, they deserve repetition again and again and again. For purposes of simplicity, they may be boiled down to one sentence—DO NOT TURN YOUR BACK ON YOUR OWN.

These are one-syllable words and can easily be committed to

memory. Retention, though, is not nine-tenths of the rule. An elected official must live up to it, as well. He must never consider the lowly precinct worker either safely in his pocket, or not worth keeping in his pocket. He must not court new allies if, in order to win them, he would have to discard true-and-tried old ones. Political reformers, rebels and opportunists, like the "sunshine patriots" of Thomas Paine's writings, will always stand by his side when a dazzling halo circles his head. But in the cold winter of misfortune, they will form his first legion of deserters. And to whom could he turn then?

XVI

Of Tammany Men
Reformers and Reformed Reformers

WHEN ROBERT F. WAGNER, JR., 102nd IN THE LINE OF SUCCESSION, abdicated his Mayoralty throne, he left no crown prince to carry on. Many considered Paul R. Screvane, President of the City Council, number two man in the city administration and a Wagner protege, as the logical heir apparent. But usurpers abounded throughout the municipal palace. No orderly procession to power loomed ahead. And no regal gathering of Democratic county leaders could be expected to thrash out the question of succession, as in the days of yore. The result was a scramble for the Democratic nomination, the likes of which had not been seen since 1937, and the equal of which had never been seen at all.

Screvane quickly threw his lance into the pit and announced his willingness to joust with the black Republican knight. So did City Councilman Paul O'Dwyer, younger brother of the late Mayor. So did Queens' able District Attorney, Frank D. O'Connor. So did reformist idol William Fitts Ryan, who had earlier backed out of a primary tilt with Wagner because he had no money in the campaign till. So did Comptroller Abraham D. Beame, number three man in the city regime, an official who considered himself *in* the Wagner administration, but not *of* it. For a while, Franklin D. Roosevelt, Jr., toyed with the idea of entering the contest, too. Then he decided to remain a spectator, apparently on grounds that the tournament was already overcrowded.

The contenders were a varied crew in terms of personal background, public record and political "philosophy." Nonetheless, each aspired to the same high office and, with the exception of Screvane, sought to attain it by demolishing, rather than building upon, the works of the present Mayor, a fellow Democrat. Such exposures of the party's dirty linen were bound to warm the cockles of Republican hearts. For all the talk of party "democracy," few Democratic stalwarts relished a bitter primary battle culminating in mid-September, just six weeks before the general election. Old-timers foresaw the lethal melodrama of 1937 being repeated— Democrat fighting Democrat while the opposition jubilantly applauded from the sidelines.

As the spectre of Democratic blood-letting beckoned, the Liberal Party plunged its own small dagger into its benefactor. During his third term, Wagner had delivered many political jobs to Liberals while deserving Democrats fretted and fumed. Now, as the Mayor sought third party support for his protege, Paul Screvane, the Liberal leadership about-faced and ran away. The group did not stop running until it reached the camp of John Lindsay. The situation seemed bizarre to many Democrats. How could the Liberal Party favor a Republican, whatever his liberal standing, whose campaign would obviously revolve around an attack on the liberal Democratic administration of which they had been an integral part?

It also seemed baffling—and a bit frightening—to many lower echelon Liberals, too. Down at the Municipal Building, a few feared that a vengeful Wagner would stage a brutal purge of his former allies. Some shrugged their shoulders. They had no voice in the decision to change sides.

As fate would have it, the candidate-selecting apparatus of the Liberal Party in the 1960s was more illiberal than had been Tammany's machinery back in the 1920s. No large aggregation of assembly district leaders, noses to the sidewalks of their neighborhoods, made their collective will known to the Liberal county leaders. Both assembly and county leaders were non-existent. Instead, a small screening committee listened to the Republican standard-bearer and to those among the Democratic hopefuls who were willing to appear before it.

A few days later, in a fashion befitting a gathering at the Roman

Coliseum rather than a political party convention, the imperial Liberal leadership regally announced its decision. The verdict was "thumbs up" on Lindsay, "thumbs down" on whoever the Democrats would eventually nominate. The sole missing element on the dais was a dazzling display of purple togas. Conservative business suits (no doubt with an ILGWU label) provided a 20th century facade for the festivities. And the ultimate purpose of these proceedings, mind you, was, in the words of the Liberal Party's vice-chairman, to save the city from the risk of "subjecting it to boss rule."

Proper lip service was paid, of course, by party leaders to the record and person of Robert Wagner. That was the least the Liberals could do for him—the very least. Oratory costs nothing.

With the Democratic primary contest barely under way, Republican candidate Lindsay had become Republican-Liberal candidate Lindsay. Now he beckoned for a second "hyphen" to round out a handsome trinity—Republican-Liberal-Fusion candidate Lindsay. Having selected the Liberal Party's State Chairman, a psychology professor, as his running mate for the City Council Presidency, Lindsay looked about for a willing Democrat to fuse onto his ticket. This was unorthodox, but not illogical. He was simply adding a new dimension to a tactic used by Fiorello LaGuardia. Back in 1933, the Little Flower (with whom the dashing Silk Stocking District Congressman was being constantly compared) had used Fusionist flavoring to neutralize the odor of his Republican tag and make himself more palatable to Democratic voters.

The man Lindsay chose to complete his ticket, however, lifted tempers as well as eyebrows. His eager running mate for Comptroller happened to be the $35,000-per-year housing coordinator in the Wagner administration. Moreover, he was privy to the campaign strategy of the Screvane camp. Or so it was said by those who denounced him as a party turncoat. Cries of "Foul!" gushed from many Democratic circles, made a few headlines, then faded away.

Such a turnabout would never have occurred in the days when Tammany held sway. Breaking from his party's ranks would have branded a man's political future for life and led to his excommunication from the political community. How this man—or any man—who held such a responsible and appointive post in one administration could justify his leap aboard the bandwagon of a candidate dedicated to ousting that regime from office is a question whose answer invariably escapes me. The terms "independent Democrat" and "Democratic independent" should clothe a man in integrity, not license an act of party treason. In defense of his conduct, all that can be said is that he felt handcuffed within the confines of the Democratic organization and sought to strike out in a new direction—any direction.

Though their former teammate's new role aroused the ire of many self-righteous and even less than self-righteous Democrats, the candidates for the city's top post were too busy drawing up their own slates to waste much time on outbursts of indignation. The "Beame Team" developed when Queens' District Attorney Frank O'Connor dropped his own Mayoral notions and accepted second spot on Comptroller Abraham Beame's ticket. Its third member, Bronxite Mario Procaccino, provided the appropriate ethnic and geographical balance.

The "Rule of Balance" also impressed the Screvane camp. His ticket was rounded off with an Irish intellectual, who traced his political loyalty to the Kennedys, and a Jewish businessman-philanthropist, who traced his lineage to one of the most famed names in New York's pantheon of heroes—the late Herbert H. Lehman. (Even reformers Ryan and O'Dwyer filled their slates with respect, if not precisely awe, for the balance concept.)

The chaotic city-wide primary was reflected in the shambles of my own district, which was not even the "Fourth Assembly District" anymore. A redistricting plan rammed through by a lame-duck session of the state legislature in 1964 had abolished it. Treasured names of neighborhood political antiquity slipped out of existence throughout the city. In their places rose consecutively numbered assembly districts. This was a convenient arrangement for orderly minds, but not for those of us who sentimentally link names and numbers with the history to which they bore witness.

A primary battle—of sorts—shaped up in the newly-mapped "Sixty-sixth Assembly District." It is noted here not because of the sparkling nature of the campaign or the arresting manner of the campaigners. Quite the contrary. It shaped up as a dull contest and deviated not a whit from expectation. Nonetheless, despite its lack of sound and fury, it signified much.

In a neighborhood where precinct captains could once direct votes to the right ballot line with the certainty of a gasoline attendant filling a car tank, the present leader, Mitch Bloom, found it vital, not merely judicious, to grasp the tailcoats of the candidate "most likely to succeed" on the Lower East Side in order to save his own leadership. This was a revolutionary phenomenon. It plucked our district's minor primary contest from the sea of more noteworthy primaries around the city and gave it ominous meaning.

Until recently, the district's captains and their leader automatically pulled in ANY candidate they pumped for in the primaries. Although Democratic enrollment here was largely Jewish, the trick was turned just as easily for a Downing or Murray as for a Goldfogle or Dickstein. Now came the ultimate abdication of power. No longer could the district leader guarantee victory for the candidate of his choice. Unless, of course, the candidate was capable of securing the triumph on the basis of his own popularity.

Such popularity on the Lower East Side was non-existent for Paul Screvane, choice of Mayor Wagner and the New York County Democratic organization, which cowered beneath his patronage whip. Informal polls pointed to a decisive Beame victory here in the face of more formal polls which pointed to a Screvane success city-wide.

Mitch Bloom now faced a dilemma in which political gymnastics counted for more than political savvy. After setting up his club in the Screvane camp, Bloom recognized that the winds of change blowing along the East River were blowing away from his man. At first, it mattered little. A Beame conquest of Mitch's bailiwick might prove embarrassing, of course. But it would have been bearable if he stuck with Screvane and Screvane carried the rest of the city. Time eventually heals the scars of any political humiliation.

Besides, Mitch's deputy commissionership would have been as secure as a safety deposit box for the next four years, assuming Screvane won the general election.

Bloom's quandary was not so easily solvable, however. Submission to a Screvane drubbing in his district was one thing. Endurance of the loss of his district leadership was quite another. And this possibility, dim at first, increasingly cluttered his mind following the endorsement given Beame by the "East River Democratic Association," a splinter group of anti-Bloomites with headquarters a bare block from Mitch's own clubhouse.

No one had taken that disorganized conglomeration of dissidents seriously until a large sign appeared outside its clubhouse windows boldly proclaiming: "VOTE FOR AND ELECT FOR MAYOR ABRAHAM BEAME." Ads were sprinkled in a neighborhood newspaper announcing that the leaders of the new club were "the only candidates for Democratic leaders in the 66th Assembly District, Part A (Lower East Side) who are actively working for and supporting the candidacy of Abraham D. Beame for Mayor."

This was no mere statement of political preference. It was a grim warning, as well. Though the outfit's candidates for the district leadership and female co-leadership were cloaked in anonymity, they stood poised nonetheless as a clear and present danger to Bloom's political future. After all, they did not have to bubble with personal dynamism or display magnetic drawing power of their own. If Beame accepted them on his slate, if the political marriage matured, if brochures, pamphlets and local ads planted liberally throughout the community publicized the union, if Beame won "big" in the district, his triumph might have swept Mitch out and his challengers in.

There were an awful lot of "ifs" involved, but Mitch no doubt wondered, then worried, about his previous commitments. As week after week passed, no competitive sign appeared outside his clubhouse windows bearing evidence of his continued devotion to Screvane. Just a bare fire escape greeted the eyes of passers-by. Some of my old friends within the Lower East Side Democratic Association were angered by Bloom's backing of Screvane. It was against their own better judgment. Now their leader's eyes slowly opened. Mitch realized that his commitment to Screvane's political future conflicted with the more personal and precious commitment to his own.

I was therefore far from startled by the rumor, reported on a late evening telecast in early August, that Mitch was on the verge of deserting the Mayor's protege and joining Beame. Hearsay became fact several days later when he publicly acknowledged his turnabout.

Political observers were puzzled, especially those pundits whose knowledge of Lower East Side affairs was limited to the axiom that the area always voted as its leader commanded, without knowing or caring about irrelevancies such as the candidates themselves. One columnist even speculated that Bloom was peeved when a $20,000-per-year deputy borough presidency post was handed by the outgoing Wagner forces to a West Side reform leader. Bloom had reportedly staked out the job for his very own.

The story, despite whatever truth it contained, was a triviality. Nonetheless, Mitch could easily have welcomed it. For although it attributed his switch to a motive far from noble, it at least conveyed no hint of his suspicion he could no longer carry his own district. It also gave no hint that the local Democratic organization was no longer the unassailable structure it had been in the days of the Ahearns. In truth, Mitch's decision was neither noble nor knavish. It was based on that most basic of motives—self-preservation.

The Screvane ticket's victory in the rest of the borough would have availed him nothing if he fought a losing battle against local insurgents seeking his job. And so it came to pass that Mitch Bloom latched his good name and future to the ballot slate led by the triumvirate of Beame, O'Connor and Procaccino. His "courage" and "independence" were duly applauded by camp followers of his new teammates. His locally circulated throwaways now proudly proclaimed: "VOTE ON THE BEAME LINE" and boasted his club was "The ONLY officially recognized and permanent Democratic Club in this area."

Mitch had safely touched home base. And all but a few diehards in the deflated opposition knew it.

Despite the cheery prognosis for Beame on the Lower East Side, Screvane's hopes were radiant in other corners of the city. He bore the Wagnerian Seal of Approval, an emblem worn by no other candidate in the primary. Democratic officeholders under Wagner owed their benefactor their jobs—if not loyalty—and how could they repay that debt better than by supporting the candidate of his choice?

Nonetheless, the City Council President had ample cause for uneasiness. For, if the Mayor's strengths were his strengths, so were the Mayor's weaknesses his weaknesses.

After 12 years of Wagner's rule, the city was suffocating in crisis. This excursion into big city politics is not the place to delve into the social and economic ills plaguing the metropolitan area. Volumes have been churned out on those perplexities. Suffice it to say that they ran the gamut from a bursting crime rate to the basics of air and water—air pollution was rising and the reservoir's water level was dropping.

Of all the aspirants for Wagner's office, Screvane alone could ill afford to prick pins in the performance of the incumbent. In return for leaning on Wagner's political influence as a crutch, he had to pay the penalty of wearing the Wagner record as a harness. It would shortly become evident that the price was too high for value received.

The Queens County Democratic Executive Committee, considered one of the three borough groups in the Mayor's hip pocket, gave faint endorsement to the Screvane candidacy. And this, despite alleged carrot-and-stick pressures exerted by Wagner on district leaders in the form of extended patronage or its withdrawal.

The same tale applied to the New York County Democratic Executive Committee—only more so. (At this point in the narrative, it should be reiterated that reference to Manhattan's Democratic organization as "Tammany Hall" would be a misnomer, nay, an insult to the memories of the Ahearns and their contemporaries.) After several delays in voting, geared to give Wagner's

agents time to do some arm-twisting, the committee came around
for Screvane. But not very far around. He received 9 and one-
twelfth votes out of a possible 16. This was certainly no smashing
triumph.

Furthermore, the dissenters were not remnants of the bygone
Tammany machine which the Mayor had arduously labored to discredit. Quite the contrary. In part, the holdouts consisted of co-
horts of Representative Adam Clayton Powell, overseer of Harlem
and a man who recognized no political superior. A far unkinder
cut inflicted upon Wagner and his heir apparent, however, was
that carved by the unreformed reformers. That wild-eyed crew
had won Wagner's ear and gifts during the preceding four years.
Now, they furled their flags around William Fitts Ryan, who had
shown himself more holy than any Republican in flaying the Mayor.

By way of contrast, the old-liners stuck to Wagner's man, albeit
reluctantly, although they had more cause than the reformers for
defection. Later, of course, Mitch Bloom was destined to become a
"drop-out."

Organized politicians were not the only source of disorganization
during the heated primary. Organized labor was similarly dis-
oriented. The United Hatters, Cap and Millinery Workers and the
International Ladies Garment Workers Union, whose bosses ran
the Liberal Party as a sideline, were already in Lindsay's corner.
This prior commitment made them mere spectators in the Democratic blood-letting match.

No such contractual obligation barred New York City's powerful
Central Labor Council from choosing sides. But that body, representing AFL-CIO unions with a membership at the 1,000,000
mark, assumed a posture of non-alignment. This neutrality was
termed a blow to Screvane's candidacy, for many observers considered the Council's hierarchy to be political helpmates of the
Mayor. As the campaign progressed, in fact, the President of the
City Council received a jolt from the head of the Uniformed Sani-
tationmen's Association. The union leader declared that Screvane,
a former garbage collector, had "gone high hat and Park Avenue."
He threw his support to Beame.

Although everyone in politics, and anyone outside of politics with a grain of common sense, knew Screvane was Wagner's choice as his successor, the Mayor's "official" endorsement was not bestowed until August 17, 1965, a month and a half after the campaign had gotten underway—and a bare 28 days before the election. The Mayor sorrowfully announced he would rather have stayed out of the fight. Probably, in his own mind, he was not quite sure whether his open blessings would help or hurt Screvane's chances more.

From Beame came the comment, "I'm not surprised. It is the Mayor's prerogative to support anyone who supports his policies." From Screvane came an expression of contentment: "The Mayor has been around a long time and has a great base of support. The endorsement of the Mayor will rejuvenate many of our campaign workers."

For better or worse, hand-in-hand with the Mayor's consecration, came the "Bossism" issue. This seven-letter epithet had been sprayed upon Wagner's own primary foe in 1961, with Carmine DeSapio being identified as the evil puppeteer behind challenger Arthur Levitt, a capable and competent public servant. Now, the same charge was dusted off after four years of hibernation and splashed on Screvane's principal foe, Abraham Beame. In place of DeSapio's were substituted the names of Brooklyn and Bronx chieftains Steingut and Buckley.

"I cannot stand by," announced Wagner, "and accept with equanimity the possibility of the nomination of Democratic candidates who, by their ties and associations with certain political bosses, would offer the Republican opposition a ready-made issue."

The Mayor thereafter injected the "bossism" narcotic into the Democratic body politic to such an extent that more timely and relevant issues were set aside. The Mayor, his advisers and whoever else had a hand in deciding to target in at the "political bosses" might have thought they were being cagey. Instead, they unwittingly caged their own candidate.

Anti-bossism had been Wagner's talisman in 1961. Following that election it should have been given a decent and respectful burial. By 1965, it was to be as valuable a luck charm for Screvane as an albatross. The reason was obvious, or should have been. Four years had elapsed since Wagner's own crusade. During that period, the only city-wide "boss" worth noting had been the Mayor himself. Back at the 1962 Democratic State Convention, he had forged and forced the nomination of a weak Gubernatorial candidate. Shoved aside were more appealing applicants for the post. Among those whose hopes were doomed by the Mayor's high-handedness had been Queens' popular District Attorney, now a candidate for City Council President on the very ticket Wagner was denouncing as boss-controlled.

The Mayor had displayed similarly dictatorial methods early in 1965. Few Democrats would forget that he overrode the wishes of a majority in his own party by pushing through his own choices for the leadership of the state legislature. Competent men they were. But so had been the men Wagner vetoed for personal political reasons. With this evidence of his own political absolutism readily available, could the "Bossism" charge be successfully renovated on behalf of his protege?

Within hours after the Mayor's declaration, deflation of this artificial issue set in.

"Mayor Wagner is the biggest boss himself—the biggest one we have had around here in a long time," retorted James A. Farley, who had entered politics while Charles F. Murphy still ran the city and state from Tammany's Fourteenth Street headquarters. Farley, a Beame supporter, contended that "the bossism cry gets a little bit silly. It all depends upon whom the boss is. If the party leader is with the opposition, it seems he's a boss. If he's on your side, he's something like a statesman."

If the damning of municipal monarchs was indeed worthy of time and energy, the Mayor and the President of the City Council seemed hardly the models to carry on the crusade. Like him or not—and, frankly, from a distance I did not—Congressman Ryan could have exploited that particular theme more honestly than the Screvane camp. That is, if Ryan had the funds, which he did not.

Ryan provided the primary campaign with a few of its more memorable moments. While many candidates have figuratively descended to sewer level, few have literally rolled up their trousers and splashed through the mud. Ryan did. At the time, he was leading newsmen on a wet safari above, along and beneath the Central Park Reservoir in search of a water leak. New York City, drying out in the midst of a water shortage, could ill afford the liquid's going down the drain. Hence, Ryan was Sherlock Holmesing for a heavy chlorine odor, a sure sign something was rotten in the State—or at least the City—of New York. And he found it.

Nonetheless, Ryan's own campaign was going down the drain. It lacked the slickness that only money can buy. His outpourings on hand-turned mimeograph machines were no match for the handsome and elegantly designed brochures of his opponents, nor for the television and radio time they could afford to purchase. Even two fellow reformist Congressmen, his ideological brethren in the Bronx, threw in their lot with Screvane. One admitted that Ryan's slim chances helped mold his mind. The other was equally candid. He stated, "The primary race is between Screvane and Beame."

As September 14, 1965, approached, Primary Day, Screvane proudly wore the tag of favorite, poll for poll, balance sheet for balance sheet. He had healthy cause for optimism, justified or not. Even knowledgeable friends of mine from Beame's own camp shook their heads and muttered under their breath that their man would win the Bronx, sizeable chunks of his native borough of Brooklyn, but little more. Despite all misgivings about the Mayor, few could truly bring themselves to believe that the Mayor's political stock had fallen so low that he could not control his own party's primary. After all, he held the trump cards.

Yet politics would be the "science" that politicians know it is not if elections were predictable and polls were crystal balls. Thus, during the wee hours of Wednesday, September 15, 1965, Abraham Beame found his five-foot-two-inch frame bloated to Mayoral proportions, and Paul Screvane began a painful adjustment to the role of lame-duck City Council President.

Screvane took Staten Island, with its insignificant vote total. He also carried Manhattan. But he took a severe drubbing in Brooklyn and The Bronx. And he was also rejected in Queens, his home base. The results in that borough no doubt shocked the candidate. If a man cannot carry his own territory, how can he expect to win in his foe's strongholds?

The turn of events in Queens probably startled Wagner, too. For the county organization there, like its Manhattan counterpart, had been commanded by the Mayor's men. And Manhattan itself had gone for Screvane by a bare 12,820 margin over his major foe—66,185 votes to Beame's 53,365. Congressman Ryan garnered 48,760 votes here, his heftiest showing in the city. Said Screvane of Ryan: "He's a spoiler . . . a good 80% of the votes he got would have gone to me."

Various causes were advanced for Beame's triumph. All were probably true, at least in part. Many centered on transitory themes, of import only to readers of that week's newspapers. In retrospect, the primary contest was not simply a test of political strength in which one candidate bested his three foes. In the history of New York City's Democratic Party, neither the winner nor the losers will leave lasting impressions. On the contrary, if the primary is remembered at all, it will be remembered as an epilogue to the Wagnerian drama.

In truth, it was not a test of Screvane's popularity. It was a test of Wagner's. The contest was really a plebiscite. Screvane served as a stand-in for the Mayor. And his defeat likely confirmed in the mind of his mentor the suspicions he harbored back in June when he reluctantly declined to seek a fourth term.

I realize it may seem strange to regard a primary election as an end rather than a beginning. But this one was. Whatever the outcome of the upcoming general election, the Wagnerian Era was over. Politically, only one question lingered past September 15th. Had the Mayor, in derailing his party foes and neglecting his party's workers, so weakened the Democratic Party structure that it could not pull together its shattered parts and defeat the Republican-Liberal challenger?

Idle speculation, unfortunately, is a luxury solely for defeated candidates and authors. Abraham Beame's triumph in mid-September provided no breathing spell for Abraham Beame. He certainly did not consider it a closing act. A homestretch drive of six weeks without respite lay ahead before the November 2nd day of Final Reckoning.

John Lindsay had campaigned vigorously—if necessarily with blinders—throughout the period of the Democratic primary. Not knowing who his eventual opponent would be, he could merely poke at the performance of the Wagner regime, sidestep personalities and hope the least dangerous Democrat would win. A Screvane victory no doubt would have led to minor modifications of his battle strategy. In a sense, Screvane had emerged from Wagner's hip. On the other hand, Beame's victory provoked major alterations. It would have been quite foolhardy for Lindsay to base his drive upon assaults against Wagner's record and nothing more. After all, Beame had been waging a vendetta of his own against the same record.

Until mid-September, Lindsay's high-plane campaign techniques deviated little from the style that had endeared him to voters of his Seventeenth Congressional District. But New York City is not the Seventeenth Congressional District multiplied tenfold. The heady approach so successful in the candidate's middle and upper class district would have fallen flat in the Nineteenth Congressional District, which habitually returned Lenny Farbstein to Washington at two year intervals. Intellectual appeals are fine—provided you are appealing to intellectuals.

It would be unfair, therefore, to condemn the handsome challenger for veering away from the high road he had so long trod. Waging a city-wide campaign is not a gentlemanly pastime.

Both Beame and Lindsay vigorously competed for the role of "underdog." Both realized it is always better to come from behind than it is to fall there. Theoretically, it should have been "no contest" for the title. Since registered Democrats outnumbered registered Republicans by about three-to-one, normal GOP candidates usually received the title by default. But, in this contest, historical statistics were meaningless.

This is not to say that New York City had finally become a two-party town. Far from it. Lindsay did not proudly wear the Republican label on his sleeve. He unstitched it and dropped it into an out-of-sight pocket. Given the circumstances, he had no choice. Time and time again, competent Republicans had gone down to defeat simply because they were Republicans, clearly tagged and unapologetic. The time was not yet ripe for New York City to adopt the two-party system. Realistically, Lindsay set out to reach a more attainable goal. He wanted to make New York a two-candidate city.

The Congressman did not publicly repudiate his party. He merely ignored it, its leaders and its national policies. The GOP elephant slipped into hibernation for the duration.

This political separation, though not divorce, repelled many an orthodox Republican. It certainly repelled a good many unorthodox Republicans. One of these, William F. Buckley, Jr., promptly stamped Lindsay guilty of treason. A talented orator, debater and writer in the espousal of conservative causes, Buckley picked up his own line on the ballot machine and set out to "spoil" the chances of the official GOP designee. No one like Buckley had ever invaded New York City politics. Probably no one like him ever will again. At best, many of his notions were original. At worst, they were aboriginal.

Campaigning under the banner of the Conservative Party, he played the theme that "Lindsay had sold out New York Republicans to the left-wing Liberal Party" and headed "a ticket which is wholly committed to the spend-and-spend, tax-and-tax welfare solutions which have brought the city to its present state of crisis."

In short, the Conservative candidate charged Lindsay with being a "bad" Republican and a "good" Democrat. By siphoning off the votes of "good" Republicans, he hoped to prevent the virus of liberalism from locally spreading in the party of McKinley and Coolidge. Few considered him a serious candidate. It is an interesting point whether among this small group could be considered himself. Early in his campaign he told reporters that if he won he would demand a recount. He merely hoped to do unto Lindsay what Ryan had done unto Screvane.

Gadfly Buckley was not alone in labelling Lindsay as a torch-bearer of liberal (Liberal) and democratic (Democratic) principles. The conservatively independent "New York Daily News" suggested Lindsay "might more honestly have not run as a Republican at all" and termed him a "bleeding heart of the first order." The paper editorially supported Beame. So did the "Journal-American," which in former days had occasionally regarded professed Democrats and sinners as branches of the same family tree.

On the other hand, the liberally independent "New York Post" turned away from the Democratic standard-bearer and backed Lindsay. So did New York City's other major dailies. "Americans For Democratic Action," an outfit rarely found in the corner of the Grand Old Party, reversed field and stuffed itself into Lindsay's gloves. So did a newly-founded group called "Democrats for Lindsay," whose brochures bore a quote attributed to the late President Kennedy: "Sometimes party loyalty asks too much."

The topsy-turvy Mayoralty campaign of 1965 saw a few departures from the traditional tactics of political warfare. Naturally, all major candidates for city-wide office—with the exception of Buckley, whose techniques were as characteristically unorthodox as his principles—trekked to Coney Island on warmer weekends for hot dogs and handshakes. Naturally, they saw and were seen at the parades of various national and ethnic groups. Naturally, they made pilgrimages to the strongholds of the various minority groups scattered throughout the city.

But no longer were either terra firma or the city limits, or even the state boundary, the borderlines for Mayoralty campaigning. For example, Lindsay went airborne to survey the New York landscape and seascape from the vantage point of a helicopter. He also journeyed to Pennsylvania's Pocono Mountains to do proper homage to members of the ILGWU before Unity House, their vacation retreat. Gone were the days when New York State's own

Catskills were the only resort area suitable and appropriate for an urban candidate's canvassing.

Lindsay's overall campaign strategy, as indicated earlier, deliberately relegated the county GOP organizations to the background. At the forefront of his drive for control of City Hall marched an enthusiastic army of volunteers—professorial reformers, collegiate reformers, high school reformers, unassorted reformers. The army's ranks included some who had rallied to Mayor Wagner four years earlier during his crusade against "Bossism." At least it contained their younger brothers and sisters. Some recruits had even cheered Congressman Ryan on during his vain bid for the Democratic nomination. Only after the Democratic primary did they switch in order to continue to fight. For the most part, many of the most eager Lindsay enthusiasts were not merely above party politics— they were completely outside of it.

Nonetheless, I would boldly suggest that, consciously or unconsciously, they set out to employ political techniques we Tammany men had followed religiously years ago. This is clearly evident from a careful reading of the "Lindsay Election District Handbook," the "Official Manual" for Lindsay workers. Lest these pure and innocent souls feel retroactively tarnished by this revelation, let me state immediately that they were not led unwittingly down any path of political sin by their more knowledgeable elders. Definitely not! There is nothing vile or corrupt in the time-tested methods their generation adapted from mine.

The pointers contained in the manual offered no magic success formula. They were well-known to any old-time Tammany man with little book-learning but a germ of common sense. Unfortunately, they were less well comprehended by the new breed of Democratic politicians who had arrogated the mantle of party leadership from their elders. That is why the party of Roosevelt, of Lehman, of Truman, of Kennedy, of Johnson, could face defeat in its most secure bastion. That is why an intelligent, articulate, upper-crust, aristocratic Yale graduate could even dare suspect that a Republican triumph was not so wild a dream as those who regarded the LaGuardia era as a prehistoric nightmare would pretend.

I realize it would be heresy for a proponent of Good Government to admit a link with Tammany practices. Nonetheless, heresy or not, parallels may be seen. The introduction to the Lindsay hand-book stated: "No candidate can win by himself, regardless of his energy and ability . . . This election will be won or lost in the election districts of New York . . . The reason for that is obvious: only the candidate himself and the District Captain will be in direct personal touch with the voters."

These sentences could have been written by Eddy Ahearn himself.

The booklet outlined the duties of the "Lindsay Election District Captain" as follows: "He must visit personally and interview every registered voter in the election district regardless of party affiliation . . . The District Captain has the critical responsibility of finding Lindsay voters and insuring that they vote on election day . . . in most cases the District Captain will be the only personal contact between John Lindsay and the registered voter. Our political experience has shown that personal contact is indispensable to winning an election."

Join "Tammany Hall Precinct Captain" with "Lindsay Election District Captain" and you have a political success story, past and present versions. In both, the "personal touch" was of inestimable value.

The Congressman's campaign workers operated out of store-fronts, not clubhouses. This physical difference was irrelevant. In a real sense, the Lindsay people had removed a page from Tammany's unwritten book—I hesitate to say "stolen" for reformers do not steal. They smoothed the edges, but the contents remained.

Several distinctions may be made between the mechanics of the former Tammany machine and its modern Lindsay counterpart. Lindsay captains carried index cards containing the names of registered voters in their districts. We Tammany men carried the names in our heads. Lindsay captains distributed campaign literature in large quantities. We did not waste paper. Lindsay captains were instructed in "How to Conduct An Interview." We instinctively knew how to speak to our people for we had grown up among them. Lindsay captains drew detailed maps of their districts. We knew every nook and cranny of ours. Lindsay captains were armed with a short biography of their candidate listing all his virtues for inquisitive voters. We never had need for such accessories.

Perhaps this last point illustrates the most basic cleavage between Lindsay's vote-chasers and Tammany men. It is so basic that all similarities are inconsequential before it. Only its disappearance from Democratic politics in recent years made the 1965 contest a close race in the first place. Our constituents cast ballots for us, not the candidates we represented. Reciting their biographies would have been a meaningless exercise. No one really cared who they were, so long as they could be depended on to perform their jobs and answer the calls of local Tammany representatives. Our political chores were year-round chores, and we provided service, not impressive biographies, for our constituents. If the men who benefited from our canvassing occasionally lacked the trappings of respectability, at least they were not caught short on humanity. Our constituents knew that we, their captains, were in a position to insure they acted in the best interests of all, whether they were bright, dim-witted or somewhere in-between.

Arrayed against the spirited, zealous forces surrounding Lindsay was a Democratic organization torn and tired, withered by dissension and desertion. The aging James A. Farley, who had known greatness in former years. and the still-young Edward N. Costikyan, who never had a chance to know greatness during his brief tenure as New York County Democratic chief, were Beame's principal managers. They issued sparkling statements, exuded confidence, presented optimistic reports, uttered bright forecasts. But they presided over a listless, muscleless skeleton. The name "Democratic Party" had lost its invincibility.

Thus far I have said next to nothing about Mayoral issues. Since elections theoretically are supposed to be decided on the basis of issues, I shall attempt to relieve myself of any sense of guilt for this omission in the next sentence. As 1965 closed, New York City needed better housing, more schools, less traffic congestion, a lower crime rate, a higher grade of administrative efficiency, cleaner air, more water, safer parks, more long-range imaginative planning, less garbage, more city services, less city taxes and a semblance of fiscal sanity and solvency.

In applying themselves to these issues, both major candidates favored the good life and abhorred the thought of municipal evil. Each said he was more eager to get on with the job of making New York City a better place to live in than his opponents. Often, both men agreed not only on where they wanted to lead their city but also on the route they planned to follow in getting there.

So much for issues. Let us return now to the politics of the campaign.

The synonymous orthodoxy of the two major foes annoyed Conservative Buckley. In fact, the shadowy "Third Man" in the race complained the only difference separating the two front-runners was "biological." Lindsay stood six-foot-three and weighed in at 180 pounds. Beame crammed 135 pounds into a five-foot-two frame. (Buckley's own measurements fell somewhere between the extreme proportions of his opponents. In this sense alone could Buckley ever be labeled a "moderate.")

At first, Lindsay regarded Buckley's candidacy simply as a thorn in his side—articulately painful, but not very serious. How else can you describe a man who turns down an opportunity to gobble up every second of his allotted time during a television debate with the comment, "I think I'll just contemplate the great eloquence of my previous remarks."?

As time wore on, though, various polls showed Buckley digging into the Congressman's strength. The thorn was becoming a shaft. Lindsay directed some of his secondary armament at the Conservative candidate. He ceased ignoring him as a "charming professional negativist." Despite unavoidable diversions, however, Lindsay trained his big guns on Beame, by far the more dangerous foe.

His biggest gun of all exploded the incendiary shell of "Bossism." This same shell had proven a dud when fired by Paul Screvane in the Democratic primary. But the public is always more willing to accept what a Republican says about a Democrat than what Democrats say about themselves. You close your ears in a family squabble. It is too embarrassing. You would rather believe a stranger.

"Beame's win represents a retreat to the political machine system," Lindsay charged the day after the primary. And he hacked away at the theme of "Bossism" and "clubhouse control" from that day forward without let-up 'till Election Day.

On television, the Republican-Liberal candidate charged "the Buckley-Steingut machine is behind Mr. Beame with its tentacles wrapped around him." He said Beame was merely a front man for a Democratic machine that planned to "stuff and stuff" city government with "politicians out of the clubhouse." Lindsay contended in pamphlets that his pledge to bring New York a non-bossed, non-partisan city administration had won him the "enmity of Charles Buckley—the Bronx boss—an architect of the Beame ticket." In newspaper advertisements, Lindsay supporters argued that "Eleanor Roosevelt didn't want bosses. Herbert Lehman didn't want bosses. But Abe Beame does."

Even the "Tammany Hall" epithet was resurrected. The Congressman's imaginative allies found it just as easy to condemn the past as flay the present. Excursions into history, especially in search of a moral, always strike a responsive chord.

As the honest and honorable politician I know him to be, Lindsay truly believed political machines were by nature evil. As a 43-year-old, his range of experience covered merely the decay in machine government. The handsome young fusionist was a schoolboy when Eddy Ahearn tore up and down the Lower East Side, with nary a concern for the clock, on behalf of his constituents.

Lindsay's knowledge of city and state politics during the era of Murphy and of district politics during the days of the Ahearns undoubtedly came from books and the memories of Silk Stocking District patricians. Such information was beyond the realm of his own personal background. If political government had been conspiratorial in those days, then nearly everyone and his brother were part of the conspiracy. There were few disgruntled outsiders. Justice and mercy often marched arm-and-arm through the briar-patch of dusty rules and red tape. Bureaucrats with libraries filled with regulations and by-laws could not ensnare guilty and innocent alike with technicalities of the law. And the clubhouse served as the clearing house where irate citizens could air their grievances and precinct captains could act upon them.

No less prominent a figure than Justice Samuel H. Hofstadter recently came to the defense of the clubhouse system. Justice Hofstadter was chairman of the state legislative investigating committee which delved into the extra-curricular affairs of the Walker administration back in 1931 and 1932. So he could not exactly be called an apologist for Tammany Hall.

In a letter to a local newspaper, the judge scoffed at the term "clubhouse loafer" as "the inelegant but picturesque designation by Fiorello LaGuardia for the men and women who serve gallantly, if inconspicuously, in the assembly district organizations—Democratic and Republican alike."

The widely-respected judge pointed out that "no one exploited these workers more in his rise to prominence than the 'Little Flower' and no one abused them more or gave them less of the rightful rewards of honorable political effort when he came to power."

I do not know Justice Hofstadter. And I do not know how many minds his wise words reached when they appeared in a letter to the editor column a few months before the 1965 Mayoralty campaign got under way. I certainly do not know whether they reached the eyes of Abraham Beame's speech writers.

Backed against the wall by a hoarse chorus of invectives, Beame was helpless to retort to screeches that clubhouse politics was bad by faintly saying it was good. Thanks to the steady dose of reformist brainwashing zeroed in at New Yorkers, any reasonable defense of the clubhouse is impossible. You might easier shield the devil at a revival meeting.

Instead, Beame limply pleaded innocent in answer to the charge he was a creature of any machine. His campaign, moreover, rotated on the axis of the same old tactic that had proven sufficient in former days. He called his opponent a Republican. Forty years ago such a revelation would have been enough to remove Lindsay from serious contention. But, in 1965, the accusation he was a bedfellow of the Rockefellers and Nixons—and even of the Goldwaters—of his party was hardly a reliable gimmick to guarantee victory. Equally futile was his effort to draw upon the Democratic Party's gallery of temporal saints—the Roosevelts, the Lehmans, the Trumans and the Kennedys. Only one man's hearty endorsement might have tipped the scales in Beame's favor. But Lyndon Johnson held back his open endorsement until October 29th— two days before Halloween and four days before the election. By then it was too late.

A few days before the November 2, 1965 election, the handwriting on the wall was beginning to take form. Already evident was the fact that the mighty Democratic organization which once could carry any rider to triumph was no more. Man for man, Beame could not keep pace with the energetic challenger. The Democrat stressed that his team had "the knowhow" to "build a greater New York." He pointed to his long years of experience in municipal government, an apparent age-before-charm pitch. This approach fell short of its mark. It only served to point out Beame's connection to the past. The Congressman was fresh. The Comptroller was shopworn.

He obviously lacked the glamour and excitement stirred up by the younger man. Abraham Beame striding down a city street in shirtsleeves did not photograph the same as John Lindsay striding down a city street in shirtsleeves. When Beame toured Harlem, he moved around with Adam Clayton Powell or J. Raymond Jones at his elbow. When Lindsay canvassed the same Negro ghetto, his companions were Jackie Robinson or Sugar Ray Robinson. When Beame exposed himself to the garment district, James Farley stood at his side. Lindsay took along Ethel Merman.

By the evening of November 2, the Final Reckoning was at hand. Lindsay polled 45.3% of the vote to 41.3% pulled by Beame. Buckley drew 13.4% of the ballots cast. Most of these were snatched from Beame rather than Lindsay, his intended target. If this surprised both Beame and Lindsay, it also did Buckley. Percentage-wise, the victor's total was the smallest since Vincent Impellitteri's upset triumph of 1950. Of 2,652,454 votes cast, a bare 102,407 separated the winner and his runner-up.

This was hardly an overwhelming mandate. It may be noted in passing, however, that John F. Kennedy's margin over Richard M. Nixon in the 1960 Presidential contest was merely a few thousand more. And 68,000,000 ballots were counted in that nation-wide race. Figures are of fleeting import. It is what an elected official does after the shouting dies down that matters.

Nonetheless, for days on end, analysts churned out charts about the Jewish vote, the Negro vote, the Puerto Rican vote, the Irish vote, the Italian vote, the white Anglo-Saxon vote, the reformist vote, the conservative vote, the apathetic vote and the vote of virtually every other bloc, apparent bloc and non-bloc in the city. Such statistical exercises, like scrabble, are interesting. But merely as a mental diversion. Their value in predicting what will happen in the next Mayoralty election is limited by the fact that time will not stand still for the next four years. No election is ever a mere replay of a preceding one.

Lengthy mathematical analyses of the Lindsay-Beame-Buckley race may be safely left to political scientists with little else to occupy their time. Suffice it to say here that in my own Lower East Side district, force of habit still prevailed. The Democrat won. All others lost.

Mayor Wagner, who was soon to become former Mayor Wagner, eagerly offered his own analysis of the returns at a City Hall press conference. For one thing, he said his party's candidate should have emphasized accomplishments of the present regime. Primarily, though, he blamed Beame's beating on "Bossism." According to Wagner, Beame had the "awful chore of carrying Charlie Buckley and Steingut and the other fellows on his back."

One knowledgeable reporter at the conference wrote that the Mayor was "purring like the cat that had swallowed the canary." Regretful, indeed, that a Democratic leader—in fact, *the* Democratic leader—in the city should gloatfully greet the defeat of his party's standard-bearer.

But it is not nearly as strange as his explanation of Beame's loss. If Beame were beaten through "guilt by association," it was his 12-year-long link to Wagnerian programs and policies which lay at fault. Proper political blame belongs, on the other hand, not on the traditional Democratic organization, but on the current Democratic disorganization. On the Mayor's shoulders rests much of the responsibility for this shattered state of party affairs. To paraphrase a rather literary Englishman, the fault lay not in the Democratic Star, but in himself. Let it not be forgotten that Beame carried the allegedly boss-ridden boroughs of Brooklyn and The Bronx. He lost Manhattan, Queens and Staten Island, where Wagner-style Democrats ruled, or at least reigned.

Republicans, half in frustration, half in envy, often point out that Democrats customarily stage violent family fights, then unite against all outsiders as Election Day nears. This was not the case in the Mayoralty campaign of 1965. Immediately after his independently-minded Comptroller had won the September primary, Wagner hesitated to back him. "There is a lot of time to think about that," he told reporters. This waiting period lasted until long after the time when the common duty of all good Democrats to come to the aid of their party had passed. When the Mayor's endorsement finally came, it recorded a faint and negative image.

As an afterthought, it may be noted here that clusters of reformers within the New York County Democratic Organization also paid scant heed to their duty as Democrats. The Village Independent Democrats voted not to endorse *any* mayoral candidate. Their leader, Edward Koch, who successfully crusaded against Carmine DeSapio in the name of building a stronger and better Democratic Party, went a step farther. He threw his support to Lindsay.

"We cannot remain silent," he said, "while the City of New York is delivered into the hands of Charles Buckley and Stanley Steingut, allies and confederates of Carmine DeSapio." Characteristically for the current crop of reformists, he made his dramatic announcement before television cameras in his Wall Street law office, not on the doorstep of his clubhouse.

Much has been made of the financial statistics released after the close of the campaign. They showed that John Lindsay's forces had spent more than $2,500,00, better than $2.00 per vote received. (Back in the days when some quarters of Tammany Hall were scolded for buying ballots, the price was cheaper. And, in jest, it might be said that the money went to needy voters on a direct payment plan, not to impersonal television stations and newspaper advertising departments.)

The winner's spendthriftiness should serve as no excuse for embarrassed Democrats. The fact remains that the three-to-one Democratic advantage in registration evaporated for reasons other than the opposition's hefty war chest. In essence, the Democratic Party was three Democratic Parties. A three-to-one advantage became a one-to-one standoff. The old-line Democratic organization had been bled dry and was too anemic to carry out its task. The Wagnerian Establishment was too incompetent to do it. And the reformist cliques were unwilling to pitch in wholeheartedly.

So much for backward glances and painful post-mortems.

The nature of grass-roots political strength being what it is, proper significance should be attached to an early decision by the new Mayor. He announced his intention of setting up "local City Halls" in neighborhoods throughout the city. Even during the heat of the campaign, he had said, "This city is too big to be run from City Hall. We're going to be running it from the local level, from the neighborhoods. These centers will give neighborhoods a direct line to me at City Hall. People could bring their gripes here, report a traffic or housing problem and know their wishes would go directly to me."

Any resemblance between the function outlined for these centers and those performed by old-time Tammany clubhouses, I am certain, were far from coincidental. It is the best way, perhaps the only way, for the man at the top of the governmental heap to know what is going on around his feet. Lest those in Lindsay's entourage blessed with aseptic respectability feel dirtied by their political inheritance from the besmudged machine system, a word of consolation is in order. Proper Victorians felt equally alarmed when confronted with Darwin's theory that man descended from the ape.

As Mayor, Lindsay has been quick to welcome the support of Democratic reformers. Their past record of defection served his cause well. In accepting them unto his bosom, his intentions were pure and good. But the road to hell is paved with good intentions, and so is the road to its political equivalent, oblivion. Any elected official may do well to ponder their recent contribution to the disintegration of their own party before assessing their potential contribution to his future political growth and the well-being of the city.

John Lindsay succeeded in making New York City a fusion town for an interlude of four years at least, and perhaps longer. But whether the two-party system will emerge is a tale that no one will be able to tell for a good many years beyond that. Since this is a book of political history rather than one of political prophecy, no attempt to hazard a guess will even be made. One point is crystal clear, though, crystal ball or not.

For the next several years, the ups-and-downs of reformers of varied political stripes—perhaps more stripes than the Tammany Tiger ever had—will probably dominate local Democratic politics. It appears quite possible they will now fuse themselves to the GOP Mayor who will dominate the city scene. As an old-timer looking at party developments from the outside, my few concluding words will no doubt be drowned by the chorus of voices belonging to the "new insiders." They are certainly an articulate crew, which may or may not be a blessing.

The story of reformist "idealism" is a tenfold-time told story. Their novel of goals and aims makes for inspired reading. On paper, they shine as a bold troop of Sir Galahads, charging the big, bad Tiger. The fact that the cat has already been de-clawed and de-fanged is immaterial. It still makes an exciting tale.

Perhaps New York City is a better place to live in now than when Tammany looked down from its perch of power. But, judging from the recurring headlines of crime and violence, not much better. Back in the days when a patrolman looked the other way at the behest of a Tammany captain while a Sunday law was being violated, New York's Finest were held in higher esteem than they are today. True, the patrolman on the beat knew his neighborhood Democratic captain—and everyone for blocks around knew that he knew him. But the symbol of law enforcement was no less respected despite this common knowledge.

Political morality, or what passes as political morality among political scientists, possibly has climbed. But surely its influence on those young people who theoretically should be impressed has been less than inspiring. Do they look now with awe and more confidence at representatives of public authority, civilian or uniformed? In "evil" Tammany's day, the streets were safer.

The reformist captains today have a better education than we had. They belong to the right non-political fraternal organizations and do not say "ain't." They may split hairs more often than they split infinitives. And they may be publicly praised for not cutting corners. Indeed, in many ways they are a different breed of politician than the Tammany captains they succeeded. But outwardly "respectable" characteristics do not make them better men.

The conflicts between the "new" reformers and the "old" reformers show clearly that a commissionership here or a deputy commissionership there are still welcome diversions no matter how glittering a man's political credo. And not a few reformist attorneys would fight just as hard for a judgeship as for a principle.

No doubt Herbert Lehman, a great man, and Eleanor Roosevelt, a great lady, were both motivated by nothing less than a desire to root all evil out of politics and instill all good. No doubt, many of the youngsters who flock to reform clubhouses, barely of voting age, share those high hopes. But these youngsters do not yet lead. They follow. As their older guides mature, they lose the spark that drove them in their own youth. It is extinguished as jobs fall vacant and they fill them.

Tomorrow, a new collection of rabid reformers will again arise—new faces, mostly lawyers. These "outs," in turn, will seek to become "ins" the traditional way, by ousting their predecessors. They, too, will band together under the banner of "Reform." What will they say of the crusaders of the 1960s? These will be denounced as false prophets and mere insurgents.

It is neither wise nor fair to lay down a flat "rule of thumb" that all reformers are good and all Tammany men are bad. Politics is not that simple. Politics is people. Not "just" people, but PEOPLE in large, bold capital letters. And political morality cannot be spoken of in terms of a collective noun. It is easy to damn all of Tammany Hall as the deepest recess in Dante's political hell, and lift all reformers to the crown of political heaven. But the Tammany Tiger had many stripes, as do today's reforming felines.

Political morality is an individual thing. It is capable of being measured only by measuring the worth of each man who plays the game. Opportunism, as well as opportunity, knocks at many doors—reformist, insurgent, conservative, liberal, regular alike. Some men grasp at one, some at the other.

The Ahearns, father and son, never had any cause to fear any stigma attached to the Tammany name. To them, the words "honor," "integrity," "loyalty," "trustworthiness" and "unselfishness" were not mere terms in a dictionary. In the service of their constituents, they strode as Tigers. Beside them, most of today's pure-striped reformist felines look like scrawny alley cats.

Index

Ahearn, Edward J. "Eddy," 10, 13, 14, 16, 32-36, 38-43, 48-50, 55-57, 59-61, 63-69, 71-74, 76, 77, 79-81, 83-88, 90-95, 97, 101-103, 106-109, 119, 126, 127, 130, 132, 134, 137, 144, 148, 172, 178, 193, 199, 209-211, 214, 216, 223, 226, 231, 232, 242, 255, 257, 285, 288, 296

Ahearn, John F., 8-10, 12-22, 24, 25, 28, 30, 33, 34, 39, 42, 45, 51, 62, 63, 65, 80, 94, 103, 109, 139, 199, 211, 213, 218, 296

Ahearn, Mrs. John F., 92, 93

Ahearn, William, 65, 92, 93, 95, 96, 108, 133, 148, 179, 180, 193, 194, 200, 211

Albano, Vincent, 226, 253

Amsterdam, Birdie, 9

Baruch, Bernard M., 87

Bayer, Walter J., 9

Beame, Abraham D., 268, 271-274, 277-283, 287-292

Bennett, John J., Jr., 150

Berger,—, 132

Birns, Harold, 9

Blaikie, Robert B., 191, 194, 195, 206

Bloom, Michael "Mitch", 213-216, 218, 219, 221-225, 231-234, 260, 272-276

Bragalini, George M., 208

Brickman, Harry, 191, 194, 197, 198, 200, 202, 203, 206, 208,212

Bryan, William Jennings, 82

Buckley, Charles A., 233, 248, 250, 251, 291, 292

Buckley, William F., Jr., 282, 283, 287, 288, 290, 291

Burkan, Nathan, 84

Byrnes, Father, 34

Chadwick, Msgr. John P., 74

Chaney, Lon, 52

Christenberry, Robert, 253

Churchill, Winston S., 246

Cleveland, Grover, 11, 105

Cohen, Louis, 173, 174

Coolidge, Calvin, 32, 57, 59, 112, 165, 282

Copeland, Royal S., 108, 118-120, 127

Corsi, Edward, 192

Costello, Frank, 94, 147, 149, 158, 159, 196, 197

Costikyan, Edward N., 217, 241, 243-245, 260, 286

Cox, Joseph A., 200

Croker, Richard, 14, 18, 59, 229

Cruise, Michael J., 74

Culkin, Charles W., 84

Curran, Thomas, 164

Curry, John F., 60-64, 66-68, 71, 72, 74, 76, 77, 79, 81-86, 96, 97, 101-103, 107, 109, 119, 127, 130, 146, 151, 175-176, 178, 179, 192, 199, 209, 241, 243

DeSalvio, John "Jimmy Kelly", 129

DeSalvio, Louis, 2, 129, 197, 226, 227

DeSapio, Carmine G., 43, 135, 147, 181, 184, 185, 190-202, 204, 205, 207-211, 213,-218, 224, 226, 228-231, 233, 234, 241, 243, 251, 265, 277, 292

Dewey, Thomas E., 108, 123, 127, 130, 131, 150, 161, 163, 204

Dickstein, Samuel, 27, 67, 68, 137, 138, 172, 219, 272

297

DiFalco, S. Samuel, 9, 177, 181
Donovan, William J., 76, 77
Dooling, James J., 88-90, 96-98, 101,
  106-113, 117-119, 127, 130, 148,
  149, 176, 178, 245
Dooling, Peter J., 97
Downing, Barney, 9, 34-36, 38, 68,
  71, 73, 86, 110, 117, 172, 272
Dunn, Philip, J., 151

Eisenhower, Dwight D., 202, 253
Einstein, Izzy, 51-53
Farbstein, Leonard, 202, 219, 220,
  235-241, 281
Farley, James A., 80, 86, 87, 90,
  94, 95, 101, 102, 106, 107, 110,
  112, 113, 131, 150, 278, 286
Farley, Thomas M., 69
Fassett, J. Sloat, 56
Fay, James H., 147, 159
Finn, Daniel, 107, 111, 135, 147,
  233,
Flynn, Edward J., 43, 74, 79, 82,
  113, 117, 132, 186, 196, 204, 205,
  233
Foley, James A., 44, 60, 63, 175
Frankel, Rabbi David, 53, 54
French, Eleanor Clark, 253
Goldberg, Arthur, 239
Goldfogle, Henry, 9, 27, 29, 272
Goldstein, Jonah J., 108-110, 135,
  136, 165, 166
Goldwater, Barry, 290
Grant, Ulysses S., 11
Greenfield, -, 53
Greeninger, Arthur, 134, 223
Griffin, Anthony J., 128
Grumet, Jacob, 9
Haddad, William, 236-238, 240, 241
Halley, Rudolph, 207
Harding, Warren F., 32, 57
Harriman, W. Averell, 195, 209, 217,
  218, 229
Healy, Martin, 245
Henry, Maurice G., Jr., 220
Hines, James J., 86, 88, 89, 102, 108,
  111-113, 118, 119, 129, 130, 135,
  153
Hines, Philip A., 153

Hoey, James J., 81, 129, 140, 142
Hofstadter, Samuel H., 289
Hogan, Frank S., 228, 229
Hoover, Herbert Clark, 57-59, 71
Hughes, Charles Evans, 20, 115
Humphrey, Hubert H., 246
Hussey, Charles H., 110, 145
Hylan, John Francis, 35, 44, 58,
  148, 149

Impellitteri, Vincent R., 59, 188-
  192, 194, 195, 197-199, 202, 204-
  206, 208, 210-212, 219, 291

Jack, Hulan, 218
Jackson, Andrew, 10
Jarema, Stephen, 2
Javits, Jacob J., 251
Johnson, Lyndon B., 236, 239, 245,
  247, 284, 290
Jones, J. Raymond, 2, 245, 246,
  251, 290
Joseph, Lazarus, 188

Kassal, Bentley, 235, 240, 241
Kazan, Abraham E., 13
Keenan, Michael J., 123
Kefauver, Estes, 196, 207
Kelly, Frank V., 113, 117, 196
Kenneally, William P., 111, 112,
  119, 120, 135
Kennedy, John F., 236, 256, 283,
  284, 290, 291
Kennedy, Michael J., 93, 147-150,
  152, 158, 159, 176, 178, 184, 196,
  201
Kennedy, Robert F., 238
Klein, Arthur G., 9, 173, 219
Koch, Edward, 260, 292
Koenig, Samuel S., 53, 56-59, 114,
  150, 151

LaGuardia, Fiorello H., 23, 45, 57,
  59, 69, 82, 83, 93, 98, 100, 101,
  103-105, 109, 110, 113, 114, 116,
  118, 120, 121, 123, 124, 126, 131,
  136, 143-145, 147, 149, 153-155,
  160, 163-165, 167, 168, 171, 185,
  192, 207, 210, 233, 258, 270,
  285, 289
Landon, Alfred, 112, 113, 116

Lefkowitz, Louis J., 9, 253, 264
Lehman, Herbert H., 76, 79, 84, 89, 90, 106-108, 110, 112, 131, 136, 144, 145, 148, 156, 168, 230, 231, 235, 271, 284, 288, 290, 295
Levine, Max, 66
Levitt, Arthur, 277
Levy, Arthur Jefferson, 22-24, 34, 38, 93, 124, 125, 162
Levy, Samuel, 64, 118, 139
Lincoln, Abraham, 11, 168
Lindsay, John V., 249, 251-254, 264, 265, 269, 270, 281-287, 290-294
London, Meyer, 27, 30
Loughlin, Edward V., 93, 159-162, 167, 174-178, 184, 188, 189, 196, 201
Lydon, Richard P., 79
McCooey, John H., 43, 44, 74
McCue, Martin G., 60, 61, 74
McGuinness, Peter J., 48
McKee, Joseph V., 58, 59, 74, 82, 83, 101, 168, 190
McKeon, William H., 249
McKinley, William, 57, 282
McLaughlin, George V., 46-50, 154
McMahon, Daniel, 62
McManus, Eugene, 180
Mahoney, David A.,107
Mahoney, Jeremiah Titus, 120, 121, 123, 127, 144-146, 148
Mandelbaum, Samuel, 68, 69
Marcantonio, Vito, 114, 164
Marinelli, Albert, 66, 67, 107, 108, 118, 119, 127, 129, 130, 135, 184
Markowitz, Jacob, 9
Marro, Joseph R., 9, 227
Mellen, Chase Jr., 58, 114, 150
Mellon, Andrew, 93
Merman, Ethel, 290
Miller, Nathan, 64
Mitchel, John Purroy, 19, 20, 103
Mollen, Milton, 248
Moran, James J., 167, 186
Morgenthau, Robert M., 243
Morris, Newbold, 165, 185, 186
Moses, Robert, 126
Mullen, John A., 135

Murphy, Charles Francis, 21, 22, 32, 35-37, 43, 45, 55, 56, 59, 97, 101, 102, 113, 123, 149, 176, 184, 185, 200, 217, 228, 241, 245, 278, 288
Murray, William J. "Bud", 132, 133, 272
Murtagh, John M., 199
Myers, Debs, 250, 251
Nagel, Percival, 131
Nasser, Gamal Abdel, 239
Neal, Clarence, 123, 130, 131, 143, 147, 150-152, 160-163, 165, 167, 171-179, 187, 190, 193, 196, 209
Newman, Bernard, 9
Nixon, Richard M., 290, 291
O'Brien, John P., 59, 77-79, 81-84, 101, 127, 131, 190, 192
O'Callaghan, Thomas, 220, 221
O'Connor, Frank D., 268, 271, 274
O'Dwyer, Paul, 268
O'Dwyer, William, 59, 136, 144, 165-168, 173-175, 177, 178, 181-183, 185-188, 190, 191, 196-198, 201, 206, 243, 254, 268, 271
Olvany, George W., 43, 44, 59, 60, 85, 97, 112, 145, 176
O'Sullivan, Raymond J., 79
Pearson, Drew, 128
Pecora, Ferdinand, 159, 190, 192
Pedrick, William J., 140-142
Perry, Harry C., 48, 66
Plunkitt, George Washington, 14
Pounds, Lewis H., 77
Powell, Adam Clayton, 276, 290
Price, Saul, 9, 200
Procaccino, Mario, 271, 274
Quinn, Elmer F., 181, 182, 198, 201, 202
Rendt, David S., 79
Riccobono, Xavier C., 9
Riegelman, Harold, 207, 253
Riis, Jacob A., 6
Robinson, Jackie, 290
Robinson, Sugar Ray, 290
Rockefeller, Nelson A., 229, 249, 251, 290
Rogers, Hugo E., 183-185, 197, 201
Rorke, Alexander I., 123

Roosevelt, Eleanor, 230, 235, 288
Roosevelt, Franklin D., 10, 49, 50, 59, 63, 68-73, 76, 77, 79, 80, 82-84, 86, 87, 95, 100-103, 105, 107, 109, 110, 112, 113, 116, 118, 120, 137, 138, 145, 147, 149, 163, 168, 231, 240, 284, 290, 295
Roosevelt, Franklin D., Jr., 229, 268
Roosevelt, Theodore, 27
Rossetti, Frank, 2, 226
Rudd, Stephen A., 128
Ruddy, Stephen, 110
Ryan, Joseph, 140
Ryan, Raymond F., 141
Ryan, William Fitts, 252, 265, 268, 271, 276, 278-280, 283, 284
Sampson, Eugene, 178
Sampson, Frank, 175-182, 184, 186, 191, 194, 194, 198-201, 206, 208
Sarubbi, Dr. Paul F., 148
Saypol, Irving H., 9
Schiff, Jacob H., 27
Schimmel, Henry S., 25, 34, 38, 124, 213, 214
Schlesinger, Arthur, Jr., 256
Schultz, 'Dutch", 102
Schurman, Jacob Gould, 135, 136
Screvene, Paul R., 268-281, 283, 287
Seabury, Samuel, 37, 69, 70
Sevareid, Eric, 162
Sharkey, Joseph T., 233
Simonetti, Angelo, 2, 226
Simpson, Kenneth Farrand, Jr., 58, 115, 116, 150
Solniker, Hyman, 9, 226
Solomon, William J., 84
Smith, Alfred E., 9, 21, 34, 44, 45, 47, 48, 50, 59-61, 71, 76, 84, 86, 87, 90, 94, 101, 102, 108, 110, 112, 119, 122
Smith, Moe, 51-53
Stand, Bert, 9, 80, 87-89, 93-96, 101, 108, 110, 111, 119, 120, 122-124, 130, 131, 133-136, 143, 144, 148, 150-153, 159-162, 165, 167, 171-182, 184, 186, 187, 190, 193-196, 199-206, 208-213, 215, 216, 219, 221-224

Stand, Leon, 9, 94
Stand, Murray W., 87, 93, 94, 122, 125, 126, 143, 144, 153, 187, 194, 205, 210, 211, 215
Steinberg, Henry, 226
Steingut, Stanley, 248, 250, 251, 288, 291, 292
Stevens, Harold A., 218
Stevenson, Adlai E., 202, 218
Streit, Saul S., 9
Strudley, Elmer E., 79
Sullivan, Christopher D., 65-67, 93, 108, 110-112, 118, 119, 123-125, 127-130, 135, 137, 140, 144-146, 149, 150, 159, 171, 176, 178, 184, 191, 201, 228
Sulzer, William, 21-23, 124
Thompson, George, 180
Trujillo, Rafael, 240
Tweed, William Marcy, "Boss", 11, 18, 56, 59, 65, 229
Truman, Harry S., 189, 218, 284, 290
Untermeyer, Samuel, 27
Viggiano, Prosper, 2, 197, 226, 227
Wagner, Robert F., Jr., 117, 205, 215, 217, 219, 229, 230, 233, 244-252, 254-258, 260, 261, 263-266, 268-270, 272, 274-278, 280, 281, 284, 291, 292
Wagner, Robert F., Sr., 21, 60, 79, 108, 118, 148, 205
Wagner, William, 73, 109, 110
Walker, James J., 32, 34, 35, 38, 44-48, 50, 59-61, 63, 67-80, 83, 88, 101-103, 109, 114, 131, 145, 165, 181, 209, 217, 243, 255, 289
Walsh, Patrick, 8
Waterman, Frank, 45
Weintraub, Samuel, 64, 65
Weiss, Daniel, 9
Weiss, Theodore, 238-240
Whalen, Grover, 35, 36, 117-120, 126
Wilson, Woodrow, 105, 115, 168
Wise, Rabbi Stephen S., 27
Wood, Fernando, 18
Yellowley, E. C., 53, 54

CPSIA information can be obtained at www.ICGtesting.com
Printed in the USA
BVOW031610020713

324841BV00002B/9/P